The Illustrated Guide to

Holistic
Care for
Horses

QUARRY

The Illustrated Guide to

Holistic
Care for
Horses

An Owner's Manual

Denise Bean-Raymond

BEVERLY MASSACHUSETTS

QUARRY BOOKS

First published in the United States of America by
Quarry Books, a member of
Quayside Publishing Group
100 Cummings Center
Suite 406-L
Beverly, Massachusetts 01915-6101
Telephone: (978) 282-9590
Fax: (978) 283-2742
www.quarrybooks.com

Library of Congress Cataloging-in-Publication Data
Bean-Raymond, Denise.
  The illustrated guide to holistic care for horses : an owner's manual / Denise Bean-Raymond.
     p. cm.
  Includes index.
  ISBN-13: 978-1-59253-457-9
  ISBN-10: 1-59253-457-0
  1. Horses--Diseases--Alternative treatment. 2. Holistic veterinary medicine. 3. Horses--Health. I. Title.
  SF951.B39 2009
  636.1'08955--dc22

                                                                    2008033067
                                                                    CIP

ISBN-13: 978-1-59253-457-9
ISBN-10: 1-59253-457-0

The Illustrated Guide to Holistic Care for Horses contains tips and recommendations for your horse. While caution was taken to give safe recommendations, it is impossible to predict the outcome of each suggestion. Neither Denise Bean-Raymond, Judy Goldman, nor the publisher, Quayside Publishing Group, accepts liability for any mental, financial, or physical harm that arises from following the advice or techniques, or use of the procedures in this book. Readers should use personal judgment when applying the recommendations of this text.

10 9 8 7 6 5 4 3 2 1

Writer and Developmental Editor: Judy Goldman
Design: Judy Morgan
All photography by Glenn Scott Photography unless otherwise indicated.
Illustrations: Gayle Isabelle Ford

Printed in China

DEDICATION

This book is dedicated to the Higher Power, to my parents, and of course to ALL the horses of the past, present, and future.

Contents

Introduction

Welcome to the world of equine holistic health-care and complementary and alternative (C/A) therapy.

The Illustrated Guide to Holistic Care for Horses is a resource guide for horse guardians intrigued by but unfamiliar with nontraditional methods of maintaining equine health, preventing and treating equine illness, and alleviating pain. This book teaches horse owners and caretakers to make informed decisions about the health and well-being of the horses in their care. It offers them a broader range of choices for maintaining health and for healing and palliative care.

Mine is a unique perspective, as I am not only an equine practitioner but also a patient of C/A therapy. I personally have discovered the powerful benefits of these modalities. Complementary and alternative methods can add to the total health plan of those facing serious illness. My experiences prompted me to give my own horses the advantages of what I had learned. Once I saw the impressive results, I felt it important to share them with others in the equine world.

C/A therapies may be integrated with traditional care to preserve physical and emotional well-being and to address imbalances or illness in our equine companions. This book is not meant to change your thoughts or opinions about traditional care but rather to enlighten you with new selections. C/A therapy is not a magical cure; rather, it is a way to encourage your horse's body to function properly and heal itself. It is not often a replacement for veterinary care but rather a complement to it.

This book is a hands-on practical guide as well as an educational tool. The spiral binding and glossy paper mean you can bring it to the barn and refer to it whenever you are working with your horse.

Chapters 1 through 4 introduce the holistic approach to horse health; Chapters 5 through 8 teach C/A therapies, including equine massage, acupressure, stretch exercise, and the use of herbs and essential oils. These are all techniques you can practice yourself on your horse. Using them in conjunction with veterinary care, you can promote continued wellness in a healthy horse, give comfort to an elderly horse, speed healing in a horse recuperating from injury or illness, and help a horse with a chronic or acute condition.

C/A therapy and a holistic approach to health have helped me through some of the most difficult times in my life. I am exceptionally fortunate to have the opportunity to combine my passions—horses and C/A therapy—and share them with you.

Here's to a more healthful lifestyle for you and your horse.

A Holistic View of Equine Health

Equine health encompasses much more than the physical wellness of your horse. *Whole health* refers to your horse's physical and emotional well-being, as well as mental acuity.

Health is not only the absence of illness but also the presence of balance and vitality. *Physical health* refers to the soundness and balance of bodily systems (skeletal, muscular, respiratory, circulatory, endocrine, digestive, reproductive) and an absence of illness or injury. As for *emotional health,* whether animals experience emotions as we, humans, do is a topic of intense debate. In this book, we define an emotionally healthy horse as one that is generally relaxed; accepts new people, animals, and objects in the environment without fear, or is quick to desensitize to them; and, given time and a positive environment, bonds with and trusts in the important humans in his life. *Emotions* have a physical as well as a psychological aspect. *Mental acuity*, on the other hand, refers to the ease and level at which learning occurs.

DIFFERENCES BETWEEN TRADITIONAL CHINESE MEDICINE AND WESTERN MEDICINE

Holistic health practices are the foundation of traditional Chinese medicine (TCM). Much of the holistic medicine practiced in the United States and elsewhere today has roots in TCM, which differs from Western allopathic medicine in some essential ways. However, the two approaches are used today in a complementary fashion by individuals as well as American medical health care professionals. Some veterinarians have also embraced certain TCM practices.

Western medicine approaches healthcare in a linear fashion. For example, a horse presents with a cough. A certain type of bacteria has entered the lungs; the bacteria causes inflammation and infection in the lungs; the lungs respond by producing a large amount of mucus; a cough, which is the response of the body to rid the lungs of the mucus, develops; and so on. The doctor responds by conducting tests to see what type of infection is plaguing the horse and prescribing drug therapy (generally a course of antibiotics) to eliminate the infection.

TCM approaches healthcare in a circular fashion and seeks a root cause for illness symptoms. A horse that presents with a cough is observed for demeanor, odor, oral health (gums), comfort level, eye brightness, overall condition, hair quality, hoof health, respiratory pattern, and temperatures throughout the body. Time of year, time of day, medical history, and environmental factors are also considered. The goal is to address the underlying problem as well as the presenting symptoms. In this example, the horse's respiratory system is treated to clear it of mucus and infection; in addition, the immune system is treated to strengthen it.

TCM can be beneficial in resolving chronic health issues that do not require surgical intervention. It is also a preventive therapy because it notes imbalances in the horse's system that may be precursors of other health concerns. If these imbalances are recorded and treated, future health problems can be averted.

A NEW VISION OF INDIVIDUAL EQUINE HEALTH CARE

Horses are herd animals, originally roaming the plains in large groups. In the process of domestication and our attempt to keep them as companions, we have compromised their ability to use their natural survival skills. We must, therefore, compensate through intense care and understanding.

A variety of problems arise for the horse because of domestication. For example, some domesticated horses have limited or no social interaction with people or even other horses. Many are parked in their garages (stalls) all day. Lack of social interaction can cause a horse to be unhealthy, unhappy, and unable to perform well.

Another problem is the lack of or limited grazing opportunities. In the wild, horses roam freely, spending most of their day (18 to 20 hours) searching out forage and grazing. When humans provide domesticated horses their forage, the horses lose the hours of exercise they would get foraging in the wild. In addition, horses, like other animals, know what ails them and often seek natural remedies.

They have the means and the ability to self-medicate in the wild, where plants with healing properties abound. Stabled horses do not have that opportunity.

The tools of domestication are unnatural to the horse and can affect his health. Stalls, saddles, shoes—these and other human interventions affect horse health and well-being. Horse guardians must nurture and support their animals' physical, emotional, and cognitive health to compensate for their loss of living as nature intended.

1

Keeping Your Horse Physically and Mentally Healthy

Each horse has his own personality, spirit, and mannerisms. Take the time to learn your horse's ways and familiarize yourself with his behavior and physical presentation. This awareness will help you distinguish both physical and psychological imbalances.

RECOGNIZING THE SIGNS OF SOUND PHYSICAL HEALTH

Be sure to inspect your horse's body for physical symptoms; grooming is a good opportunity to do so. Paying attention to and learning your horse's body language and behavior can also help you assess his general mood and health. Is your horse not able to salivate on the bit? Is your horse not free and loose in his movements? Is your horse listless and hiding in his stall instead of eagerly coming over to greet you? Each of these behaviors, or lack thereof, indicates a horse's "dis-ease." Understanding your horse's communication system is an important element in determining his physical and emotional states. (See Appendix A.)

Outward signs of physical health include bright eyes (no discharge, weeping, swelling, or tenderness); a shiny, gleaming coat; full mane and tail; tidy, intact feet; defined, clean joints (no swelling or disfigurement); clean, filed teeth and pink gums; healthy appetite and gut sounds; and proper weight.

WARNING SIGNS OF ILL HEALTH

It is important to monitor your horse's vital signs—and to know how to interpret them. Checking vital signs when your horse is well allows you to establish a baseline of your horse's normal body functions. If you suspect your horse is unwell, check the following and compare them to the baseline. (See Appendix C.)

▸ *Breathing pattern*—Your adult horse should breathe 8–16 times per minute. A newborn foal usually breathes 60–70 times per minute. Track breathing by watching your horse's side, or barrel, move in and out and counting the number of breaths taken in 1 minute.

▸ *Pulse*—Take your horse's pulse when he is at rest. If the horse is excited or has recently worked, you will not get a proper reading. Check the pulse by placing your fingers in the groove under your horse's chin. Count the pulse for 30 seconds and then multiply that number by 2. Healthy pulse rate, measured in beats per minute (bpm), depends on a horse's age:

newborn = 80–120 bpm

foal = 60–80 bpm

yearling = 40–60 bpm

adult = 28–40 bpm

Note: If your horse's breathing pattern is faster than his pulse rate, he is seriously ill.

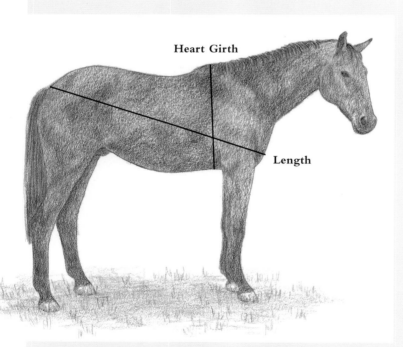

Heart Girth

Length

Measure the horse's heart girth and body length. (HG).

Determining your horse's approximate weight is easy with a tape measure and a calculator.

1. Measure your horse's heart girth (HG) by placing the tape behind your horse's elbow, bringing it over the withers, down the other side, across the belly, and back to where you started. Record the measurement.

2. Measure the length of your horse's body (L). Place the tape at the point of the shoulder and measure to the point of the hip. Record that number.

3. Use the following equation: HG x HG x L = Total. Divide this total by 330. The result is your horse's approximate weight.

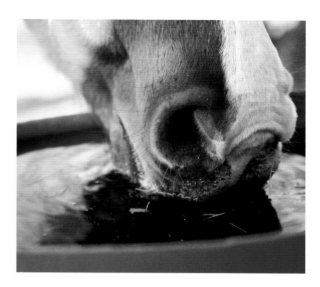

▶ *Temperature*—A horse's temperature normally runs about 100°F (38°C) but can vary through-out the day from 99.5°F (37.5°C) to 101.5°F (38.6°C). Use care and caution when inserting the thermometer so you do not get kicked; move slowly so your horse is not startled.

▶ *Skin*—Monitor your horse's skin for dehydra-tion. Skin should be pliable and spring back into shape quickly and easily. Grab a section of skin on your horse's neck or shoulder and release. It should retain its elasticity and quickly return to its original condition. Skin that re-mains misshapen and tight or takes a while to return to normal indicates dehydration. Skin color is another helpful sign in determining ill-ness. For example, if your horse's skin appears to be giving off a yellowish glow or tint, jaundice is indicated; a yellowish discoloration of the skin may indicate liver malfunction.

▶ *Gums*—Check your horse's gums by raising the lips and observing the gum color, which should be pink. Pale gums indicate anemia; red indi-cates problems such as mild shock or toxicity from enlarged capillaries; blue indicates inad-equate blood flow through your horse's system.

Teeth—Your horse's teeth should be intact and have smooth edges. The mouth should be clean-smelling, with no bad breath. If teeth are loose, chipped, or missing, or the breath is foul, contact an equine dentist. Teeth with sharp edges can cut your horse's gums and cause abscesses to form; chipped or missing teeth can inhibit chewing, causing uneven wear; and a foul odor can indicate infection.

Bodily functions—Horses generally produce about 5 quarts (3.5L) of urine per day. The color of the urine ranges from yellow to brown. Your horse passes manure about every 2 hours. Manure is generally tan to dark green in color. It is defined in ball shape formations. If the manure is loose and shapeless, presenting as diarrhea, contact your veterinarian. Horses can dehydrate quickly if they have diarrhea.

Hooves—Examine your horse's feet often. The front feet should be symmetrical to one another, as should the hind feet. All four feet should be clean and free of cracks and chips. Severe breakage can lead to unsoundness. Grasp each hoof and pick it up for further investigation. Press along the coronary band. This area should not be particularly sensitive, nor should it be terribly soft or wet. If it is, infection or disease may be present. Check your horse's soles and frogs. The soles should be intact and free of dark patches. Localized dark patches may indicate bruising. The frogs should be free of odor, symmetrical, and elastic to the touch. Odor may indicate thrush. (For more on thrush, see page 18.)

MAINTAINING PHYSICAL HEALTH

A holistic approach to equine physical health requires not only tending to your horse physically but also addressing environmental factors that can affect health. Making the practices below part of your routine will yield lasting benefits.

Veterinary Practices

Horses need proper routine veterinary care. Inoculations, nutrition, worming, dentistry, hoof condition, and overall health should be discussed regularly with your veterinarian so your horse can be placed on an appropriate maintenance schedule to achieve optimum health. Veterinarians are an essential part of a horse owner's network of equine professionals.

- *Facial symmetry*—Is your horse's face symmetrical in appearance when you look at him face on? Eyes, ears, and nostrils should be even. An uneven face may indicate uneven muscle development or skeletal deviance, either of which may cause undue exertion on facial muscle tissue and sharp edges to develop on the teeth.

- *Muscle symmetry*—Is the cavity and muscle tissue surrounding the eye bigger on one side than the other? This imbalance indicates that your horse is favoring one side over the other when chewing. This results in the teeth wearing unevenly.

- *Incisors check*—Do your horse's molars have jagged edges? Using care not to get bitten, run your fingers along your horse's molars. If you feel jagged edges and your horse pulls away from your touch, this indicates the jagged edges are digging into his cheek.

- *Chewing motion*—Does your horse chew in a circular pattern or in an up-and-down motion? The correct pattern is circular. If your horse is chewing up and down, this may indicate the teeth have formed uneven edges, inhibiting his ability to chew.

Dental

Be sure to have a professional equine dentist examine your horse's teeth once or twice each year. Some dentists use power tools, while others work by hand. Some dentists use both methods, choosing one or the other depending on the situation. The choice to have work done by hand or mechanically should guide your choice of a dentist. Ideally, you want your horse's experience to be as pleasant as possible while achieving optimum results. Observe these points when monitoring your horse's dental health:

TIP

Tea Tree Oil

You can apply tea tree oil to scrapes on your horse's body. This oil is an antiseptic. Disguise scrapes on the white portions of your horse by applying the tea tree oil and then lightly tapping baby powder over it. Tea tree oil can be toxic if ingested, so use it with caution. See Appendix B.

Grooming

Grooming aids in circulating the blood, removing dead skin cells, maintaining muscle tone, keeping the pores open and clean, and removing debris from your horse's coat. The skin's natural oils are brought to the surface and spread, resulting in a shiny coat. In addition, grooming is a wonderful opportunity to inspect your horse's body for lumps, bumps, cuts, scrapes, skin issues, cracks in feet, and other changes. Grooming also desensitizes your horse to human touch, necessary in caring for and handling him.

Some grooming products on the market—wipes that contain natural herbal extracts such as lavender and chamomile; grooming stones that stimulate circulation while removing debris and dead hair; natural sponges for bathing; and flexible curry combs with long, pliable extensions—promote circulation, encourage natural oil production, and support skin health.

Hoof and Foot Care

Horses' feet must be examined and maintained regularly. If your horse's feet are diseased, infected, or in otherwise poor condition, your horse cannot be healthy. Those feet carry the weight of a heavy animal and, at times, a rider, and they transmit the energy created by their own movement.

Your horse's hoof functions as a defense mechanism, and it contains many intricate internal structures. Hooves are made up of varied skin. They grow continuously, like your fingernails, so they must be trimmed regularly. They are subject to cracks, chips, and splits, just as your nails are.

Begin by ensuring your horse has a clean, dry surface on which to stand. If your horse is continuously exposed to wet, untidy conditions, his feet are more susceptible to disease and infection.

Inspect your horse's feet every day so you become familiar with the way they normally appear, making it easier for you to distinguish changes or abnormalities. Each hoof should be similar in size and shape. Your horse's front feet are round, while the hind feet are a bit oval. The angles of your horse's limbs and feet reflect weight distribution. Most horses bear approximately 60 percent of their body weight on their front limbs and about 40 percent on their hind limbs, though this varies by breed.

Treating Thrush

Dirty, wet conditions are common causes of thrush, a hoof disease. Feet that are not cleaned out daily are more prone to it. Thrush presents with a foul odor and a dark-colored discharge. It can be treated with an iodine solution, a natural remedy of tea tree oil, or commercial products designed for thrush. A farrier may need to trim away dead tissue in the center of the foot (the frog) first.

To Shoe or Not to Shoe

Horseshoes support the feet, and corrective shoes address foot problems. On the other hand, horseshoes inhibit natural wear, harm the hoof through concussion, weaken the growth pattern, provide an ideal home for bacterial growth, and reduce essential blood flow.

The decision not to shoe comes with a commitment to appropriate exercise, correct trimming, and a healthful diet, and it is a decision you must make for each individual horse after consulting with your veterinarian. The transition from shod to shoeless should be made slowly and carefully

A shoeless horse must move about freely on all sorts of terrain, as an abrasive environment is what keeps a shoeless hoof in good condition. Shoeless hooves should also be exposed to footing similar to the surface on which your horse is asked to work so his feet can adapt and strengthen accordingly. Barefoot horses exposed regularly to varied terrain can strengthen and wear down their feet naturally. Trimming is required about every five weeks. Horses confined to stalls or small paddocks generally do not wear down their feet or strengthen them so are not good candidates for shoelessness.

Horses with conditions including laminitis, navicular syndrome, and arthritis may improve with proper barefoot hoof care. Hoof boots and pads are sometimes used on shoeless horses in certain situations.

Whether or not your horse wears shoes, work with a professional natural farrier to monitor and maintain your horse's feet appropriately.

Check the feet for cracks, chips, bruises, sensitivity, foreign objects, abnormal growth patterns, heat, swelling, odor, and discharge. Also note if your horse is particularly sensitive about a foot being touched or examined. Keep a watchful eye, as sensitivity in one foot may indicate a problem. Discuss your observations with your veterinarian and your farrier.

Clean your horse's feet daily. Note any changes on the underside of the foot. Horses' feet are often exposed to urine, manure, mud, and varied footing—an ideal environment for bacterial growth. If the underside of the foot does not receive enough oxygen, bacteria thrive and infect the foot, a condition commonly known as *thrush*.

When cleaning your horse's feet, hold the hoof securely. You do not want to risk dropping the hoof on your own foot or onto the ground, startling the horse. Be cautious when cleaning near the frog, which is soft and sensitive. Do not pick directly into the frog. Pick out the debris starting at the heel and moving downward toward the toe; this keeps the debris from flying up toward you. Clean out each foot thoroughly, as leftover debris can harbor bacteria, leading to infection.

A flat thrush pick makes it easier to clean out debris, but a plain old pick will do. Brass picks are easy to hold, long-lasting, and sturdy.

Inoculations

It is necessary to immunize your horse to prevent disease. However, if you are concerned about your horse reacting negatively to a vaccination or being overly vaccinated, ask your veterinarian to conduct an antibody titer test. This blood test determines the presence and level of antibodies to a particular disease in your horse's blood. In turn, this reflects your horse's exposure to an antigen or substance the body recognizes as foreign. The test reveals the strength of your horse's response to its own tissue in the presence of disease and whether or not the last vaccination created a strong and continuing protection from the disease being tested. If the antibody titer test reveals enough immunity to a disease, your horse does not need that particular vaccination.

Required or recommended vaccinations vary regionally; be sure to discuss them with your local veterinarian. If your horse is in competition or travels, additional vaccinations may be required. Laws vary from state to state and country to country. Make sure your horse is immunized for the region in which he resides and for any areas through which he may travel.

Horses are commonly vaccinated for rabies, tetanus, Eastern (the most deadly) and Western encephalomyelitis (sleeping sickness), rhinopneumonitis, influenza, rhino/flu combination, strongles, Potomac horse fever, and West Nile virus. In addition, many competitions require proof of a Coggins test, a blood test for equine infectious anemia.

All horses, whether or not competing, traveling, or working, should be vaccinated or titered. Many diseases are highly contagious yet preventable.

Worming

As a general guideline, worm your horse every eight weeks and rotate the worming product, being sure the effective ingredient differs each time.

Worms are found in pastures, forage, and manure. Insects can transmit worms. Excessive worms in a horse's system can cause weight loss, colic, and even death. Many types of parasites can infest your horse. These include ascarids, lungworms, pinworms, roundworms, tapeworms, and strongyles.

Traditional and holistic approaches to parasite control are available. Choose the most appropriate, safe, and effective means to manage the problem.

Preventing Worms

The keys to a successful worming program are prevention, consistency, rotation, and targeting. Worms develop resistance to medicines. Therefore, the program must include changing not only to a different worming product each time but also to one with different effective ingredients. This ensures that a different worm is targeted each time a worming medication is administered. The most common active ingredients found in chemical products are fenbenazone (which kills ascarids, large strongyles, lungworms, and pinworms), pyrantel (large strongyles, pinworms, roundworms; also tapeworms when the dosage is doubled), and ivermectin (common parasites in their adult phase). Chemical pastes, powders, and pellet feeds are available for parasite control.

Before using these products, have your veterinarian test your horse's manure to determine the types of worms that are present, allowing you to administer the most appropriate chemical. If you live in an area that experiences seasonal changes, you may decide to use chemical wormers less frequently in winter, as parasites are less numerous in colder temperatures.

Natural worming products contain ingredients that strengthen immunity, promote digestion, and eliminate parasites, including diatomaceous earth, clove oil, glycerin (vegetable extracts), grapeseed oil, kelp, probiotics, and sage. Wild horses "treat" worms with diatomaceous earth, which has antiparasitic properties. Clove oil is a digestive aid. Grapeseed oil has antioxidant properties. These products can

TIP

Titer Tests

Antibody titer tests eliminate unnecessary vaccinations. Equine influenza, encephalitis, herpes, and viral arthritis; Potomac horse fever; rabies; tetanus; and West Nile virus are all diseases for which antibody titer tests can be conducted.

be hard to find and are generally more expensive than commercial wormers. However, they do not contain chemicals that must be processed by the liver, reducing the risk of overtaxing the organ. Also, they promote digestion, whereas chemical products inhibit digestion by destroying gut bacteria. (You may want to administer probiotics to your horse for a week after giving him a chemical wormer in order to restore gut bacteria.)

Follow these guidelines below no matter which approach, traditional or holistic, you use.

▶ Implement a consistent insect control program. Insects transmit parasites.

▶ Monitor your horse's manure regularly. If you can see parasites or their eggs, have the manure tested by your veterinarian.

▶ Monitor your horse's behavior. Constant tail rubbing may indicate worm infestation.

▶ Keep all areas of your horse's living space clean and free from manure, which is a prime environment for parasites. Remove manure from stalls, paddocks, and pastures daily, and rebed stalls weekly. Do not feed your horse near manure-infested areas.

▶ Have your veterinarian perform fecal egg counts. This test determines the level of parasitic eggs in your horse's manure. The manure is tested before and after worming to determine its effectiveness.

Barn and Stable Maintenance

Most traditional stabling practices do not support the well-being of a horse. If you can't allow your horse to roam freely, consider these points:

Air Quality

Breathing clean air is crucial to overall horse and human health. Equip your barn with safety windows, fans, doors, and rooftop ventilation. Remove dust, excessive heat, and odor from the stable. Install and weatherproof windows, vents, fans, and doors according to climate so the stable does not become too warm or cold and does not flood or leak.

Stalls

Generally, the average size of a stall is 12 feet square (1.1 m²). Mares in foal and large horses require extra space. The horse needs enough room to eat and drink, lie down, and pass manure and urine. If the space is too small, the horse has no choice other than to trample waste into the bedding. This is unhealthy for the horse's feet, food ingestion, and general emotional state; it makes stall cleaning more difficult and means you have to discard most or all of the bedding daily when cleaning the stall, which is neither cost, nor time, effective and generates excessive waste.

Stall walls should be at least 5 feet high (1.5 m), and the overall height of the stall should be at least 10 feet (3 m). Dividing walls should be built high enough that horses cannot reach over them; you do not want them confronting other horses and thus risking injury. Concrete should not be used for dividing walls. (If concrete is unavoidable, line it with rubber stall mats for cushioning.) Instead, use a thick, sturdy, animal-safe, chemical-free wood. Check the walls for splintered or broken pieces and protrusive objects such as nails and broken hardware.

Examine stall windows; make sure they are intact, clean, secure, and built to prevent cuts or injuries. Note how high each window is and how it operates. The most common protective mechanism for stall windows is metal grilles or bars. Place the bars so your horse cannot access the actual window but still benefits from the light and ventilation. Set the bars a safe distance apart; you do not want your horse getting his nose caught between them. Horses can easily break unbarred windows and get injured. Be sure windows open and close properly.

The stall floor should be level, sturdy, clean, and free of holes, divots, rot, and harsh materials. Rubber mats can be helpful; be certain to install them securely so they cannot shift and allow debris to build up underneath them.

The stall door should be at least 4 feet (1.2 m) high so the horse's head, hoof, and leg cannot get caught underneath, through, or over it. The door must close securely.

Ideally, the stall should be furnished with an automatic water system that dispenses fresh, clean water on demand. If using buckets, attach them to the walls with hardware that is free of sharp edges and corners. Be sure the buckets cannot fall off when the horse is eating or drinking out of them. Place the buckets close to the door so you need not enter the stall when feeding and watering, as many horses are aggressive at feeding time.

Do not place feed buckets on dividing walls because if horses can see one another at feeding time, they may become agitated and aggressive.

Muck out stalls daily, and pick them out in the evenings. Inspect and clean all buckets daily. Always look in the buckets before feeding time and remove manure, insects, rodents, and foreign objects.

Inspect stalls daily for damage, protrusive objects, broken boards, foreign objects, and splinters.

Bedding

Bedding should provide cushioning, absorb urine, and retain manure. It must be clean, free of debris and dust, and animal-safe. Read all labels to check for toxic materials and allergens. Be sure the bedding is not a substance your horse might be tempted to eat. Good bedding choices include wood shavings and peat moss. Avoid straw, as it packs down and becomes urine-soaked quickly. Bed stall floors 3 to 5 inches (0.9 to 1.5 m) deep. Provide additional bedding where your horse stands and urinates. Older horses and horses with soundness issues may require additional bedding for comfort. Be aware that even small amounts of black walnut wood residue in horse bedding can cause laminitis.

Emergency Procedures

Keep an up-to-date, well-stocked first aid kit for you and your horse available at all times (see photo below). Post emergency numbers (police, fire, veterinarian, farrier) near all phones in the stable, along with clear directions to the farm. Develop an evacuation plan that explains and diagrams the safest, most efficient routes out for horse and human, and post copies near all phones and exits. Mark electricity, gas, and water controls—valves and circuit breakers—and post their locations.

Post a large street number in front of the farm so it is visible day or evening coming from either direction in the roadway. It is best to maintain an easily accessible, clean, serviced horse trailer and

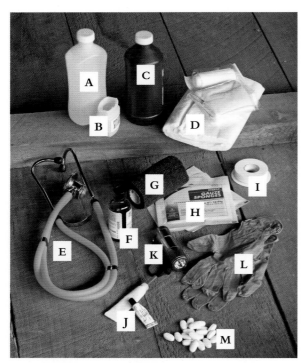

Pictured are common items that may be included in a first aid kit.

(A) rubbing alcohol; (B) petroleum jelly; (C) hydrogen peroxide; (D) poultice wraps; (E) stethoscope; (F) tea tree oil; (G) wound wrap; (H) gauze; (I) medical tape; (J) triple antibiotic ointment; (K) flashlight; (L) medical gloves; (M) equine antibiotic pills

vehicle at all times so if your horse must be transported to an equine hospital or another facility during a natural disaster, you can do so immediately.

Finally, check on the horses and the property every evening. Make sure all horses appear alert, bright, and healthy; doors, windows, and gates are secure; supplies are put away; lights are turned off; and the property and barn are in general order. This is also a good time to top off water buckets and feed the final hay ration for the day.

Fire Safety

Do not store flammable hay and bedding near the horses; keep it in a separate structure if at all possible. Install electrical wiring, fire extinguishers, alarm systems, smoke detectors, and sprinkler systems in compliance with fire code regulations, and keep them in working order. Place lightning rods on the building. Multiple, well-marked exits; emergency phone numbers, posted near working phones; and easy access to a water source are essential. Inspect all electrical outlets and lighting fixtures regularly, control the rodent population, and do not use portable heaters. Do not allow smoking on the property.

Other Areas

Horses spend plenty of time outside the barn. Be sure they are safe.

Paddocks

Keep footing tidy and free of debris and holes. Rocky, hilly, or muddy terrain and manure, urine, and standing water are unsanitary conditions that can cause health problems. Be sure paddocks have sufficient drainage, and keep all gates secure and in good working order. Check that the junctions of gates and fences are intact and spaced properly, protecting your horse from injury or escape. Provide clean, easily accessible water in an animal-safe, secure container. Fencing should be at least 4-feet (1.2 m) high and constructed of durable material that is intact, free of sharp corners or edges, nails, and broken areas or splinters.

Riding Areas

Your own facility or your boarding facility may offer an indoor arena, an outdoor arena, trails, fields, or a combination thereof in which to ride or drive your horse. Maintain all riding areas properly. Address footing, lighting, drainage, size, and climate control. Footing material may consist of sand, stone dust, or recycled rubber. Be sure arenas are well lit for safety in the evening.

Keep riding arenas free of waste, dust, and leaks. Manure, poor drainage, and constant use all contribute to the breakdown of arena footing. Drag and wet the footing to reduce dust, maintain level ground, and prolong the life of the footing material. Clear rocks and vegetation, especially toxic plants.

Storage Areas

Prevent cross-contamination by designating storage areas for specific items. Do not store machinery that runs on fuel in the same area as feed. Keep all areas clean, free of hazards, easily accessible, and protected from the elements.

CARING FOR AN AILING HORSE

Sometimes an owner spends less time than normal with an ailing horse because he is not riding or working him. However, recuperation is a time when your horse needs special attention. He will benefit from your society as he undergoes the taxing experience of ailment or injury and his body is trying to heal.

Keep a daily log of your observations concerning your horse's behavior, energy level, emotional interactions, and habits. Is your horse eating and drinking normally? Is he passing manure and urinating regularly? Does he express curiosity when you visit, or is he lethargic and uninterested in you? What does his overall condition look like—gaining or losing weight, bright or dull eyes? This log will help you to assess his progress, or lack thereof, and detect complications.

Horses are usually banned or limited from work and turn-out when in recovery. Your horse may be confined to his stall or a small paddock. He may only be allowed out if you hand-walk him. Your interaction with him is vital to ease his monotony. If you can walk him or bring him out to graze, he will appreciate the change of scenery, time away from the confines of his stall or paddock, social time with you, and physical movement.

Grooming may ease his discomfort. Your presence in general, your voice and touch, are soothing and comforting to your horse. Use these to their utmost.

Massage, acupressure, and stretching encourage the healing process and ease the stress of the recuperation period. Check with your veterinarian before implementing these therapies.

DEVELOP AND MAINTAIN YOUR HORSE'S EMOTIONAL HEALTH

Horses have an emotional life, albeit a bit different from that of humans. Horses display fear, pleasure, curiosity, anger, depression, excitement, pride, and aggression.

An emotionally well-balanced horse is content and happy to interact with humans as well as other horses. He has a friendly demeanor, is alert and sociable, and his ears are forward and eyes soft. He is comfortable with the human touch. Curious by nature, he approaches humans rather than turns away. If your horse has bonded with you, he will often greet you with a nicker. Your horse has developed trust in and respect for you. When you talk to him, he should find your voice soothing and comforting.

Horses need physical contact as much as humans do to thrive. If a horse is isolated from other horses, he loses or never develops adequate social skills. When a poorly socialized horse finally runs with other horses, he may be bullied until he learns his place in the pecking order. Keeping horses in separate yards and stables does not allow them to groom each other, feel comfortable enough to sleep lying down, or learn important social skills for herd living.

To maintain the emotional health of your horse:

▶ Arrange to trailer your horse to a friend's property and ride together. If you are unable to trailer, invite your friend and her horse to your property to ride together.

▶ Arrange an informal group ride in your area, using a beach, trail, riding arena, or other venue, and set a date for you and several of your horse friends to ride together.

▶ Obtain a companion animal, such as a goat or pony, to keep your horse company.

▶ Trailer to local clinics or horse shows. You can often trailer to a local show and ride on the property while the show is being conducted without actually competing.

▶ Join a local equine group, such as a regional council, to become integrated with other horse owners and to meet people who own horses and property in your area. You may be able to trailer to events with them if you do not own a trailer.

▶ Post a listing in your local tack shop or on a local website inviting other "one horse only" owners to get together with you and ride.

▶ If you live near a farm that has a riding arena, arrange to use the arena weekly or monthly. This gives you and your horse the opportunity to work in a different setting and in the company of other horses and people.

Spending time to bond and develop mutual trust and respect are key to promoting an emotionally stable horse. Social animals, such as horses, feel vulnerable when left alone for long periods. For your horse to thrive emotionally and mentally, take the time to develop a true relationship with him outside of a working or training situation.

The act of grooming can be a wonderful bonding experience. Talk to your equine companion while grooming him. He will grow accustomed to being touched on all parts of the body by human hands; this desensitization to human touch is necessary in caring for and handling your horse.

Foster a trusting relationship with your horse. Let him know you never hurt or frighten him. Convey this by treating him kindly. Perhaps you could sit in your horse's paddock and read a book while your horse is turned out. Speak in a calm, soothing voice when you are working with your horse. Touch your horse's body gently all over. Praise your horse and tell her vocally how you feel about her. Encourage your horse when she is afraid or having difficulty performing a task. Always use both vocal and physical praise (patting). Kindness and consistency aid in gaining trust.

Horses learn, adapt to, and are comfortable with routines. If you follow routines in the time you spend with your horse, he will become familiar with them and decrease his fear of the unexpected. For example, if you scratch your horse's withers before you place a saddle on his back, he will soon learn that saddling is a pleasurable experience.

If your horse bonds with and trusts you, many situations are more easily negotiated. For instance, your horse may be anxious when the veterinarian comes to the farm, but if you are there to hold and comfort him, he may settle and behave calmly for the veterinarian, knowing his trustworthy companion is by his side.

OUTSIDE INFLUENCES ON THE EMOTIONAL STATE

Be cognizant of all external factors that can affect your horse's emotional state. If your horse seems unusually unsettled one day, check the weather forecast, as horses often experience a mood and behavioral change when a storm is impending. If your horse is confined to stall rest due to illness or injury, the resulting restrictions on movement, socialization, and work are certain to affect mood. Your horse may become agitated when other horses in the facility are turned out and he is not.

Have you recently moved your horse to a new farm? This change of environment will affect your horse mentally and emotionally, as he must adjust to his new surroundings. Allow your horse several days to acclimate before asking him to focus and work for you. Has your horse lost an equine friend or been separated from the herd? He will certainly feel

TIP

Creative Bonding

Be creative in finding ways to bond. If you are working in the barn, stop and eat your lunch in front of your horse's stall. If you live in an area where pasture is available, lead your horse to grass, letting him graze a few minutes while you stand alongside chatting. Simply taking your horse for an easy, quiet walk, demanding nothing other than companionship, goes a long way in bonding.

disturbed and vulnerable and so may act out when you are working with him. Moving another horse or a companion animal near your horse may ease his loneliness. Has your schedule with your horse changed? Have you begun seeing him at a new time of day? Horses love routine, so yours will certainly notice you are visiting at a different time of day.

Make an earnest effort to be aware of all the factors that can affect your horse's emotional life. Do not, however, overanalyze or try to justify any dangerous or domineering behavior on the part of your horse; this type of behavior is unacceptable. Do, however, be aware and open-minded. Consider the whole picture of your horse's life. This holistic approach will help you find answers, solutions, or improvements that enhance your horse's quality of life and resolve problems that arise.

WARNING SIGNS OF EMOTIONAL UPSET OR IMBALANCE

Horses communicate emotional distress in a variety of ways. Watch your horse's signaling. Is he often agitated, aggressive, or downright dangerous? Biting and kicking, though they shouldn't be tolerated or justified, can indicate emotional and mental "disease." Consider changing your horse's career. If you try to force a horse into a job he is not physically, emotionally, or mentally capable of doing, you will see signs of distress. Watch your horse's general demeanor. Does he hide in the back of his stall when he sees you? Is he resentful when the tack is brought out? Has his attitude changed? Is he generally uncooperative while working or training? If so, alter your plans for this horse.

Undesirable Behaviors and Their Causes

Behavior: Eating feces (coprophagy)
Possible Reasons: Protein, fiber, or other nutrient deficiencies
Additional Information: Foals often eat their mares' feces, possibly acquiring beneficial microbes for gastrointestinal development.

Behavior: Eating dirt, hair
Possible Reasons: *Dirt:* Self-medication or supplementation; lack of minerals; digestion assistance through microorganisms found in the dirt; sedation of digestive problems via absorbent activity of clay; boredom
Hair: Trace minerals are found in tail hair. Horses lacking these minerals in diet may self-supplement by eating tail hair.
Additional Information: Horses normally eat the occasional mouthful of dirt.

Behavior: Chewing wood
Possible Reasons: Lack of fiber; boredom; lack of movement or socialization
Addtional Information: Horses in the wild gnaw on wood, especially in fall and spring. The bark of trees contains copper, which is good for their coats.

Behavior: *Cribbing:* Grasping and holding onto something, usually wood, with the incisor teeth, arching the neck, tensing neck and facial muscles, and taking in air
Possible Reasons: Stress; anxiety due to boredom; loneliness; physical problems such as ulcers or other intestinal disorders; genetic predisposition to chronic stress; high-concentrate diet
Additional Information: Horses naturally need to nibble and graze often. When they are not allowed to do this at will, they may develop this undesirable behavior.

Behavior: *Weaving:* Continuously shifting weight from one front leg to the other, making a rhythmic rocking motion
Possible Reasons: Lack of consistent exercise; excessive food ingestion; mimicking other horses that do it; anxiety

Additional Information: A companion animal may soothe a weaver. An equine toy (such as an equine ball), hung in the path of the weaver, may curb the habit. Providing plenty of turn-out in a large area may also help.

Behavior: *Wind sucking:* Like cribbing, but without grasping an object
Possible Reasons: Boredom; lack of exercise; addiction to endorphin release in brain triggered when this act is performed; an inherited condition or an equine form of obsessive-compulsive disorder; digestive disorder—the horse is attempting to rid himself of elevated stomach acid levels resulting from concentrated feeds

Behavior: Running the fence
Possible Reasons: Separation anxiety, often when a horse he is socially involved with is removed from the paddock; general anxiety; anxiety about being out of the safety of the stable; desire to be brought back into the barn; insects
Additional Information: In the wild, horses do not have this issue because they do not live in fenced-in regions. They have vast amounts of space in which they can roam or flee. In general, if horses are turned out in a group and one horse flees, the other horses will flee also.

Behavior: Refusing to eat when no physical problem is present
Possible Reasons: Loneliness; depression. If your horse has recently undergone a change (perhaps the death of a pasture mate), change of owner, or change of living area, he may become detached and express his discontent by refusing to eat.
Additional Information: Horses may be subservient to more domineering horses. The dominant horses may eat, taking food from the horses that are lower in the social order. The subservient horses may develop fear when it is time to eat.

Other Undesirable Behaviors

Calling certain behaviors *vices* or *bad behaviors* is anthropomorphic—that is, it attributes human characteristics to animals in an attempt to understand their behavior. Horses have no moral or ethical values. So-called vices are better referred to as *undesirable* (to humans), *dangerous* (for horse and human), or *unhealthful* (for the horse).

Behavioral problems can result from dietary or environmental deficiencies, boredom, or lack of exercise or companionship. Some of what we consider problem behavior is normal behavior for horses. These behaviors may be the products of the tools of domestication—stabling, saddles, bits—and the protocols of domestication—limited movement, socialization, feeding or grazing time—not natural to *equus caballus*.

Three common causes of undesirable or unhealthful behaviors are boredom, diet, and internal system disorders. Horses that spend most of their time in a stall or small paddock tend to develop habits out of boredom. Some horses are fed grains that are easily ingested, leaving them with nothing to do once they have eaten. These horses may become wood chewers, cribbers, or dirt or hair eaters. If your horse is a wood chewer or cribber, implement an exercise plan and apply anti-chewing solvents to the places he chews.

One positive way to respond to boredom behaviors is to use food-dispensing stable toys as feeders. Your horse must move the toy, often a ball, in order for the feed to be dispensed. This feeding method can occupy a stabled horse that has little or no pasture time and lengthen his eating time.

EQUINE STRESS MANAGEMENT

Domesticated horses are subject to a tremendous amount of stress. Several contributing factors include living conditions, work schedules, quality of care, and aging. The work schedules we create, whether for pleasure or competition, place demands on our horses mentally, physically, and emotionally. Quality of care, no matter how efficient and effective, can never replace the benefits to a horse of a natural lifestyle.

Many practices can help you reduce and relieve your horse's stress level. Here are some you may want to try:

▶ Music therapy has been shown to lower blood pressure, alter mood, and ease pain in humans. Why not apply it to your horse? Play soft, easy music in the barn. Keep the volume low so it is audible but soothing.

▶ Create and maintain a daily feeding and turn-out routine. Horses respond well to routine.

▶ Always make a forthright effort to make your experiences with your horse positive. If you are ill-mannered, unnecessarily loud, or physically rough with your horse, he will always be uneasy in your company.

▶ Pay attention to other people in your barn. If you see someone treating your horse inappropriately, speak up. Your horse needs you to defend him.

- ▶ Factor a day of rest into your horse's work schedule so he mentally, emotionally, and physically has a break from the weekly routine. Rest is as important as work.

- ▶ Plan sufficient daily turn-out time for your horse, time to escape the confines of the stall and wander, roll, and play as a horse should. Plan according to local weather conditions.

- ▶ Spend silly time with your horse weekly. This is time for grooming, walking, grazing, chatting with, and feeding treats to your horse—time when you both enjoy one another's company, placing no demands on each other.

- ▶ Organize and orchestrate your horse's schedule strategically. If your horse is due to see the veterinarian, farrier, and C/A therapist, book the appointments separately so he is not worked on by all of them on the same day. Horses are not machines; they are living, breathing creatures.

- ▶ Every now and again, plan a quiet time to ride, a time during which no other horses or riders are in the arena (perhaps an early morning or evening) so you and your horse can have each other's exclusive attention.

DEVELOPING MENTAL ACUITY

A horse's mental acuity is measured by his level of curiosity, the rate at which he learns, and the level of learning he can attain. Horses learn best in a positive environment that provides challenging and varied activities. The horse's brain is the same size as a human's and has a well-developed cerebral cortex and hippocampus, both of which have many folds or convolutions. Basically, the more folds, the more intelligent the being.

Foals are especially curious and need an enriched environment and exposure to a variety of people, places, and things.

Create a Positive Learning Environment

When working with your horse, no matter the task or goal you are trying to achieve, or whether it is short-term or long-term, work slowly, patiently, clearly, and consistently. Create a positive learning environment and offer praise for honest effort.

Balance this positive approach with an authoritative and respectful but firm demeanor. Do not settle for dangerously defiant or disobedient behavior. However, if your horse seems to be defying or disobeying you, consider the circumstances before declaring him out-and-out defiant. Could the problem be one of communication or rider error? Is your horse in pain? Is your horse fearful of something in the environment—maybe something you do not readily notice? Is your horse too hot or tired to work? Again, be firm, but see yourself more as the benevolent leader than as the boss.

The worst but most effective punishment for a horse within a herd is isolation from the others in the herd.

Use positive reinforcement:

▶ Provide praise, petting, massage, or food when your horse behaves in the desired manner.

▶ Do not provide such rewards when he does not.

Offer praise or other positive reinforcement for correct responses. Refrain from physically challenging (striking, yelling at) your horse.

Set Up Your Horse for Success

Create conditions appropriate to your horse's learning style and level of learning to increase his chances of success.

Before you begin working or training, make sure weather, time of day, the training environment, and physical factors such as pain or saddle/tack discomfort are not at issue.

Work in simple, small steps when teaching your horse a new behavior; do not attack the entire task, making it overwhelming. Break the task into individual behaviors that, taken together, achieve the desired goal. If your horse gives you an incorrect answer but makes a legitimate effort, acknowledge his attempt to cooperate.

If you are training your horse to complete a task, such as walking over a ground rail, set up only one rail, allow the horse to examine it before you mount, and then encourage the horse to step across while following behind another horse. Once your horse steps across the ground rail, immediately offer praise. Repeat and ask your horse to step across without another horse leading the way. Consider positioning a helper on the other side of the rail holding a bag of treats; make sure your horse can hear the crinkling sound of the paper bag, which he probably associates with treats. Your horse will likely step over the rail willingly, hoping to receive a treat for doing so. Have your helper offer a treat immediately. Next, remove the helper and ask your horse to step over the rail again. Once the horse steps across, offer enthusiastic vocal praise and pats.

Create a Challenging and Varied Learning Environment

The ideal environment for your horse is open pasture in which he can gallop, graze, and play with other horses. The ideal terrain includes places to explore, rock outcroppings, trees, brush, and hills. You may not be able to provide this ideal scenario, but you can easily enrich your horse's present environment, often at little cost, in small ways to encourage and facilitate learning and strengthen mental acuity.

A variety of durable equine toys is available. To enrich your horse's environment and encourage exploration, build confidence, and affect learning, offer him large balls with handles for grabbing with the mouth, tug toys, and toys that dispense a treat after the toy is rolled or moved.

Teaching your horse tricks using positive reinforcement is another way to engage his mind. Teach him to bow down on one knee with his head between his legs, take a blanket off his back or a tied cloth off his leg, or pick up a cloth and have him hand it to you while you are seated on him. This fun training deepens your bond with him and encourages brain activity. The more your horse learns, the more he is capable of learning.

Introduce Variety into Training

Most professional riders today realize the value of training within their discipline as well as across disciplines. Reining horses—in fact, horses in almost any discipline—can benefit from dressage. Jumpers can benefit from practicing correct hunt-seat form.

Dressage horses can gain a lot from working with ground poles.

Give your horse plenty of opportunity to trail ride. In addition, offer variety within your horse's environment so he remains sharp, bright, attentive, and focused.

Here is a list of activities you can schedule into your horse's regimen:

▸ *Simple riding session*—Schedule a day on which you simply sit on your horse's back and hack throughout your property. Do not ask anything of your horse other than to explore the property with you. Ride in areas you do not normally work in, providing it is safe to do so. Simply walk along and take in the sights and sounds of the area.

▸ *Obstacle course*—Be as creative as possible when setting this up. Arrange safety cones in a pattern for your horse to maneuver around. Lay a tarpaulin on the ground and walk your horse over it. Assemble a small stack of ground rails and ask your horse to step across them. Create a narrow channel using ground rails and walk through the channel. Vary the setup of the obstacle course.

Consider setting up a course of ground rails only. Research courses used in prominent equine competitions, such as state or regional championships, or seek suggestions in books, magazines, websites, or videos. Recreate courses used in past Olympic games using ground rails instead of actual jumps. This will provide a challenging pattern without overwhelming you or your horse.

▸ *Basic dressage test*—Memorize and practice a basic dressage test. An introductory level test may be appropriate for starters. As you and your horse improve, vary the degree and difficulty by choosing other tests.

▸ *Lunge session*—Lunge your horse for a day. Practice transitions, circular size changes, and straight-line tracks. You and your horse will both benefit from honing your lunging skills. You may want to lunge your horse at a show prior to riding to gauge his mood and energy level, on a day you have limited time, or if you cannot ride one day.

▸ *Group ride*—Arrange riding time with other horse owners in an arena, on a trail, in a field, on a beach, or at a suitable, safe area. This encourages socialization and a change of scenery.

▸ *Stretch ride*—Practice mounted stretches with your horse. Work in the walk only and concentrate on your horse's range of motion, flexibility, and overall ability to respond to each stretch. End the session with a loose-rein, relaxed walk, allowing your horse to move loosely throughout his body. See Chapter 3 for examples of stretches you can do while riding your horse.

▸ *Off-property ride*—Periodically arrange to ride at varying locations. Seek designated equine areas that allow schooling in fields, parks that provide trails, or beaches that allow riding. Riding off-property creates interest for and stimulates your horse.

2 Equine Nutrition

As more populations became less dependent on the horse for work and transportation and the horse became more of a companion animal, horses lost their place in the economy as a commodity. As a result, emerging large animal nutritional research focused on meat-producing animals such as cows and pigs. However, with increasing interest in horses for pleasure and especially for sport, equine nutritional research has finally come into its own. The research has produced a dizzying array of findings, some of which are contradictory, though some areas of consensus are emerging.

Although little research has been done on equine holistic nutrition, if one can generalize from the holistic studies done on humans and small animals, then it is safe to say that high-quality nutrition is essential for health—both physical and mental— affecting both the body and behavior.

EQUINE DIGESTIVE SYSTEM AND EATING HABITS

A general understanding of the horse's digestive system and eating habits is essential to any discussion of nutrition.

As it does for humans, the horse's digestive process begins in the mouth. The teeth are an essential part—the better the teeth, the better the chewing, and, therefore, the better the release of the food's nutritional value. It is important to provide your horse regular dental care, which should include filing or floating the teeth. Sharp points often develop on a confined (or mostly confined) horse's back teeth, where the food is ground, because eating hay and grain does not demand as strong and full a jaw sweep as grazing. These sharp points can render chewing inefficient and, as a consequence, lead to loss of nutritional value from food. Address overbite and underbite problems, which also affect how efficiently the food is utilized.

As the horse chews, his saliva mixes with the feed, moistening it to aid in swallowing. The muscles of the esophagus move the food into the stomach, where acids continue the digestive process. The small intestine is responsible for digesting most of the carbohydrates and fats and all of the amino acids (the end products of protein). The cecum breaks down remnants of undigested feed, especially long-stemmed fiber.

The Digestive System of a Horse

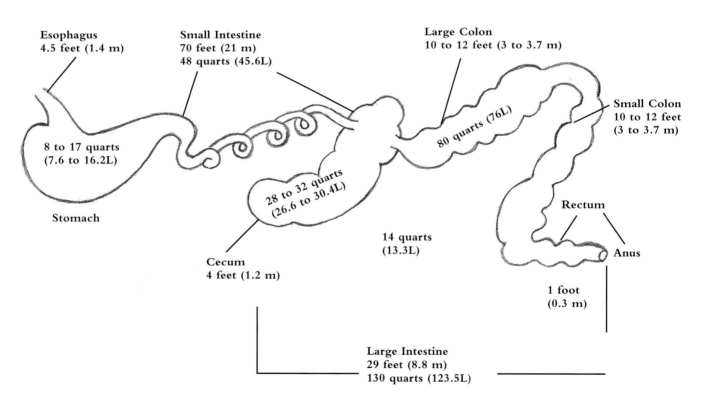

Esophagus
4.5 feet (1.4 m)

Small Intestine
70 feet (21 m)
48 quarts (45.6L)

Large Colon
10 to 12 feet (3 to 3.7 m)

Small Colon
10 to 12 feet
(3 to 3.7 m)

8 to 17 quarts
(7.6 to 16.2L)

80 quarts (76L)

Stomach

28 to 32 quarts
(26.6 to 30.4L)

Rectum

14 quarts
(13.3L)

Anus

Cecum
4 feet (1.2 m)

1 foot
(0.3 m)

Large Intestine
29 feet (8.8 m)
130 quarts (123.5L)

The practice of feeding horses twice a day only is a primary cause of digestive problems. In their natural state, horses eat small amounts of roughage all day long. This is due not only to their small stomachs but also to the function of the cecum. A steady stream of feed and fiber must be moving in and out of the cecum at all times. If the cecum sits partly empty for a time, waiting for the next feeding to introduce more fiber for processing, digestive problems such as colic can result.

In the wild, horses spend 18 or more hours a day grazing. Continuous grazing is crucial to proper stomach function. Proportionate to the horse's size, his stomach is small and can hold only a small amount of food. Horses are non-ruminant animals, so, unlike cows, they do not regurgitate. When horses overeat, they cannot vomit to relieve themselves and the stomach can rupture.

The digestive process is negatively affected by the stress of illness, confinement, performing in spite of pain, overvaccination, and too-frequent deworming.

Feeding Schedule

Five or six feedings or even more each day can help your horse's digestive tract work as nature intended. Constant pasture grazing is the ideal. The act of eating helps prevent boredom and keeps undesirable behaviors from developing. Your horse will thrive on a daily feeding routine that approximates the free-feeding pattern of the wild horse.

Grazing in the wild not only nourishes but also keeps horses on the move. Stimulation of the hoof and locomotion cause a horse's stomach to contract. When he stands in a stall all or most of the day, a horse's natural digestive processes are impaired.

Do not work, exercise, or ride your horse immediately before or after feeding. The horse's system needs time to digest the food, cool down, and relax. Exercising too quickly can result in digestive disorders such as colic.

Portion and Feed Adjustments

When feeding your horse, measure and feed by weight rather than volume. A certain volume of one type of feed provides different amounts of nutrients than the same volume of another type.

Horses have delicate digestive systems. Make any change in feeding—amount or type of feed—gradually and incrementally over several weeks. Otherwise, your horse risks colic, digestive problems, appetite fluctuation, and general loss of health.

During high exercise or work periods, your horse will need more and possibly different types of feed than during periods of low energy output. Feeding a nonworking horse the same amount of feed you give him during times of work can lead to health issues, one of which is *azoturia*. The quantity of food taken in by your horse should relate directly to his weight and current level of activity.

A diet healthful for one horse may not be for another. Variables such as age, present work level, health issues, lifestyle, and pregnancy affect dietary choices. The following examples illustrate how these variables affect dietary choices. *Note: These examples are not meant to prescribe. Each horse has his own dietary needs. Always consult your veterinarian when planning or changing your horse's diet.*

The Older Horse

Horses live longer than ever before—30 years or more. As horses age, factors such as decreased digestive efficiency, dental decline, decreased activity, and disease demand a change in diet.

Generally, an aged horse requires a high-protein, low-carbohydrate, high-fat diet featuring lots of easily digested fiber. Provide your older horse many small meals a day rather than the standard two. Older horses also need increased amounts of phosphorus in the diet and, therefore, increased calcium to keep the two minerals in correct proportion. Too much calcium can cause kidney stones, so it is wise not to oversupplement.

An alfalfa-grass mix is high in protein and balances overall alfalfa consumption, which can lead to problems. Old horses tolerate grains such as barley, rice, and oats well. They also do better with cracked and rolled rather than whole grains; these are more easily ingested and digested.

Fats and oils provide energy with less weight gain in a diet low in carbohydrates. High carbohydrates provide plenty of energy but can add unnecessary weight to the relatively inactive aged horse. Use vegetable oils or stabilized rice bran to provide fats and oils.

Roughage in the form of young, leafy hay with tender stems is ideal for the elder horse. Avoid mature, stemmy hay, which is hard for an old horse to ingest and digest. Feeding chopped or cubed hay may be a better option for senior horses. Whole flax seed is an excellent source of supplemental fiber as well a source of omega-3 fatty acids. Beet pulp can supplement fiber in the diet.

Dietary needs vary not only with age but also with health. If a horse has health issues involving the liver, kidney, or thyroid, for example, his diet should reflect this. For example, a high-protein diet is not advised for an older horse with a liver problem.

Always introduce changes in diet slowly over time. Never change your horse's diet without consulting your veterinarian, who can work with you to determine the best diet for your particular horse's needs.

Mares in Foal

The overall condition of the pregnant mare, proper nutrition for embryo survival, and adequate milk manufacture all rely on proper nutrition. Mares must be at a healthy weight to undergo the stress of pregnancy and, once expecting, the mare's system requires nutrients to support both mare and foal. Once the foal is born, the mare must be healthfully maintained so she can recuperate from pregnancy.

It is no longer considered a problem if a mare suddenly gains weight in the second trimester. Excessive weight gain overall is no longer considered unsafe for mare or foal.

The second trimester is crucial to fetal development. The mare must consume 2 to 2.25 percent of her body weight in feed daily to increase the fat reserves she needs for nursing.

Calcium and phosphorus levels and ratio are particularly important during pregnancy, as are selenium, manganese, copper, and zinc levels. Do not oversupplement in the first trimester; in fact, dumping a lot of vitamin and mineral supplements into your pregnant mare without proper understanding can harm rather than help by causing an imbalance in her system. Although vitamins and minerals are important, the ratio or balance between them is the crucial variable. Increased protein is also necessary.

Lactation

The greatest nutritional demands on a mare are made when she is nursing. Lactating mares need as much or more energy in their diet as hardworking performance horses. A lactating mare's energy needs increase overnight.

The nursing mare's energy needs are double what they were in her second trimester and three times what they were in the first. Her protein, vitamin, and mineral needs are at least 25 percent higher, too. Without sufficient calories in her diet, a lactating mare's hipbones and ribs may become visible. That indicates her body is breaking down its reserves to produce milk.

A mare's daily needs for water, high-quality grass hay and whole grains (approximately 3 percent of her body weight), protein, and vitamins and minerals increase substantially during lactation, but the increases must be made incrementally. Begin a week or so prior to foaling so the mare slowly builds up to lactating levels. Every few days, increase the amount of grain, and maintain that level for a few days before increasing again. This will avoid such complications as colic.

WEIGHT MANAGEMENT

Underweight

Underweight horses present with little or no energy, poor coat and skin quality, and obvious bony protrusions. Ribs, hips, and backbones are often quite visible. Horses may become underweight because (1) they are not being fed enough, or the quality of the feed is poor; (2) they have a metabolic disorder, parasite infestation, or dental problems; or (3) the demands on their bodies exceed their energy/caloric/nutritional intake during times of hard work, heavy exercise, or pregnancy. Fortunately, most of these problems can be fixed.

It can be hard to get a horse with a poor appetite to eat enough food to maintain his health. Poor appetite may be a sign of vitamin A deficiency. Feeding alfalfa hay can be an option, as it may appeal more than grass hay to your horse. You can also give your horse healthy treats such as carrots or apples, in sensible amounts. Tempt your horse by combining several types of feed; the variety allows your horse to choose what is appealing. Ask your veterinarian and an equine nutritionist for more ideas.

Sometimes a horse that normally eats well suddenly stops eating his feed. Reasons can vary: The horse may have an internal illness or condition, such as colic; an oral or dental problem, such as ulcers; or dislike a new feed. Evaluate all circumstances surrounding the change in appetite and contact your veterinarian.

Overweight

Obese horses are generally overfed in quantity or richness and often underexercised. They have a loss of muscle definition, large round barrels, and low endurance. The extra weight strains their hearts, joints, and limbs.

Avoid using sweeteners, such as molasses, simply because your horse likes the taste, as they may encourage him to eat more than he needs. Choose treats that are low in sugars, starches, and fructans, as these carbohydrates not only contribute to weight gain but also are implicated in colic and laminitis as well as insulin resistance—a rising trend in horses. Ask your veterinarian to test insulin levels and blood glucose, as a high insulin level or a low glucose-insulin ratio calls for a change of diet to ward off such problems as laminitis.

If your horse is overweight, purchase weight tapes from a supplier so you can estimate your horse's weight and monitor it (see chapter 1, page 14).

Reducing caloric intake and increasing activity help an overweight horse trim down. Do not, however, deprive your horse of food; very low food intake can cause a fatal secondary condition called *hyperlipemia*. This occurs when fat reserves enter the bloodstream rapidly, stressing the liver. Horses lack gall bladders, so the constant flow of bile released by the liver into the small intestine breaks down the fats. A compromised liver cannot break down fats and, therefore, cannot utilize them.

EQUINE DIETARY NEEDS

A holistic approach to equine health recognizes that the nutritional needs of every horse are unique. A horse's basic dietary needs are roughage (hay, pasture), concentrates (grains), and vitamin and mineral supplements.

It also recognizes that whole is better. Living, healthy plants and whole grains are the ideal for a horse, as they carry the energy meant to sustain life. Highly processed or extruded feeds lose this life force in the manufacturing process. The more processed the feed, the more likely necessary bacteria and enzymes are lost. Unless a horse's health or age necessitates extruded feeds, avoid them.

Hay

Consider the chemical herbicides and fertilizers used to grow hay you feed your horse. Unlike human food production, animal feed is not closely regulated. Toxins in feed adversely affect the natural bacterial environment in a horse's gut. If possible, have your horse's hay tested periodically for nutritive content and the presence of toxins.

Many factors affect the growth and production of hay and of hay quality itself. Examples include geographical region, rainfall, sunlight exposure, and soil fertility. Quality is also contingent on actual plant content and on when and how the hay is harvested.

Hay deprived of adequate water as it grows will be stunted. Overwatered hay may be exposed to diseases that destroy the leaves of the plant. Also, if hay is cut and baled while retaining too much liquid, mold will grow on it—and mold is poisonous to horses.

When evaluating hay for nutritive content, look for hay consisting of the following: young plants; high green-leaf content; a fresh, clean, scent; and little or no debris. Avoid hay that consists of mature plants and seeds with few leaves or leaves that are discolored and bleached, a musty mold odor, and debris.

TIP
Hay's Nutritional Value

If possible, get your hay tested for minerals, vitamins, and nutritional value. The concentrates and supplements you give your horse are meant to balance what he gets from his hay.

Feeding Hay

If your horse has plenty of grazing time on well-managed pastureland, his energy needs are being met. If you live where grazing is not possible, grazing land is poor, or winter weather cuts down grazing time, high-quality hay is essential.

Hay is the sole source of nutrition for some horses. In this case, feed your horse baled hay flakes (individual sections of hay that make up the bale) rather than hay cubes (compressed hay), as the cubes usually lack the long-stem fiber needed to keep the digestive tract working properly. Additionally, horses tend to eat cubes faster than they do traditional hay; eating quickly is detrimental to your horse's digestive system and gives him more time with nothing to do. Remember: A horse's life in the wild centers on eating, sleeping, and procreating, with the most time spent searching for and eating grasses.

Pasture Grass

Pasture is another form of roughage. Nutrients vary with the type of grass, time of year, and geographic regions. Research the pasture in your area through the local agricultural department so it can be cultivated to meet the proper nutrient level for your horse.

As grass matures, its nutrient content decreases. Generally, you want a pasture that is a mix of grasses and legumes. Consider whether the pasture is used for grazing only or for riding as well. Some types of grass are more durable than others.

Whole foods are the best source of necessary vitamins and minerals for your horse. When hay is cut, it loses nutritional value; living plants are far superior. If you maintain your pastureland properly, it will provide the essential nutrients.

Remove manure consistently to reduce the parasite population. However, properly applied composted manure, along with other organic byproducts, enhances the soil quality of grazing lands by increasing organic content, improving moisture-holding capacity, and supplying valuable nutrients. Dragging your fields and properly composting the manure for pasture enrichment is a much eco-friendlier and less expensive approach to pasture cultivation than clearing the land and hauling away the manure.

If you live in a climate that experiences spring and its rich new-grass growth, monitor your horse's intake, as overeating this grass can cause colic and founder.

If your horse is new to grazing on pasture, allow him to eat for a short period only; feed hay to supplement. Gradually increase the allotted grazing time until eventually the horse can graze freely throughout the day. Observe your horse's stool. If the manure is loose, he may be eating too much grass. Manure should be well formed and ball-shaped.

Several Types of Feed Hay: (A) Alfalfa; (B) Timothy; (C) Canadian

Above all, do not use toxic chemicals to manage your pastureland.

Forage, especially organically grown forage, is much more nutritionally balanced than stable diets of oats and cut hay or forage grasses grown on soil that has not been nurtured properly. Good pasture must be properly cultivated and managed.

If the pasture is never allowed to rest, it will become depleted and fail. Allow your horse to graze in particular sections of pasture so you can rest other areas. Weed control, irrigation, rotation, drainage, altitude, pest control, and parasite control are all vital to maintaining a nutrient-rich, prosperous pasture. Mowing the land encourages fresh growth and aids in the removal of undesirable plants.

TIP

Planning Pasture Size

Calculate the amount of pasture needed for the number of horses that will be grazing on it. Allow approximately 1 acre (0.4 ha) per horse.

Process for Soil Enrichment

Soil Sampling Procedures

Performing a soil test is the first step to a successful organic fertilization program. Here's how to do it. Check with your local lab for more specific instructions or variations in collecting samples. Tell the lab the land is being tested to prepare it for equine forage. Universities with agricultural programs are resourced for soil testing.

1. Test the soil (see below) to determine what you are dealing with chemically. Take random samples throughout the fields, ideally 12 to 15 per acre (0.4 ha).

2. Send the soil sample to a commercial lab. Many universities have testing labs.

3. Your next move depends on the results. Most properties need liming. A pH range of 6.5 to 6.8 is needed. The type of lime you need depends on the pH reading. Most kinds are low in calcium and high in magnesium (dolomic lime). For pasture-lands, just the opposite is needed: soil high in calcium and low in magnesium (calcidic lime). The balance affects a horse's nutrition.

4. Apply organic fertilizers. Because composted manure doesn't supply enough nitrogen, organic fertilizers are needed to supply this vital nutrient. Your horse can eat immediately after the application of the fertilizers, provided they are organic.

5. Spread the composted manure; top-dress at ¼" to ½" (0.6 to 1.3 cm). (Often, horse owners pay good money to have manure trucked off the farm, then pay good money to get it back in composted form.) On average, one horse provides 50 pounds

(23 kg) of manure per day. Be sure the composting area is away from water or an area that might be washed away by rain. Though it takes work to set up a system for composting, which involves turning and aging the manure, the effort is well worth it.

6. Check the amount of organic matter (this is part of the post-testing). It should read at 5 percent. Organic matter holds the nutrients for the plants, especially important in sandy soil, which doesn't hold nutrients as, for example, clay soil does.

7. Use the appropriate pasture seed mix. Red clover, for example, is not good for horses, whereas it is for cows. Horses need white clover. Orchard grass from New Zealand (Pekapo) is desirable, along with Festolium. Do not plant rye or fescue; these are good for residential lawns because they control surface-feeding insects, but they can make a horse ill and even sterile.

8. Irrigate well initially. This encourages a strong root system. The organic approach strives to achieve this strong root system, which in turn yields a drought-tolerant pasture.

9. Periodically submit samples of the pasture forage for analysis. Track the progress of the plants to assure adequate amounts of protein and minerals in the feed. Forage quality varies widely due to variations in genotype, maturity, season, management, and anti-quality components. Because of all these factors and their interactions, static tables of forage quality and nutritive value are unlikely to provide complete or useful information about particular forage.

Concentrates

Concentrates are feeds that have been reduced in volume and made pure, resulting in an elevated energy level and a reduced fiber level in comparison to roughage. These feeds consist of various types of grains. Many horses are fed a grain ration; however, not every horse needs it. Hay quality, hay nutrient content, and your horse's age, condition, and work program determine whether or not he requires grain in his diet.

Grain Concentrates

▸ *Corn*—Corn is high in carbohydrates and, therefore, a high-energy food. It is unique in that it contains vitamin A. Corn is low in protein and amino acids. High-quality corn feed has a pleasant aroma and is free of mold. The individual corn kernels should not be broken and should be distinctly separate. Variations of feed corn include cracked corn and rolled corn. These types are easier to digest.

TIP

Corn Poisoning

When feeding corn, beware of a toxin produced by a fungus called *fumonisin*. This toxin can cause a condition referred to as *moldy corn poisoning* (equine leukoencephalomalacia). Always check for findings of fumonisin in the area where the corn is grown.

Horses afflicted with this poisoning present with lack of coordination, suppressed appetite, and uneasiness, and usually die within 24 hours. There is no antidote for this poisoning, though gastrointestinal protectants such as activated charcoal and/or laxatives may be administered to assist with the elimination of the toxin. Fluids and dextrose may be given to supply hydration and energy to the ailing horse. Be sure to remove contaminated feed from all other animals.

► *Oats*—Oats are higher in fiber than other grains, and they appeal to most horses. Oats tend to keep well. High-quality oats are primarily intact, lustrous kernels, with minimal husks, free of dust and debris, and fresh-smelling. Weight measurement is an important factor; more nutrients are present in heavier oats. Oats with a low ratio of husks to kernels weigh more than oats with a higher ratio of husks to kernels. The more intact kernels are present, the more nutrient content per unit of weight.

Oats are available in several forms, including whole, crimped, rolled, and crushed. They are more easily digested when not eaten whole; however, the nutrient content of broken oats decreases over time. Oats contain a higher level of phosphorus than calcium. Therefore, they should be supplemented with hay that is abundant in calcium.

► *Barley*—Barley has less fiber content than oats. It is fed in processed form, either crimped or rolled. It should smell clean and have a fresh color. It is often used in place of oats because it offers a higher level of energy mass per unit of volume. Barley is usually fed combined with other grains, as it tends to be dusty.

► *Milo*—Milo is classified as a heavy feed, so it should not be fed alone but rather combined with a substantial feed, meaning a bulky feed, such as oats, to help digestion. Milo is usually processed so the horse can chew it more easily. It is a high-energy grain.

Other Concentrates

► *Beet pulp*—Beet pulp is a source of high energy, roughage, and calcium. In general, avoid beet pulp with added molasses. Feed beet pulp to horses who struggle to maintain their weight. For some, molasses may be necessary to encourage eating.

► *Molasses*—Molasses is a common ingredient in many feeds because it is inexpensive and reduces dust content in grains. It is also used to increase the palatability and energy density of the diet without increasing the volume of feed. However, unless you need to make feed palatable for a horse that is not eating or you need to raise a horse's energy level without increasing his feed, avoid molasses. As is true of all soluble carbohydrates, lots of molasses can cause hyperactivity, colic, and laminitis.

► *Fats and oils*—Fats and oils are used for energy and dust reduction, and they help in maintaining weight on horses that are underweight (so-called hard keepers). Reminder: Horses do not have gallbladders; oils and fats are processed in the intestinal ducts, affecting the absorption of vitamins A, K, E, and D. This, in turn, can affect calcium levels, leading to joint problems. Do not use animal fats. Some studies find soybean oil better than corn oil for horses in training, possibly because of its higher omega-3 fatty-acid content. Essential fatty acids are important in a horse's diet; flax oil is an excellent source. Consult your veterinarian before feeding fats and oils, or try an alternative approach, such as whole flax seed or beet pulp.

Supplements

Supplements provide nourishment to your horse beyond that in the feed. They are divided into four categories: vitamins, minerals, protein (amino acids), and a blend of these three. Your geographic region may be known for certain deficiencies. Your local agricultural agency and your veterinarian can determine if a horse needs supplementation.

Vitamins

Vitamins are a group of organic substances essential in small quantities for normal metabolism. A healthy equine digestive system and a nutritious diet should meet the horse's vitamin requirements. Unfortunately, the digestive system of many horses is not healthy. Giving these horses supplemental vitamins is not the whole answer because an unhealthy digestive system will not utilize them properly.

The goal is to strengthen and maintain the bacterial and enzymatic environment in the horse's intestinal tract. Giving your horse probiotics is one way to begin the process. Stress reduction and a healthful diet go a long way in maintaining the bacterial health of the intestinal tract.

Vitamins are divided into two categories: water-soluble (vitamin C and the B group) and fat-soluble (vitamins A, D, E, and K). Water-soluble vitamins are not stored in the horse's system; therefore, your horse must manufacture them or receive a supplement daily. Fat-soluble vitamins are stored in the fat cells and in the liver; serious complications can arise if excessive amounts are stored. Horses get vitamins from their food and manufacture them within their bodies. As a result, they commonly do not lack vitamins. Horse owners often administer vitamins to their animals, thinking they are deficient; however, too much vitamin content in the system can be harmful.

TIP

Equine Supplementation

Discuss all supplementation with your veterinarian. The popularity of equine supplements has grown tremendously over the past several years. However, the effectiveness of some supplements is still controversial. The decision to supplement or not should be well thought out and informed. If you decide to add a supplement to your horse's diet, track your daily observations. Include the date the supplement was first introduced, and date all observations. This will help you decide whether to continue using or to terminate the product. Always follow the manufacturer's instructions and keep your veterinarian up to date with your supplementation program.

Several Types of Grain: (A) high-fiber pellet; (B) extruded feed; (C) low-protein pellet; (D) hay-replacement pellet

Several Types of Equine Supplements: (A) Chondroitin; (B) Glucosamine; (C) Yucca; (D) Methylsulfonylmethane

▶ *Vitamin A*—This vitamin is stored in your horse's liver. Therefore, if the horse is being fed high-quality forage, he should have a sufficient amount in his system. The cells that line the tissues of your horse's body, including the eyes, skin, and respiratory system, are kept healthy by vitamin A. Both vitamin A deficiency and excess create serious health problems for your horse. Night blindness, inhibited hoof growth, poor hair and coat, open skin wounds, and respiratory infections are all signs of a deficiency. Brittle bones or abnormal thickening of bone tissue can be signs of excess. Sources of vitamin A include fresh, green forage and fish oils, should your veterinarian decide your horse needs supplementation.

▶ *Vitamin B*—The 10 vitamins in this group are called *B-complex vitamins.* Horses produce B vitamins in their colon, and they are also present in high-quality feed. Horses that are fed poor-quality feed or are experiencing severe anxiety may require supplementation. Signs of B-vitamin deficiency include decreased appetite, anemia, and poor attitude. Vitamin B can be administered by injection or by adding brewers yeast to the feed.

▶ *Vitamin C*—Horses produce vitamin C in the liver. Neither deficiency nor excessiveness has been recorded in horses. The benefits of this vitamin to horses are not established.

▶ *Vitamin D*—Vitamin D, a fat-soluble vitamin, comprises vitamins D2 and D3. It is found in sun-dried roughage and is produced in the body when the sun's ultraviolet rays convert a compound found in the skin into vitamin D. If your horse is not exposed to sunlight or receives poor-quality feed, he may be lacking this vitamin. Consult with your veterinarian before supplementing, as elevated levels can lead to calcium deposits in soft tissue, leading to deterioration of heart, muscle, and kidney function.

▶ *Vitamin E*—Not much information is available about a horse's need for this fat-soluble vitamin. Current wisdom links it to muscle function. As a result, it is often administered to horses with azoturia. Sources of vitamin E include wheat germ oil, hay, and green plants.

▶ *Vitamin K*—Vitamin K is required in blood coagulation or clotting, so a deficiency results in the failure of blood to clot when an injury occurs. Too much vitamin K can cause blood cells to rupture. Requirements for vitamin K in horses are not well documented. Sources include green feeds and natural production in a horse's colon.

Minerals

Minerals are inorganic elements necessary for proper bodily function. They are divided into two categories: macro (including sodium, calcium, and potassium) and micro (including iron, iodine, and selenium). Mineral ingestion must be monitored closely, as too much or too little can lead to stunted growth, appetite loss, muscle breakdown, collapse, and death.

Soil quality and feed quality play a vital role in mineral supply. An imbalance may be due not to the horse's diet but his inability to absorb certain minerals. Also, deficiency in one mineral affects another, as minerals work together.

Some holistic veterinarians suggest that horses be given free-choice minerals. This is based on anecdotal evidence that horses know what they need and adjust their intake accordingly.

Macro Minerals

▸ *Sodium*—Sodium (or salt) is vital to muscle motion, fluid regulation, nerve action, and acidic balance. Actual salt requirements vary according to each horse and his environment. Horses lose sodium through perspiration; therefore, they should be given free-choice salt, offered in block or loose granular form. Horses naturally seek and ingest the proper amount, unless they are highly deficient in it or are not provided proper hydration (water). If a horse does experience a salt overdose, it may present with loose stool, loss of movement in the hind limbs, colic, and excessive urination. Signs of deficiency include poor hair coat, decreased milk production, loss of appetite, and retarded growth.

▸ *Calcium*—Calcium is vital for skeletal (bone) health. Requirements vary according to the age and state of the horse. For example, younger horses need extra calcium because they are growing and developing, older horses because they retain less, and pregnant mares because their systems need extra support. Calcium deficiency can inhibit bone growth, while excess can cause bones to become fragile.

▸ *Potassium*—Potassium is an electrolyte. It is linked to many bodily functions. Lack of potassium can result in muscle fatigue because this mineral is needed for nerve-muscle contraction. Low potassium levels can contribute to muscle loss.

Micro (Trace) Minerals

▸ *Iron*—Iron is found in the red blood cells of horses. It is vital to biological processes. Iron deficiency is rarely a problem for horses. If your horse is tested and found to be anemic, an iron supplement may be necessary. Symptoms of iron deficiency include lethargy. Excessive iron in foals can be fatal. Iron is an essential component in hemoglobin; it gives blood its red pigment and supports its job of transporting oxygen throughout the body.

▸ *Iodine*—Iodine, found in the thyroid gland, is necessary in the production of certain hormones. Iodine deficiency results in thyroid gland enlargement. The gland attempts to capture more iodine for thyroid hormone production, forming a goiter. The condition is resolved by feeding iodized salt. Both low and high iodine levels present with goiters, hairless foals, deceased foaling.

▸ *Selenium*—Selenium is involved with antioxidant production and thyroid hormone levels and is necessary for proper metabolism. Selenium is included in high-quality feed. Deficiency appears only when vitamin E is lacking. Grains, brewers yeast, and wheat germ are all sources of selenium. Signs of deficiency include breakdown of muscle tissue, impairment in breathing, loss of strength, and inability to swallow efficiently. Excessive selenium levels present with loss of vision, hair loss in mane and tail, hoofs shedding, and inability to move.

Water

Horses consume 8 to 20 gallons (30 to 76L) of water per day. Water intake varies according to weather conditions, exercise program, pregnancy, and dry-matter ingestion. Horses should have access to clean water at all times, with one exception: Do not allow a horse that is hot, having just come in from exercise, large quantities of water. This can lead to laminitis. Give horses that have just been worked small amounts of water until they have cooled thoroughly.

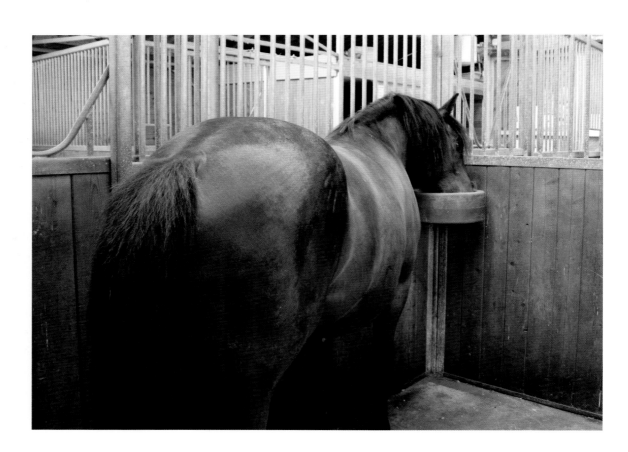

New automatic watering systems for stables, paddocks, and pastures allow your horse to drink fresh, clean water on demand. If using buckets, clean them daily to keep them free of debris and fungus. Have your water tested, as in some barns the water source is not safe for people. Horses should drink water of the same quality humans do. If necessary, buy a filter or invest in a filtering system.

Large paddock buckets must be drained and cleaned to prevent the formation of algae. Blue-green algae is toxic to horses. It can cause labored breathing, stomach pain, and liver problems. Strategically place water containers in paddocks. Do not place them in a corner, where other horses can box your horse in, possibly leading to injury. Never separate a water bucket with a fence; your horse could become entangled in the fencing when attempting to drink. Last, do not place water buckets under trees or plants. Debris from the trees and plants will drop or blow into the water and contaminate it.

Isolate standing water in your horse's turn-out area so your horse does not have access to it. Standing water is a breeding area for fungus, bacteria, disease, and insects.

In cold climates, check water periodically throughout the day as it will freeze, preventing your horse from drinking. Be sure no sharp edges of broken ice are left that can injure or cut your horse. Many horses will not drink very cold water, so you may need to provide lukewarm water in bitter weather. If your horse is not drinking enough water, he may not be getting enough salt in his diet. Signs of dehydration include decrease in or loss of appetite, weight, and skin elasticity.

Fats/Carbohydrates

Energy is supplied to your horse through fats and carbohydrates. The amount of energy your particular horse needs depends on his condition, work program, and daily living conditions. Factors in determining energy needs include exercise, reproductive cycle, and stage of development. A working horse needs more energy than one that doesn't. Stallions and mares require increased levels of energy during breeding season. Mares that are nursing require a high energy intake; their need may be double as they produce milk and recover body weight. Horses that are developing require energy to support the growth process; however, overfeeding can negatively affect the young horse's skeletal and digestive systems. It is important to monitor the youngster's development closely. If your horse is overweight or underweight, or hyperactive or lethargic, change his diet by adjusting the amount of fat and carbohydrates.

Protein

Protein (amino acids) is essential for a horse to develop, grow, form skin and hair, maintain healthy hooves, build muscles, and repair bodily tissues. Amount and quality of protein are vital. High-quality hay and grain, fed consistently, meet the protein requirements of the average horse. Increased water consumptions is a sign of excessive protein intake. Protein deficiency results in poor hair/coat, poor hoof growth, and loss of muscle.

Treats

Feed healthful treats to your horse, all in moderation: carrots, apples, fruits, vegetables, and homemade natural treats. Err on the side of vegetables; feed fruit in moderation, as it is high in natural sugars. Avoid candy and sugar.

When giving your horse a treat, place it in his feed bin rather than feeding by hand, as you can quickly create a biter. The horse will learn to nip at your hands or clothes searching for a treat.

Be sure to discuss your choices with your veterinarian. If your horse is prone to allergies, founder, or colic, do not vary his diet. Options that provide antioxidants include bananas, mango, broccoli, green beans, sweet potatoes, and wheat germ oil. Wash all produce thoroughly to remove pesticides. Give all treats in small amounts and in moderation.

It is best to feed treats at the end of your visit with your horse. If you feed treats the moment you see your horse, he may become, greedy, distracted, and unruly. You do not want your horse's focus to be treat obsession.

HEALTHFUL AND TOXIC PLANTS

Beneficial Plants

Horses in the wild instinctively know what they need when they are sick or infirm, so you would be wise to provide free-choice opportunities for each individual horse to heal and maintain health.

Some healthful plants you can grow around the barn and along fence lines are chamomile, comfrey, rosemary, marjoram, dill, thyme, sage, marjoram, parsley, mint, nettle, sorrel, rosehips, dandelion (not the common variety), fennel, sorrel, and oats.

Poisonous Plants

Literally hundreds of plants are toxic to your horse. These vary from region to region. Educate yourself about toxic plants in your area. Obtain a current list of regional toxic plants from your local agricultural society. Constantly check your pastures and hay for toxic plants. By recognizing them, you can remove them before your horse has a chance to ingest them. These plants may grow in your pasture, be baled into your feed hay, or be part of a decorative presentation. They can spread into your field from adjoining properties.

If there are poisonous trees in the area that cannot be removed, be sure to isolate them properly so your horse cannot get near them. Check your property after windy weather or storms, as branches and leaves may blow into areas where your horses can eat them. If you find a poisonous plant, dig it up, taking care to remove its root system. Check the area thoroughly for other plants. Treat the property with an animal-safe herbicide to remove further growth. If you want to turn out your horse into a new or unfamiliar pasture, check the property before placing the horse in the area.

While amounts of toxic plant material intake vary according to plant, as little as 1 pound (0.45 kg) of certain species can be lethal to a horse. Signs of poisoning include loss of coordination, difficulty breathing, muscle spasms, diarrhea, constipation, elevated pulse, excessive thirst, excessive urination, drooling, sweating, dilation of pupils, abdominal discomfort, blistering of skin, and collapse. If you suspect your horse has ingested a toxic plant, contact your veterinarian immediately.

TIP

Vinegar as Weed Killer

Vinegar is an inexpensive, environmentally safe means of killing weeds. Pour undiluted household vinegar in a spray bottle and saturate the weeds. Seedlings less than two weeks old will be killed entirely; older weeds will have their top-growth killed but not the roots, so they will regrow.

TOXIC PLANTS

The following is a list of common toxic plants found in the Unites States. It is wise to research which plants are common to your region or country. Please read through this list carefully, and view each image so you can familiarize yourself with these plants. Prevention is the key when discussing plant toxicity.

American yew (*Taxis canadensis*)

Bracken fern (*Pteridium aquilinum*)

Black walnut (*Juglars nigra*)

Oak tree (*Quecus petraea*)

Red maple (*Acer freemanii*)

St. John's wort (*Hypericum perforatum*)

Oleander (*Nerium oleander*)

Patterson's curse (*Echium plantagineum*)

Rayless goldenrod (*Solidago* spp.)

Avocado (*Persea gratissma*)

Larkspur (*Delphinium menziesii*)

List of Toxic Plants

Note: The treatment regimens listed here are for general information only. A veterinarian should always be consulted when treating for toxic plant poisoning.

Bracken fern (*Pteridium aquilinum*)

The bracken fern is found worldwide in pastures, forests, and fields. This green plant with triangular leaves averages 2 to 3 feet (0.6 to 0.9 m) in height. The fern may be the only green plant available in a forest or pasture in early spring or late fall.

Toxic element: Thiaminase

Information: Horses usually ingest this plant when grazing or mixed in with feed hay. Thiaminase reduces thiamine, which helps the functioning of your horse's nervous system. After four to eight weeks of consistent ingestion, the horse may drop weight and lose the ability to coordinate his body, resulting in an arched neck and feet spread widely apart. The horse pushes his head into objects and staggers. The horse may go down and be unable to get back up. This poisoning is fatal if not treated immediately.

Treatment: Administering vitamin B1 (thiamine) in horses is highly effective if diagnosis is made early. All horses that have been exposed to the bracken fern (even if not yet presenting with symptoms), should be given vitamin B1 as they can develop signs days or weeks after removal from the source of the bracken fern.

Oak tree (*Quecus petraea*)

The oak tree is found throughout North America.

Toxic element: Gallotannin

Information: Horses usually ingest the leaves or acorns of the tree while grazing. Horses present with abdominal pain and constipation, followed by diarrhea (occasionally bloody), excessive urination, general weakness, and increased pulse rate.

Treatment: The horse should be removed from the tree immediately and administered activated charcoal and fluids to treat dehydration and acidosis.

St. John's wort (*Hypericum perforatum*)

St. John's wort is commonly found in depleted areas where soil is not fertile. Pastures that have been overgrazed and property that has not been managed are ideal places for this plant to grow.

Toxic element: Hypericin

Information: Hypericin, the toxic element, is triggered by a light source (the sun), resulting in a chemical sunburn, usually within 24 hours after the plant is eaten, on unpigmented skin patches. Excessive itching and ulceration of the skin can cause permanent damage.

Treatment: Horses that present with symptoms of photosensitization must be moved out of sunlight and into areas of shade. Your veterinarian may administer antibiotics and an analgesic for peeling skin. (See Chapter 8 for herbal and essential oils treatments for skin therapies and pain management techniques.)

American yew (*Taxis canadensis*)

The American yew plant can be found in the northeastern and north-central regions of the United States.

Toxic element: Taxine

Information: This highly toxic plant is often used in landscaping. Taxine, the toxic element in the plant, interferes with the electrical current of the heart muscle. This causes the horse to experience muscle tremors and collapse. This poisoning is fatal.

Treatment: not available

Black walnut (*Juglars nigra*)

The black walnut tree is found in Canada and the northeastern United States.

Toxic element: Unknown

Information: The shavings from this tree might be accidentally mixed in with your horse's bedding. Ingesting low quantities can produce poisoning. Symptoms usually appear soon after the horse is exposed to the bedding. They include loss of appetite, fluid build-up in the legs, laminitis, lethargy, fever, and colic.

Treatment: Remove shavings from your horse's stall. Your veterinarian may administer analgesics to reduce pain and swelling. Bathe your horse's legs to reduce any further absorption of toxin and stand him in a cold-water bath to reduce inflammation and pain.

Red maple (*Acer freemanii*)

The red maple tree is often used ornamentally for landscaping property in Canada and the eastern United States.

Toxic element: Unknown

Information: The leaf of the tree is highly toxic and can kill your horse. Red blood cells are damaged, causing oxygen deficiency in the bloodstream. Horses' mouths and eyes become dark, and they no longer want to eat. Urine may become discolored, and the horse may suffer abdominal discomfort. The horse can die within hours of ingestion.

Treatment: Large quantities of intravenous fluids and possibly blood transfusions are treatment options.

Oleander (*Nerium oleander*)

Oleander can be found in the southern United States. It is used in landscaping.

Toxic element: Cardiac glycosides

Information: Horses usually ingest this plant when branches fall into their paddock or if they are able to reach the leaves on the tree branches. This plant possesses a toxic cardiac glycoside that can cause

colic, loss of coordination, labored breathing, excessive perspiring, muscle tremors, and cardiac failure.
Treatment: If caught early, horses can be given activated charcoal to inhibit further toxin absorption and anti-arrhythmic drugs to aid in stabilizing the heart muscle.

Patterson's curse (*Echium plantagineum*)
Patterson's curse can be found throughout the southern United States.
Toxic element: Pyrrolizidine alkaloids
Information: This plant is sometimes inadvertently mixed in with feed hay. The toxic elements can cause liver failure. Weight loss, lethargy, jaundiced membranes, and neurological problems are all signs of this poisoning.
Treatment: If poisoning is recognized early, removing the source may lead to a full recovery. It is important to implement a diet that will aid in the liver's recovery. Advanced stages of recovery involve continuous monitoring of condition, and possible admission to an equine hospital.

Rayless goldenrod (*Solidago* spp.)
Rayless goldenrod can be found in southern Colorado, western Texas, New Mexico, Arizona, and northern Mexico.
Toxic element: Trematol
Information: Poisonings usually take place in summer and fall. Ingesting this plant can be fatal. Symptoms of poisoning include muscle weakness, cardiac arrhythmias, trembling (indicates swelling of the nervous system), and excessive sweating.
Treatment: There is no treatment for this poisoning. Your veterinarian may choose to administer drug therapy including purgatives, smooth muscle stimulants, and activated charcoal to alleviate symptoms.

Avocado (*Persea gratissma*)
Avocados are found in California and Florida.
Toxic element: Persin
Information: Horses usually ingest this toxic plant when grazing and exposed to the branches, leaves, or fruit. Mares are primarily affected, presenting with mastitis and colic.
Treatment: Your veterinarian may administer anti-inflammatories, diuretics, and antibiotics to control infections of the mammary gland.

Larkspur (*Delphinium menziesii*)
Larkspur can be found west of the Mississippi River.
Toxic element: Diterpene alkaloids
Information: Horses may ingest this plant if minimal vegetation is available. The toxic elements in the plant cause neuromuscular paralysis. Signs of poisoning include general weakness, excessive salivation, muscle tremors, colic, and convulsions. Heart failure or respiratory distress can occur, resulting in death.
Treatment: Your veterinarian may administer drug therapy that may reverse some of the effects of the poisoning. Anti-bloat medications and medications that reverse neuromuscular paralysis can be helpful. Recovery and survival depend on the amount of larkspur ingested.

3

Equine Exercise

Horses are meant to move and roam. Long periods of confinement in a stall or paddock undermine all aspects of health. Horses need to be exercised consistently, safely, and moderately. The more consistently your horse is exercised, the more fit he becomes. Consistency is not to be confused with quantity. Hours of strenuous work drains him not only physically but also emotionally and mentally. Horses that can exercise strenuously are horses whose stamina has been built up slowly, step by step, over time.

The caliber of work will vary according to your horse's age, condition, lifestyle, and career. For example, a horse in training for strenuous competition will exercise differently from a horse used for light trail riding.

Each horse will benefit from an exercise program tailored to his needs. An elderly horse may have some limitations, but some exercise is better than no exercise. Physical fitness in horses varies just as it does in humans. You want your horse to be physically fit no matter his career or age.

BENEFITS OF EXERCISE

Exercise Builds and Strengthens the Human-Equine Relationship

Exercise can be an important ingredient in equine-human relationships. It determines who the dominant personality is, who has the most tenacity, and what kind of work ethic exists between the horse and the human.

If your horse controls the sessions and ignores your requests, you may need to seek professional assistance from a trainer or instructor. Horses, being such large creatures, must respond to their owner's requests for safety's sake. On the other hand, if you are harsh or unkind toward your horse, you will either create an animal that is fearful and timid, losing its own spirit and identity, or an angry, aggressive horse that protests and defies you, trying to preserve its existence.

A well-thought-out exercise program helps both horse and human understand how the other thinks and operates. Exercise provides a working element to the bond between you and your horse. Many horses behave one way on the ground and an entirely different way when asked to work.

Working together is uplifting for you and your horse. Exercise sessions allow the horse to burn off energy, receive reward, and condition his body. They allow you to strengthen your leadership skills, use and strengthen your body, hone your creativity, sharpen your focus, and emotionally retreat from outside stressors. How wonderful to see a rider praising her horse as he arches his neck and holds up his ears proudly—horse and rider both smiling!

Exercise Strengthens the Body

Exercise has important physical benefits. It builds muscle, strengthens the heart and lungs, builds endurance, and increases stamina. It stimulates the body by increasing circulation and elevating the endorphin level in the horse's system. Exercise activates the mind, keeping it sharp and aware. If your horse is not exercised, his physical state suffers, leading to emotional and mental loss as well. Many horses are brightest and most content when working.

Exercise Activates the Mind

Exercise allows the horse a change of scenery, a purpose, and awareness of his own physical capabilities. It challenges his mind, forcing it to focus. The more the mind is active, the more able it becomes.

PLANNING AN EXERCISE PROGRAM

Be aware of these points when designing and using an exercise plan.

Assess and Monitor Fitness

Before you begin the exercise program, assess your horse's overall health, looking for healthy horse signs and becoming familiar with his vital signs. Refer to Chapter 1 to determine and implement a realistic and suitable exercise program. Obtain your horse's history from a previous owner, if possible, so you have a better sense of his fitness level.

Physical appearance can be telling. A horse that is generally fit has solid muscle definition, proper weight, an alert demeanor, and bright eyes. He does not perspire excessively nor become terribly winded after exercise.

Monitor your horse's vital signs, including temperature, pulse rate, and respiration, after an exercise session. Compare them to the horse's normal readings to determine his physical fitness level (refer to Chapter 1, page 14).

A horse that has walked and trotted for several minutes generally has a pulse of 60–80 beats per minute. As the work increases, the pulse rate elevates. However, after ten minutes the rate should begin to decrease and after approximately twenty minutes return to 60–80 beats per minute. If your horse's pulse rate has not decreased sufficiently after twenty minutes, he may not be ready to work at the level you are requesting.

Respiration levels should average two or three heartbeats to one complete inhalation and exhalation. If your horse is taking one breath for each heartbeat, it is a sign his body has been overly taxed. Consult with your veterinarian.

Your horse's temperature may increase to approximately 106°F (41°C) after he has been exercised. However, temperature, pulse rate, and respiratory rates should all return to normal within one hour after exercise. If they don't, contact your veterinarian. As you continue your horse's fitness schedule, his pulse rate should reach 100 beats per minute to aid in strengthening heart and lungs. As his fitness level improves, this pulse rate may be increased to 160 beats per minute.

Create an Ideal Environment

Ideally, you want to create an environment that is safe, social, and stimulating for your horse. If your horse feels he is in danger, alone, or just bored, he will not be happy.

Horses enjoy routine; it gives them a sense of security. Your horse will welcome daily scheduled exercise. Horses are intelligent, observant beings and learn routines quickly. If the times of daily care such as feedings and turn-outs are fairly consistent, your horse soon adapts, and his internal clock will let him know when he will be turned out or brought in and when he will eat or exercise. He might even remind you when it is time for regularly scheduled activities by vocalizing.

Schedule Exercise Sessions

If feasible, plan your sessions at a time when distractions are minimal and your energy and focus are optimal for the work. If you are exhausted, numerous other riders are in the arena, or your horse is hungry because it is feeding time, your session may not go well. In reality, some days you will have to work in less than ideal conditions, but try not to make excuses and discontinue the session. You and your horse should be able to adapt to the circumstances. You both must learn to be comfortable and to work in a chaotic environment. The only way to achieve this is by practice.

Be sure to schedule one day of rest each week for your horse. The rest day may include a hand walk, a day of ground stretching, or a light hack around the property, asking for nothing more than quiet exploration time from your horse. This day of rest and relaxation is just as important as the days of exercise. It allows your horse to rejuvenate and strengthens the relationship between the two of you. It is time shared that requires nothing more than companionship.

The important thing is the consistency of the exercise program, not how long or how hard it is.

Create Routine Beginnings and Endings

You and your horse need mental and physical time to warm up and prepare for an exercise session as well as time to settle and relax at the end of one. Begin each session with a routine, and always end with praise.

For example, when you mount your horse at he beginning of a session, pat him on the neck and tell him what a good horse he is. Next, ask him to stretch his head and neck to the right and left several times before you begin the actual exercise. At the end of the session, after you have cooled your horse properly, ask him to halt and then to back up several steps.

Set the Mood

When you begin to exercise your horse, do so in a positive, clear manner. If you are negative, harsh, or overly demanding, your horse will not respond honestly and intently. Conversely, if you do not send firm, concise signals to your horse, and if you allow him to do whatever he wants, he will not progress.

Your horse's exercise program must be realistic, incremental, simple, clear, and varied, and it should reflect your long-term and short-term goals. Focus

on the small achievements made each day. This positive attitude will transmit to your horse and allow for progress. If you work the horse continuously, never resting it and never interacting using touch and voice, you will create an animal that has no interest in seeing you, feels no love for you, has no want to please you, and will most likely become resentful and angry toward you.

An equine exercise program should be divided into three phases: beginning, intermediate, and maintenance. Raise the level of performance requests on your horse incrementally.

Think of exercising as you and your horse sharing together-time in a positive, beneficial way. Obviously, you and your horse are living, breathing beings that experience changes in mood and energy levels each day, so sessions will vary. Certainly, some exercise sessions will not go as well as you would like. Although those sessions will undoubtedly occur, you must focus on moving on.

Develop an Effective Tone of Voice

Use a light, positive, encouraging tone when asking your horse to do something, praising him because he has responded correctly, and encouraging him when he has at least made an effort to do so. A firm, deep tone should be used when making a correction. Absence of voice can also offer correction as your horse begins to associate positive vocal praise with success and no response as an indication that his attempt was not successful.

Make Adjustments

If your horse is having difficulty focusing or performing one day, adjust the session. Go back to something he is confirmed in doing and review that for a bit before moving to the task of the day. You may want to reschedule the task to the following day. Let's say you are asking your horse to perform lateral movements one day but notice that his head, neck, or hip is stiff. You might do mounted stretching exercises to loosen those body parts before asking again for the lateral work. If you see your horse is still not up to the task, then reschedule the lateral work for another day.

Address Limitations

You may find a particular exercise is physically challenging for one or the other of you. Think about what you are trying to accomplish and how each of you is put together. It is helpful to have in mind multiple ways to achieve the same outcome.

other work. Do not move from one level to another before your horse is secure in the present level. Moving ahead before your horse is ready will only contribute to an emotional and physical breakdown for both of you. Do not let anyone else judge you. This experience is between you and your horse.

Seek advice from a professional trainer or instructor, attend clinics, and read books by respected professionals. As you learn more and more, you will feel more confident in your work and have a better sense of when it is time to increase the degree of difficulty.

Avoid Repetition

Excessive repetition can overtire your horse physically and drain him mentally. He may become bored to the point of agitation if forced to repeat the same task many times. Once he has performed the exercise several times correctly, or made the effort to do so, during an exercise session, move on to something else—preferably an easier, more enjoyable exercise. Your horse is still reaping the benefit of exercise while doing something less demanding and more enjoyable, ending the session on a positive note.

Keep It Simple

Simplicity is crucial to success. If tack or task is overly complicated, it can lead to confusion and negativity. Simplify each exercise so it is clear enough in your mind to teach it to your horse efficiently and effectively. Break down exercises into logical, simple, individual steps or behaviors that, when taken together, yield the desired result. Make the exercise simple to achieve even though it may be complicated when looked at as a whole.

For example, say you are introducing lines to your jumping horse. (Lines are a combination of jumps placed in a row, with several strides between each, such as two or three fences.) Begin by

If your horse is having difficulty traveling straight on, set some ground rails close together, forming a narrow channel through which to ride. These rails will guide your horse and encourage straightforward movement.

Determine When to Move to the Next Level

Patience is key. Do not rush or force yourself or your horse too quickly. You both must feel comfortable, have a thorough understanding, and be confirmed in the exercises before moving on to warming up over a groundrail. Once your horse is loose, focused, and consistent, school him over a low cross-rail (perhaps 18 inches [45.7 cm]). Next, work over a line that consists of a groundrail and a cross-rail, placed to allow multiple strides between the two (perhaps eight strides). Once your horse is doing well, change out the groundrail for another low cross-rail. This will allow your horse the practice of jumping a line that consists of two actual jumps. As your horse progresses, you may create lines of varying difficulty by changing the style and height of the jumps, the number of strides between the jumps, and the track of the line.

Keep It Positive

Always praise your horse for any honest effort made, especially when you are asking for an exercise or movement that is particularly difficult. Likewise, if your horse ignores your request or responds with disobedience or protest, immediately correct with a firm tone of voice and clearly signal again what you are asking him to do.

Vary the Exercise Program

Be creative when planning and executing the exercises, and vary the program throughout the week. Use ground work, lunging work, mounted exercises,

---

TIP

Communication

Do not punish your horse severely with whip, spur, or bit. You do not want to break his spirit and have him performing tasks out of fear. Often it is the handler's error or miscommunication or the horse's fear or pain causing protest or disobedience. Consider these explanations first when your horse is not compliant.

---

and stretches. Plan a day of rest when you and your horse spend pleasure time together, taking a leisurely trail ride or just hanging out.

BASIC EQUINE EXERCISES

Equine exercises can be performed from the ground or while mounted. They differ from simple riding or hand-walking in that they are specific in their applications and are seeking defined results.

Each horse performs exercises differently according to his condition, health, and capability. As your horse becomes more physically fit, more mentally aware of what is being asked, and more emotionally responsive to your praise, he will be able to perform the exercises with improved accuracy.

The idea is to keep the exercises simple for both you and your horse so you will accomplish each goal easily, without confusion or frustration. You must be fully aware during your daily work sessions with your horse so you can note and enjoy the daily accomplishments you are both achieving. Of course, you will have long-term goals; however, the daily short-term goals are the foundation to achieving your long-term goals.

Do not expect your horse to automatically and immediately understand or be able to accomplish the exercises. Each honest effort your horse makes should be praised and built on. Exercise should be worked on incrementally—that is, add a new short-term goal to the program only when your horse is confirmed in his response to his present task.

Always review previous exercises your horse has learned well. If he has completed an exercise and you move forward to other exercises without asking for the original exercise ever again, it may be forgotten. Incorporate older exercises with newer exercises.

All of the exercises described in this section assume the horse is relatively quiet and well trained and the handler is experienced.

Ground Exercises

These exercises are performed while you are standing on the ground. Your horse is dressed in a halter, with a lead rope attached. Maneuver your horse by holding the lead rope while performing each exercise as described below.

You will need a halter, a lead rope, proper footwear, riding gloves, a dressage whip, and a clean, safe, open workspace for these exercises. Though not required, wearing a safety helmet is always recommended.

Hand-Walking Up and Down Hills

If you are fortunate enough to live where the terrain includes inclines and declines, take advantage of this.

1. Start by standing on the left side of your horse's body, securely holding the lead rope, and briskly hand-walk your horse up and down the hills. The change in landscape means your horse must engage and work his hind-end muscles to move up and down the hills. He also must balance his body and focus on the exercise so he can safely navigate the terrain.

The key to this exercise is walking briskly so your horse is actively in motion and stimulating his mind with work that necessitates his full attention. You might vary this exercise by walking across the terrain in a diagonal or left-to-right pattern so you are not always tracking straight up and down the hill. This varies the pattern for you and your horse, again maintaining focus, requiring balance and co-ordination, and working multiple muscle groups.

2. Walk in both directions (up and down, left to right) so you work both sides of your horse's body equally.

Hand-walking up a hill

Reverse the Motion

This exercise involves your horse taking multiple steps backward, slowly and consistently. Like human bodies, the horse's body is primarily used for forward motion. Exercising your horse by asking him to move backward increases range of motion, opens areas of tightness, and strengthens tissues. These benefits are achieved when you require the body parts to do something different. Reverse motion also strengthens the trust between you and your horse, as many horses are cautious about backing up.

The more your horse performs this exercise, the more adept he becomes and the more relaxed he will be about doing it.

1. Begin by standing directly in front of your horse, so you and he are face to face. Hold the lead line with one of your hands positioned just below the lead's snap attachment and the other hand closer to the bottom of the lead. Never allow the lead to drag on the ground, as you or your horse could step on it and become entangled.

2. Vocally tell your horse to back while simultaneously pushing your body weight and the lead backward into his chest area. Your horse should begin to reverse motion and step backward away from you. Follow along so your horse will continue the reverse motion. When you are asking the horse to back up, be sure to ask for multiple steps. One or two steps are not sufficient; try for five to ten. You may only be able to get one or two in the beginning, but gradually increase the number as you work this exercise. Praise any and all efforts.

Hip Movements

This exercise requires you to place your flat hand directly behind your horse's hip and push the hip so the horse moves the hip and hind leg away from you. Hips are often tight, tender, and locked. This movement allows the horse's hip joint to open and free itself.

Use caution, as your horse may become agitated when you first attempt to touch the hip or be unwilling to move away from your hand. This is an ideal moment for your horse to kick you. Do not do this exercise until your horse is comfortable with you touching his hip area. Desensitization to touch can begin with grooming, riding, massage, and acupressure.

TIP

Walking Backward

Reverse motion can prove tremendously helpful in several areas of your horse's life. For example, many horse trailers require a horse to walk backward to exit. Many horse shows require a horse to back up during a class or test. In everyday barn affairs, you often need to maneuver your horse back for various reasons. If your horse is used to backing up, daily activities become much easier.

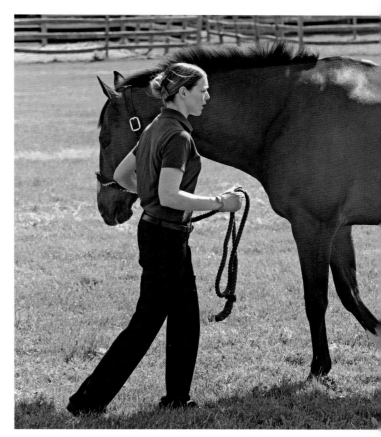

Walking the horse backwards

Praise your horse the moment he allows you to touch his hip. Then praise him when he makes an effort to step away from you. Finally, offer abundant praise when he actually crosses the hind leg closer to you in front of the opposite hind leg.

1. Start on the left side of the horse's body. Face his hip area. Begin by talking soothingly to your horse.

2. Lay your hand flat behind your horse's hip, palm down. Simply rest your hand there a few moments.

3. Apply pressure to the area by leaning your body weight into your flat hand. This will encourage your horse to step away from you. Ideally, you want your horse to cross the hind leg closer to you in front of the other hind leg as he steps away from you.

This may not occur in the beginning phase of this exercise. If your horse simply shuffles away from you without actually crossing his hind leg over the other, the stretch is not as effective. You may need to hold a long whip in your pressing hand so you can press the hip and simultaneously rest the tip of the whip against the lower portion of the hind leg (near the hock and hoof). Thus, when you apply hand pressure, the whip also applies pressure, encouraging the horse to cross its entire hind leg in front of the other. If your horse is having difficulty crossing the hind leg, you may need to move your hand to the long digital extensor muscle and press it away from you so the horse clearly understands what you are asking.

4. Once the horse steps away and crosses the leg over, praise him. Now ask again, this time placing your hand on the original area behind the hip, and see if the horse steps away and crosses over the leg. If not, simply do not offer any praise. Return your

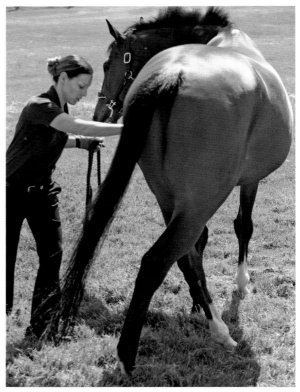

Pushing the horse's hip to move the hind leg

Using a long whip to encourage the hind leg to cross over

Pressing on the long digital extensor to encourage the hind leg to cross over

hand to the long digital extensor and press into it once again for the crossover of the hind leg. If your horse achieved this, offer abundant vocal praise and repeat the request once again, placing your hand flatly behind the hip area. Eventually, your horse will understand that he is praised when he crosses over properly but gets nothing but silence when he doesn't.

Lunging Exercises

Lunging refers to exercising your horse by attaching him to a lunge line, standing in an area, and having him work in a circular track around you. Hold the lunge line in the hand closer to your horse's head and a lunge whip in the hand closer to the horse's hind end. Stand still as your horse exercises around you while on the line. The lunge line is secured to a halter, bridle, or lunging cavesson.

Before You Begin

You will need the following items: a lunge line, a lunge whip, proper footwear, a safety helmet, riding gloves, and a halter, bridle, or lunging cavesson.

A lunge line is a cotton or synthetic piece of material about 20-feet (6.1 m) long and 1-inch (2.5 cm) wide. It resembles a very long dog leash. It has a snap on one end so it can be attached to the horse. Lunge lines vary in length and width. Some have snaps on the end while others have a length of chain and then a snap. Some have a small, round, hard rubber piece called a *doughnut* attached to the end of the line. The doughnut prevents the line from slipping out of your hand. Do not hold a line with an open loop on one end because if you get your hand caught in the loop, you may be dragged by your horse.

A lunge whip is a 4-foot (1.2 m) whip with a leather or synthetic string-like piece on the end. This piece is usually about 4-yards (3.7 m) long. This length allows you to make contact with your horse from a distance as he works on the circle. You can stand in the center of your lunge circle without having to step toward your horse in order to wriggle, move, or raise the whip. The whip is commonly used along the ground, raised in the air (similar to casting a fishing line), or even cracked for sound effect. Usually the presence, positioning, and sound of the whip encourage the horse to move forward. It is not common practice to actually touch the horse's body with the whip.

You need to wear gloves to lunge properly and should consider wearing a safety helmet. The gloves prevent chafing from the lunge line, and the helmet protects you if your horse accidentally kicks you in the head.

Securely outfit your horse with a properly fitting halter, bridle, or lunging cavesson (a specially crafted head collar with ring attachments for a lunge line).

Proper Lunging Technique

The lunge line should be free from knots or entanglements. Hold it loosely gathered in your hand so you can feed it out to enlarge the circle or reel it in to decrease the size of the circle. Never wrap the line around your hand.

Lines should be equipped with secure snap attachments but should not be worn in any open areas, as they can break and your horse can escape. Keep the distributed line fairly taut so it cannot drag on the ground and become wrapped around your horse's feet or legs. Hold the remaining line wrapped loosely in a circular shape (similar to when you wind a garden hose) so it does not hang and allow you to step on it or become entangled in it.

Basic Lunging

Attach the lunge line to your horse. Stand in the center of what is going to become your lunge circle. Hold your lunge line in the hand closer to your horse's head and the lunge whip in the hand closer to his hind end. Bend the lunge-line arm at the elbow, offering elasticity in the joint, and keep your whip-hand low and cautious.

Feed out the line and encourage the horse to move away from you by placing the length of the whip between you and your horse, near his hind end. Be cautious, as your horse may kick out at the whip. Stand still so your horse can create a circle

around you. Do not to follow your horse around. If you randomly walk around the area, you will never be able to determine the size and shape of the circle. Your horse will never learn to focus and respect this exercise. Remember that your horse is focusing on the placement of the whip. Do not make sudden gestures or flail with that hand. This may scare your horse, and he could attempt to pull on the line and flee.

The concept of lunging is that the lunge line functions like reins and the whip functions like your legs. You are the center stabilizer; therefore, you want to keep your horse between the lunge line and lunge whip at all times. Never use the whip near the horse's face, as that only creates anxiety and resentment. Use the whip near or behind the hindquarters to encourage the horse to move forward.

Circular Pattern Modifications

After you have taught and established the traditional circular pattern while lunging your horse, add variety to the exercise. Vary the size of the circles throughout your lunging session. Large circles allow the horse to warm up and move forward loosely. Smaller circles are more challenging, as they require additional focus and physical effort. The degree of balance required is greater, as well, when the workspace is limited and the circle smaller.

1. Begin the lunging session with large circles to the left. As your horse warms up, gradually decrease the size of the circle by reeling in the lunge line a bit at a time. Work back and forth throughout the exercise so your horse spends a few moments working the larger and smaller circles in each gait. Practice this exercise in both directions so your horse lunges equally to the right and to the left. Smaller circles are more challenging for horses, as they require additional balance and joint flexion. Do not reduce the circle size so much that your horse experiences tremendous difficulty moving forward. Do not work your horse excessively on a small circle.

Feeding out the lunge line to establish a circle for lunging

Lunging on a straight track

2. Change the shape of the circle by adding sections of straight line patterns to the session. Simply walk in a straight line for several steps, allowing your horse to travel straight alongside you on the lunge line. After you have walked in a straight line for multiple steps, stop and return to a circular pattern. This may be especially helpful after your horse has worked for a few moments on a reduced-size circle, as the straight pattern will give him a rest from circling.

Teaching Voice Commands

Lunging can be a wonderful tool to teach your horse voice commands. Be sure your commands are behavior-specific—that is, always use the same word to request a particular behavior and no other. If you want your horse to walk forward, always say "walk" clearly and firmly. If you want your horse to come

to you, however, use a different command, such as "right here" or "come here."

When a horse is trained to voice command, you can use your voice when riding, when loading and unloading the horse trailer, and when working in the aisle and stall with your horse. When your horse understands and willingly responds to your vocal cues when you ask him to move forward, back up, and stop, he is easier to handle.

Lunging provides an opportunity to teach your horse to stop, walk, trot, canter, gallop, and come to you by consistently using the same terminology for the same request. Do not overlook the halt command. Many people never teach their horses to stop on the lunge line and then have difficulty with control.

Enhance the voice commands by attaching other terms. For instance, you might use "up, up" when requesting your horse to increase speed in a gait. Simultaneously raise the lunge whip or move the lunge whip back and forth on the ground.

You can use the word "easy" when you are requesting your horse to slow down in a gait. At the same time, lower the whip or hold it still and gently offer resistance several times through the lunge line by taking back and giving forward the line through your bent elbow. Introduce a new gait to your horse with a specific word before the gait change. That way he learns that when you say the transitioning word, a gait change will follow.

Be aware of your vocal tone, clarity, and use. Your horse should respond to your request promptly. Constant repetition eventually leads your horse to lose focus, zone out, and ignore your vocalizations. People off-lunge their horses while making a clicking noise the entire time to encourage the horse to move forward, but meanwhile the horse is going along at his own pace and exhibiting no change in speed.

Be just as aware of your horse's response or lack thereof. Each voiced request should be answered by effort on the part of your horse and with your praise according to effort. If your horse does not make any effort, increase your volume and raise the whip or move it along the ground. Voice, lunge line, and lunge whip should work together.

Use lunging as you would any other exercise—to achieve goals and set the tone for proper work. Set a variety of goals beyond taking the edge off your horse's energy level each time you lunge.

Alter the order in which you ask for gait changes. Do not always walk, trot, and canter in the same order. Vary the session so your horse must focus on you because he does not know what you will ask next.

Ground Rails Work

Adding ground rails to your lunging sessions periodically gives your horse something different to focus on, no matter his career, discipline, or work program. Ground rails work can teach your horse balance, focus, flexibility, and confidence.

1. Place a single rail down in your lunging pattern. Work your horse in varied gaits over the rail. Lunge your horse over the rail in both directions.

> ▸ If your horse rushes over the rail, practice halting before and after it.

> ▸ If your horse tries to go around and avoid stepping across the rail, set other ground rails on each side vertically, creating barriers and encouraging your horse to travel straight across the original rail.

> ▸ If your horse stops in front of the rail, set it so it meets the wall or fence if working in an enclosed area. This will automatically block that side so the horse cannot escape from the rail on that blocked side. Use another rail to block the open side. Use your voice and raise the whip or move the whip along the ground to encourage your horse to step across the ground rail.

2. Once you have worked your horse over a single ground rail successfully, try placing several ground rails throughout your lunging track. Be creative in your placement and pattern.

Mounted Exercises

The mounted exercises below are discussed in simple, general terms. They are written with the assumption that you are schooled in riding. If you do not understand the exercises, seek additional information from an instructor. Mounted exercises are for people experienced in the saddle working with quiet, well-trained horses.

Lunging over a ground rail

Flexion Requests

This exercise can be performed in the halt, walk, trot, and canter. It should be introduced at the halt and then requested at the walk, trot, and canter sequentially once it is confirmed in each gait. If your horse cannot complete this exercise while walking, do not expect him to be able to do it while cantering.

1. Mount and begin to walk the horse on left rein. Ask the horse to halt. Once the horse has halted, slowly draw your left rein back, directly toward your own left hip. Simultaneously, place your right leg back behind the girth several inches, applying light pressure with your lower leg. Your right rein should be taut and positioned close to your horse's neck.

As you gradually increase the degree of left bend, be sure your bent right elbow is flexible so it offers elasticity in the right rein. Your right leg will hang long at the girth with light pressure. The concept of this exercise is that your horse bends his head and neck to the left but does not move the rest of his body. Your right leg and rein prevent him from moving to the right. Your left leg prevents him from stepping in.

2. Perform this flexion request to the right also. Your right rein draws back toward your right hip asking for the bend. Your right leg hangs down at the girth while your left leg rests behind it.

Position the left rein against your horse's neck while maintaining elasticity in the left bent elbow. You will immediately notice a difference in the ability, range of motion, and demeanor of your horse when comparing sides. Your horse will be more willing, capable, and able to flex in one direction than the other. The horse may flex calmly to one side but become agitated or protest when asked to flex in the other direction. It is important to request flexion from both sides each time this exercise is performed so you can maintain the stronger side and strengthen the weaker side.

3. As your horse becomes more proficient in these flexion requests, ask him to move his hindquarters away from the direction in which he is flexing by increasing the pressure of your inside leg, encouraging him to step over toward your outside leg.

Reminder: When flexing your horse to the left, your inside (left) leg is positioned at the girth while your outside (right) leg is positioned a few inches behind it. Conversely, when you are flexing your horse to the right, your right leg is positioned at the girth (functioning as an inside leg), and your left leg is positioned a few inches behind it (functioning as an outside leg).

Straightness Matters

For a horse to move correctly and efficiently, he must carry himself straight—that is, when you are looking directly at the horse, from the front or back, each hind leg is behind its respective shoulder and the head and neck are positioned straight between the shoulder blades.

Left flexion at the halt

Left flexion with hindquarters moving right

When mounted, you should feel each hind leg moving directly behind and underneath you; each shoulder should be directly in front of you, and you should be able to see both of your horse's eyes, nostrils, and ears evenly and equally. A horse's hind end is his power source or engine. If the hind legs are no longer directly behind the horse but rather listing off to one side, power, inertia, and motion are lost.

That being said, horses generally do not travel in a straight line when ridden because they are compensating for some imbalance. In response to areas in his body that are weaker, deficient, or painful, the horse compensates with crooked or contorted movement. Most horses have a stronger, suppler side and a weaker, stiffer side. Your horse will move his body accordingly.

For example, if your horse's right hind leg is weaker, he will often travel with his right hind leg off to one side, no longer behind and underneath his body. He will also compensate by overloading the diagonal shoulder with weight—in this case, the left shoulder. This shoulder may become difficult to move, as it is bearing excessive weight and exertion as it functions on behalf of the weaker right hind leg.

If a horse's body is somewhat crooked when he travels, the weaker parts will not improve and the stronger parts will face overexertion as they compensate for the weaker muscles.

Straightness Exercise #1

After mounting, begin this exercise by asking your horse to halt squarely. Plan where you would like to stop by visually picking out an area. Walk the horse forward to the area; slow the motion of your hips, elbows, and back; sit down into your seat bones; press down into your heels; and stop the motion of your hands while sitting up tall and inhaling. Lightly maintain the pressure from both of your legs evenly and consistently.

As your body parts slow, transfer your weight into your seat bones and inhale. Your horse will learn to interpret these signals as stopping aids. It is important to lengthen your leg, deeply flexing downward into your ankle joint, so you can continue to apply leg pressure as your other body parts are stopping. Your legs will encourage your horse to step his hind legs underneath himself to find his own balance. As a result, when he halts, he is balancing his whole body rather than merely shutting down his power source (hind end) and leaning his body weight into your hands, looking for you to carry and support his body weight.

When trying to achieve straightness, sit evenly in the saddle, each leg long and pressing equally, your spine stretching up and centered, your hips open and pressed a bit forward so neither is collapsing off to the side or forward, and your shoulders, elbows, hands, and reins symmetrical, creating an even, equal feel on each side of the horse's mouth, neck, and shoulder.

Once your horse has halted, look down at his ears, nostrils, shoulders, front feet, and hind feet. All body parts should be even and symmetrical. All four feet should form a square underneath you—hence the term *square halt*. If your horse is standing with his feet spaced unevenly, use your leg pressure and rein connection to position him squarely. Once the horse stands squarely, offer lots of praise and patting.

Straightness Exercise #2

When introducing this exercise, begin by setting up several safe objects (ground rails, safety cones, plastic jumping blocks) in a formation that encourages the horse to halt squarely. For example, place two of the objects vertically next to one another, leaving just enough space for the width of your horse's body to fit between them, and place a third object horizontally across the top of the two vertical objects, closing off the formation.

After mounting, walk the horse forward into the formation slowly and ask him to halt. The formation visually and spatially limits the amount of space he has to work in, thus encouraging straightness. Eventually you will be able to remove the formation and ask for a straight, square clean halt and achieve it.

Straightness Exercise #3

Once you have worked on a straight halt, it is time to ask your horse to move forward into the walk, carrying his body straight from head to tail, each side evenly and symmetrically placed. Monitor, feel, and look for straightness.

Begin by halting squarely and then asking for only a few straight steps in the walk. If you should lose the shape and the horse moves head, neck, shoulders, or hind legs off to one side or the other, halt and ask again. Correct any crookedness with your leg and rein, and always return the horse to straightness.

If you need more help achieving straightness, place two ground rails along each side of the arena, forming a square chute, so you can walk along through each chute creating, monitoring, and

Using ground rails to encourage a square halt

Using a ground-rail chute to encourage straightness at the walk

returning to straightness. Match the straightness of the pole on either side to the straightness of your horse's body. Once the horse advances, introduce the trot and canter to this exercise, and then begin to eliminate one chute at a time so your horse eventually halts, walks, trots, and canters straight along each side of the arena.

Exercises Off the Rail

It is important to exercise off the rail equally as often so you and your horse can practice without the wall or fencing functioning as a crutch.

Visually and spatially, the arena wall acts as a support your horse can lean into or away from. However, using a barrier can alter your own judgment, as it is more difficult to feel where your body and your horse's are aligned with a barrier on one side. A barrier can cause you or your horse to cut corners as the corner barrier visually looms ahead.

Spend each exercise session working several feet in, off, or away from the rail throughout the arena, along the straight areas as well as in the corners. This work allows you to feel where your horse places his body parts and where he tends to lean in and fall out. It also gives you a chance to see where your signaling is more or less effective as your horse and you rely on one another, rather than the rail, for navigation.

Before you begin, place a safe visual object, such as an orange traffic cone, in each corner and along the center of each long side. This will help you draw an imaginary line from section to section so you can practice riding from object to object in a straight line.

Begin by asking your horse to move in several feet from the rail and remain on that track throughout the exercise. Be particular so your track around the arena is similar in shape and size—in other words, stay the same distance away from the rail as you work.

As you and your horse become more proficient, increase the distance from the rail and then begin varying it. Practice riding several more feet in from the rail—first 3 feet (0.9 m) in, then 6 feet (1.8 m) in, then back to 3 feet (0.9 m). Make sure your horse does not simply fall out and bounce back over to the rail when you ask him to step away from your inside leg. Your horse must step his whole body out in one piece, completely straight, such that he is stepping over to your outside leg and rein but not beyond them.

Working off the rail allows you to move your horse off your legs and reins. Vary the exercise by asking the horse to remain straight along the long sides of the arena and asking for flexion in the corners. Ask your horse to flex to the inside in the corners, and then ask him to flex to the outside through the turns so you stretch him to each side.

Difficulty with a Particular Exercise

If you are having difficulty with an exercise, you can do several things.

▶ Break down the difficult exercise into its simpler composite behaviors first. Horses often learn better if tasks are divided into their simplest parts.

Return to a simple, confirmed exercise. Practice this exercise to restore focus and confidence. Then request one of the difficult exercise's composite behaviors. When your horse makes an effort to answer, praise him and return to the simpler exercise. Do not go any further with the difficult exercise until the next session.

Begin the next session in the same manner with a simple, confirmed exercise followed by two new behaviors of the more difficult exercise. Continue in this manner, adding composite behaviors for several sessions before requesting the entire new exercise.

▶ Seek advice from an educated friend or trainer. Your cues may be incorrect or confusing. Perhaps you are asking for the exercise clearly and correctly but unconsciously sending a conflicting message at the same time. A helper can see this and point it out to you.

▶ Enlist the help of an educated friend or trainer to guide or sit on your horse and work through the exercise while you watch. Compare the results; watching a demonstration is a wonderful way to learn. Videotape the session, if possible.

▶ Read more books or articles. Do online research. Talk to your horsey friends, and discuss the exercise with an equine professional. You may need someone to clarify the concept of the exercise.

Starting Simple

Circle exercise: If you want your horse to be able to work on a small circle in all gaits, while bending his body right or left, begin by working in a slow gait on a large circle, asking for a small amount of bend. As your horse becomes confirmed in this, ask him to complete this task while working in the trot. When that goes well, work this task in a canter. Once your horse is capable of working comfortably on the large circle in all three gaits, bending right and left, gradually decrease the circle size. Then, add the trot and canter again. Then slowly increase the amount of bend. Again, introduce each new phase (circle size, gait change, bending requests) slowly and individually. This exercise should develop over time; do not rush or overpractice it.

Human Exercises

If your mind, body, and spirit are anxious, lacking confidence, pained, or imbalanced in any way, your sensitive, intuitive horse will pick up on it. Prepare yourself before approaching your horse to exercise. A few simple exercises can help you relax and prepare physically and emotionally to work with your horse.

Simple Stretching

Standing upright, raise one arm toward the ceiling, fingers pointing and reaching upward. Simultaneously, lift the heel of your foot (on the same side as raised arm) and press down deeply into floor. Inhale, exhale, and reach the arm and fingertips upward while pressing your toes into the floor. You will feel your shoulder soften, your arm lengthen, your fingers stretch, your rib cage open, your leg extend, and your ankle stretch. Repeat this stretch on the opposite side. You will feel your frame lighten and open as the stretch is completed. Hold this posture for 1 minute on each side, and repeat it two or three times per side.

Breathing Awareness

When you first mount, stay in place. Put one hand on your lower belly and hold the reins with the other. Practice breathing in deeply and slowly, trying to fill your belly with air so it expands outward into your hand. Holding your expanded belly, slowly exhale, releasing all of the air from your lungs. Feel the belly collapsing away from your hand and pressing deeply backward into your spine.

Repeat this exercise for 5 minutes before beginning your equine exercises. This breathing exercise allows your mind and body to soften, loosen, and relax, setting the tone for the equine exercises.

Simple opening stretch for the human

Equine Exercise Reference List

Daily Equine Exercises

Ground Exercises
Reverse the Motion
Hip Movements

Mounted Exercises
Flexion Requests
Straightness Matters

Weekly Equine Exercises

Ground Exercise
Hand-Walk Up and Down Hills
Lunging: Voice Commands

Mounted Exercise
Exercise Off the Rail

Monthly Equine Exercises

Ground Exercises
Lunging: Circular Pattern Modifications
Lunging: Ground Rails

Cardio Lunging

Whenever you work your horse on a lunge line, take advantage of the time to warm up your own body. Perform this exercise only with horses that lunge well and quietly and do not spook easily.

Once you have begun lunging your horse safely and efficiently in the traditional circular pattern, move him off the circle by walking briskly next to him along the long side of the arena. Take large, brisk steps. Begin in the walk to allow your horse time to become comfortable with this exercise and to build up your own endurance. You can do this as often as you feel appropriate for the day's session.

As you and your horse become comfortable, try the cardio lunging while your horse is trotting. As your horse trots down the long side, you may need to move into a light jog to keep up with him. This will increase your circulation and breathing pattern, allowing your body to warm up and prepare for your equine exercises. It also provides time for the horse to work in a straight line for several moments, easing the strain of continuous circular work.

Cardio lunging

4

Overview of Complementary and Alternative Therapy

Complementary/alternative therapy (C/A) is a broad term that encompasses several healing modalities primarily derived from ancient and Eastern medicine. When these therapies are used in conjunction with traditional veterinary medicine to assist in maintaining health and preventing, managing, and resolving health problems, they are referred to as *complementary*. When used as substitutes for veterinary care, they are referred to as *alternative*.

The decision to use any of these therapies as alternatives to veterinary care is not to be taken lightly and should be made only under the guidance of a C/A veterinarian or certified professional. The decision to forgo veterinary care and provide treatment yourself without professional help is not recommended. You should not substitute these therapies for veterinary care. If your horse appears ill or injured, contact your veterinarian immediately.

As preventive measures, you should use these modalities only if you have a thorough understanding of and experience with the therapies and their applications. Although anecdotal evidence in support of particular therapies in a specific situation is abundant, researchers have yet to determine, in controlled scientific studies, how safe or effective many C/A therapies are. Controlled studies are under way to determine their safety and efficacy.

Many types of therapy fall under the C/A umbrella, the most notable of which are acupressure, acupuncture, chiropractic, physiotherapy, aromatherapy (essential oils), chakra therapy, chromatherapy (color therapy), herbal therapy, homeopathy, magnetic therapy, massage, and reiki. These therapies can be used individually or in conjunction with one another. They may be applied to humans and animals.

All of these therapies share several core concepts. All complementary therapies seek to create, maintain, and restore balance within the body. If

> ## TIP
> ### Body Language
>
> When an imbalance occurs in a bodily system, horses in the wild are known to self-medicate. This energy of alertness and awareness can be channeled to offer comfort and relief. Horses let you know what they are feeling without inhibition. They clearly signal discomfort—and positive change—through their body language.

bodily systems have balance and harmony, health is achieved and maintained. If a system is blocked or out of balance, health problems arise and the body becomes deficient in its ability to heal itself. Balance and harmony imply open energy circulation, proper blood flow, strong immunity levels, mental clarity, emotional stability, proper nutrient production and utilization, and freedom from toxins and stress.

C/A therapies are holistic treatments in that they are individualized based on all aspects of the patient and his environment. The patient's mental, emotional, and physical states are all considered when determining the most appropriate therapies to use and the most effective methods of delivery. The practitioner considers life circumstances, exposures, and history so the condition is managed and treated properly. These therapies do not simply look at a health concern as a localized problem; rather, they consider the patient as a whole.

These therapies address each patient as an individual to set realistic goals. Each body behaves differently and specifically, and each patient's history and emotional and mental states also differ. C/A therapy seeks to encourage each client's system to function at its own optimum ability. If a client has chronic multiple health problems, each problem is addressed individually *and* as part of a system. These therapies encourage the body's own healing capabilities.

C/A practitioners seek to identify the root of a health problem before determining protocols to resolve or effectively manage it. If the actual cause(s) can be determined, the problem can be resolved or managed much more accurately than by simply addressing the presenting symptoms. Likewise, these therapies can be used as preventive medicine; if the whole body is functioning at its best, health issues are less likely to occur. These modalities can maintain health and well being.

Case Study: Easing Discomfort

An Appaloosa gelding was purchased and shipped across the country to his new owner, who took the horse to a competition after several weeks of ownership. The horse was fine on the first day of the horse show; however, he came up "off" on the second day of the competition, presenting with discomfort in his right hind leg. The horse had traveled extensively, recently undergone a new shoeing experience, and was living in a new climate, in the care of a new owner, presently at a competition, and currently in a new work program. Essential oil therapy and massage therapy were implemented. The horse had undergone numerous disruptions over the past several weeks, so calming oils of lavender and chamomile were offered as inhalants; a complete body massage was offered to restore overall balance, promote relaxation, locate the pain source, and eliminate compensatory mechanisms; and an essential oil blend of peppermint oil and grapeseed oil was applied to the skin in the areas of muscular discomfort around the horse's right hip, which appeared to be highly sensitive. The goal was to ease the discomfort and relieve mental fatigue. The horse was sound the next day and able to compete at the horse show.

BENEFITS OF THERAPY

The therapies offer myriad benefits. Each is unique and applied in a manner specific to the patient and problem being addressed.

Generally, all of the therapies provide relaxation; mental focus; emotional release; physical pain management; mental, physical, and emotional rejuvenation; energy restoration; and amelioration of physical conditions or symptoms. In addition, they often lighten the mood and lift the spirit, resulting in a positive mindset.

Nervous, grieving, aggressive, distrusting, or fickle horses often settle down and relax during a therapy session. Horses that are sick, injured, or in pain are usually open and receptive to therapy— they can sense your good intentions. They instantly let you know whether or not they like what you are doing.

C/A therapies are often successful in decreasing recuperation time after an injury or illness. The horse returns to wellness sooner than if therapy had not been offered.

CANDIDATES FOR THERAPY

When considering the use of these therapies, always consult your veterinarian. It is vital to determine if your horse is an appropriate candidate. Certain therapies are not appropriate for certain conditions. For example, herbal remedies should not be given to horses that tend to have allergic reactions to certain substances.

When discussing the therapies with your veterinarian, you are not asking about her personal beliefs; you are simply asking if it would be safe to apply a particular therapy to your horse. If you feel a certain therapy would benefit your horse and your veterinarian determines it is safe, then by all means try it.

THE POWERS OF THERAPY

C/A therapies help physical function by encouraging circulation of bodily fluids including blood, nutrients, and oxygen; stimulating healing properties; and releasing endorphins. They promote emotional balance by providing an empathetic, nurturing, caring, calm energy that radiates from the practitioner or horse owner providing the therapy. Mental clarity results, as the therapies are given in a quiet, distraction-free, comfortable setting. When physical systems are balanced, mental acuity is strengthened. Stress is reduced as your horse settles into the session. Stress from the environment, as well as stress stemming from a health problem or simply trying to maintain health in a domestic setting, is released.

MISCONCEPTIONS ABOUT THERAPY

Misconceptions about C/A therapy abound. Here is a list of the most common:

▸ *C/A therapy is a substitute for veterinary care.* In most cases, C/A should be thought of as complementing veterinary care or as options when veterinary care has been exhausted. Your horse must be seen and treated regularly by a veterinarian to maintain health. If your horse presents with an illness or injury, contact your veterinarian immediately. Once your horse has received proper medical care, C/A therapy may be considered. In every situation involving your horse's health, always contact your veterinarian first.

▸ *C/A therapy is simple.* All C/A therapies require thorough knowledge and proper application. Each therapy is applied logically and sequentially and is based on thousands of years of accumulated knowledge and use by professionals. If you are truly interested in learning and applying them to your horse, you should attend clinics, study professional texts, and consult with a professional. The more education you receive and the more practical application you perform, the better you will become at administering the therapy and thus the more effective and lasting the results. This is a lifelong learning process.

▸ *C/A therapy is magical and resolves everything.* These therapies are not cure-alls. They are applied to encourage your horse's body to function and heal as well as it can. Results can vary from one horse to another. C/A therapy can help manage certain medical conditions and maintain or restore health. However, it does not resolve everything. Further, you should not expect your horse to improve after a single treatment. Multiple treatments plus maintenance are often required. The number of treatments and length of the treatment program vary according to the horse's condition and the particular therapy. The key is consistency. On the other hand, if you have been offering treatments thoroughly and faithfully and do not see any changes, accept that your approach is not working. Try a different therapy or a combination of therapies. Apply all treatments in moderation and with the genuine intention of helping your horse.

▸ *C/A therapy has not been scientifically proven; therefore, it is useless.* These therapies are rooted in thousands of years of application with results, and thus they speak for themselves. Each person has a right to his own beliefs and opinions. The final decision is yours to make.

▸ *C/A therapy is easy to apply.* These modalities require knowledge, skill, mental focus, physical energy, analytical thinking, and endurance. You must think outside the box when determining conditions and applications. You must hone your senses and intuitions and be acutely observant of your horse's body language. As a horse owner, you must practice so your sense of touch is heightened and you tune in to your horse's energy. You must learn how your horse conveys likes and dislikes and what areas of his body are consistently most reactive. If you are considering any of the C/A therapies for your horse, it is highly recommended that you experience the therapy yourself first. You will not only be a more effective practitioner because of your firsthand experience but also because the balance and harmony you experience through therapy will transmit to your horse.

DEFINITIONS OF COMMON C/A THERAPIES

Acupressure, acupuncture, aromatherapy (essential oils), chakra therapy, chromatherapy, herbal therapy, magnetic therapy, massage, and reiki are the most common C/A therapies. (See Resources, page 211, for more information.)

▶ *Acupressure*—A branch of traditional Chinese medicine involving the manipulation of bodily energy. It is noninvasive and performed through touch.

▶ *Acupuncture*—Similar to acupressure, except it is invasive. Acupuncture needles are inserted into the skin to stimulate energy flow within the body.

▶ *Aromatherapy*—Based on essential oils that have been used for thousands of years to address health issues. The oils are derived from plants and flowers. They are inhaled through the nostrils and can be applied topically.

▶ *Chakra energy therapy*—An ancient healing approach from India. It concerns the energy whirlpools that exist within the body and relates to mental, emotional, and physical health. Chakra energy can be felt through one's touch.

▶ *Chromatherapy*—Commonly called *color therapy*. China, Egypt, and India all embrace the use of color and light to stimulate healing and promote wellness. Color and light may be applied through prisms, aromatherapy, and hydrotherapy.

▶ *Herbal therapy*—This approach has been used globally for thousands of years. It is the external application or internal ingestion of natural herbs to promote healing, boost immunity, and flush toxins from the system. Herbal remedies can be used for a multitude of conditions, including wound treatment and insect control.

▶ *Magnetic therapy*—Use of magnets for health dates back thousands of years. Magnets are applied to the body to reduce pain, stimulate the immune system, and encourage soft tissue repair. Magnetic blankets, boots, and wraps can be found in many equine catalogs.

▶ *Massage*—A noninvasive therapy involving muscle tissue manipulation. It is performed using one's hands and applied through strokes and sequences of strokes.

▶ *Reiki*—A Japanese healing art in which the practitioner uses hand positions to channel healing energy throughout the body.

Any or all of these therapies may be applied to horses after consulting with a veterinarian. You may find that one works well for a particular problem while another works better for a different concern. You may use one or a combination as preventive therapy. Essentially, C/A therapy provides additional options in caring for your horse.

TIP
C/A Therapy Reality

C/A therapy works differently on each horse, depending on the person offering it and the horse receiving it. Remember, C/A therapy is not always about curing health problems; sometimes it is about managing them.

OTHER HEALING CONCEPTS

Below is an exploration of additional healing concepts in C/A therapy. (Refer to the Resources section, page 211, to learn more.)

Equine Chakra Energy

Chakra is a term derived from an ancient language of India called Sanskrit. It translates as "wheel" or "disk." It symbolically refers to one of seven energy points within the body. There are numerous energy points; however, these seven are accepted as the main chakras in the body.

The chakras invigorate the physical body and stimulate mental and emotional states. Chakra energy points whirl and draw in chi (energy) to maintain the balance of mental, emotional, and physical well-being. In traditional Chinese medicine, chakra locations relate to acupoints. If the chi is unable to circulate through the chakras properly, the resulting imbalance affects health.

In horses, chakras correlate with organ function, emotional stability, and mental health. A horse's mental and emotional states filter through the chakras in the physical body. If a horse is injured, traumatized, or ill, working along the appropriate chakras can lead to restoring whole health.

Treatments for various health issues involve the laying on of hands and the repetition of mental affirmations. The core concept is that the human's healing energy transmits to the horse's energy through the hands, and the repetition of mental affirmations positively influences the energy being transmitted.

The seven chakras in a horse's body are the Crown, Brow, Throat, Heart, Solar Plexus, Sacral, and Root chakras. Each chakra is associated with a color, bodily organ, element, symptom, and function (see page 91).

Equine Chromatherapy

Equine chromatherapy uses color and light to restore mental, physical, and emotional balance in horses. Aside from our natural dependence on light for survival, it is thought that all cells within living beings give off light. Colors emit energy vibrations, which affect the healing process. Your horse may find healing, relief, or balance by being exposed to these vibrations. Colors may be introduced to your horse in several ways:

► *Equine chakra therapy*—Each chakra is associated with a color. You can use this information to apply the appropriate colors in therapy for your horse.

For example, if your horse is a nervous type, always anxious and fearful, you can introduce the color red into his environment. Red aids in overall health, boosts strength, and encourages survival. You can shine a red light in your horse's living space, add red essences to his drinking water, or make a conscious effort to purchase red barn supplies such as buckets, feed tubs, halters, and blankets. Also, place your hands over the root chakra, associated with the color red, consistently and envision your horse being calm and at ease.

▶ *Direct application*—Once you have determined the appropriate color for your horse's needs, shine a colored light directly on the area of your horse you are trying to stimulate. Do not shine the light directly into your horse's eyes, and do not leave the light unattended. Shine the light on the area for several minutes and log your horse's reaction. Slowly increase the minutes as needed.

▶ *Equine clothing*—When purchasing equipment and clothing for you and your horse, be mindful of the colors that offer the most appropriate vibrational effects on your horse and purchase accordingly. For example, if your horse is generally anxious, purchase a blue blanket, as blue is associated with calming vibrations.

▶ *Color essences*—Color essences may be purchased and put into your horse's water. As with any ingestion therapy, discuss this with your veterinarian before offering any and begin with a minimal amount and slowly increase over time. Never increase the dosage beyond the supplier's recommendation.

▶ *Equine interior design*—Choose the most appropriate colors when purchasing your horse's buckets and bins. Consider the wall color of your indoor arena and inside your trailer and barn. Pick colors that promote balance.

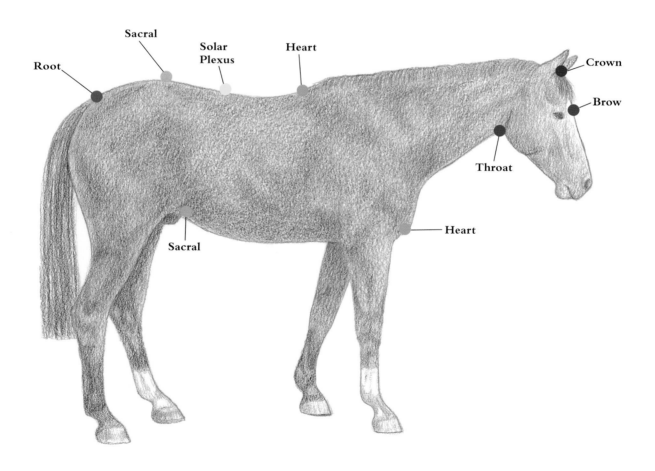

Equine Chakra Chart

	Location	Governs	Color	Contribution	Element	Symptoms of Imbalance
The Brow Chakra	Center of the forehead	Brain—especially the left side—left eye, ears, and nose	Indigo, dark blue, purple	Intuition and mental clarity	Silver	Inability to focus, deficient eyesight
The Crown Chakra	Top of a horse's head, between the ears	Brain—especially the cerebral cortex and the right side of the brain, central nervous system, spine, right eye, and right facial region	Violet	Wisdom, calm, and universal harmony	Gold	Depression and disinterest
The Throat Chakra	Just below the jaw, flowing along the throat region	Throat, mouth, thyroid, lungs, and respiratory system	Light blue	Communication and hearing abilities	Ether	Inability to communicate
The Heart Chakra	Center of a horse's chest	Heart, circulation, immune system, and thoracic vertebrae	Green	The emotions of love, forgiveness, and tolerance	Air	Anger, grief, and heart prolems
The Solar Plexus Chakra	Center of a horse's back	Liver, kidneys, stomach, nervous system, and lumbar vertebrae	Yellow	Emotional release, physical energy, and the will to survive	Fire	Anger, digestive disorders, poor eating habits
The Sacral Chakra	Abdominal region, near the reproductive organs	Pelvis, large intestine, small intestine, reproductive organs, sacrum vertebra, and the lymphatic system	Orange	Emotional security, physical sexual drive, and general release	Water	Reproductive challenges, bladder issues, lumbar discomfort, and jealousy
The Root Chakra	Point where the horse's tail begins	Legs, colon, anus, hooves, spine, and tail	Red	General health, strength, survival, and the mechanism of self-preservation	Earth	Fear, anxiety, aggression, bowel disorders

DIFFERENCES BETWEEN VETERINARY AND C/A APPOINTMENTS

Neither type of professional visit is more acceptable or correct than the other. The two kinds of practitioner simply take different approaches to resolving problems. Generally, an appointment with a veterinarian focuses on the current health concern and often results in treatment through drug therapy. The health issue is viewed as localized and treated accordingly.

A C/A appointment focuses on the horse as a whole entity, addressing its demeanor, condition, emotional vitality, history, and overall health presentation. The practitioner seeks the root of the health problem and any variables affecting or exacerbating it so the cause is addressed, thus resolving the presenting symptom.

Eastern and Western medicine have different views about treatment, so they often work well when used in conjunction. C/A therapy is not a substitute for veterinary care. If your horse appears ill or injured, contact your veterinarian immediately.

DECIDING WHO SHOULD PERFORM C/A TREATMENTS

If you are interested in offering treatments to your horse, consult with your veterinarian first. If you receive clearance from your veterinarian, offer the therapy yourself. Begin with the technique you feel most comfortable with and your veterinarian believes is most appropriate for your horse's condition. You will become more effective with each application.

Do not offer to treat horses not your own. You do not want to assume liability for others' animals.

Local and federal laws vary. Know the laws in your area pertaining to C/A therapy. Then research local therapists. When choosing a professional therapist, ask questions regarding her experience, education, qualifications, references, insurance, and clientele. If possible, talk to clients of the therapist and see what their experiences have been. If the therapist offers clinics, lectures, or demonstrations, attend them. All of these efforts maximize the chances that the professional you choose is one you can trust.

INTEGRATING C/A THERAPY INTO YOUR HORSE'S LIFE

It is better to introduce C/A therapy incrementally. Refer to the chart in this chapter, which lists options according to time schedule. Begin with something simple, perhaps one of the modalities listed under "10-Minute Therapy Session." See page 95. As you become better educated, you can move on to more complex techniques. The idea is to keep the intention, treatment, and goal clear and uncomplicated so the treatment will be effective.

The Healing Properties of Colors

Red	rejuvenates the liver, eases laminitis, promotes bravery
Orange	promotes skeletal strength, settles muscular spasms, promotes stoicism
Yellow	encourages digestion, promotes a bright demeanor
Green	combats infection, restores muscle, promotes emotional harmony, soothes
Blue	aids in skin disorders, disperses anxiety, promotes self-assurance
Purple	eases discomfort, calms, regulates body temperature

TIP

What to Do When You Do Not See Results

If a treatment does not yield results, you can:
- Offer several additional sessions.
- Try another form of therapy.
- Seek the assistance of a professional therapist.
- Discontinue all therapy.

KEY ELEMENTS IN AN EFFECTIVE C/A TREATMENT

One of the most important factors in a therapy is full awareness of your horse's reactions to and communications with you. If your horse is agitated, angry, or uncomfortable, you may choose to move on to another area of the body or to end the session. You and your horse will need an adjustment period to familiarize yourselves with the therapies—you as the provider, and your horse as the receiver. Conversely, if your horse relaxes, settles, and seems content, spend a few more moments working in that area or repeat that therapy sequence in another session. Often, horses begin the sessions concerned and alert until they begin to feel the positive effects of the therapy, at which point they quiet and relax into the sequence. Let your horse tell you what he needs.

CHOOSING THE NUMBER OF TREATMENTS

The number of sessions depends on the type of therapy (see the C/A therapy chart in this chapter). Offer chakra, massage, and acupressure therapies once a week, every other week, or once a month, depending on your goals for your horse. Stretching exercises may be performed more frequently—several times a week or even daily, if time allows. Equine herbology, aromatherapy, chromatherapy, and essential oils therapies may be applied as needed.

TIP

The Power of Intuition

Trust your intuition, feelings, and skill when applying therapy to your horse. As you practice, your awareness sharpens and you gain confidence in your abilities. Always listen to your horse. If your horse is communicating discomfort, lighten your application or move on. If your horse is relaxing and enjoying the therapy, spend a few extra moments on that body area.

Ideas for Session Plans

10-Minute Therapy Session

EQUINE MASSAGE

Cheek

Wither

Chest

Extensor Carpi Radialis

Long Digital Extensor

ESSENTIAL OIL THERAPY

Aromatherapy★

Skin Application★

★ Essential oil therapy blends must be made before beginning for a 10-minute session.

EQUINE HERBAL THERAPY

Ingestion

Compress

EQUINE STRETCHING TECHNIQUES

All the equine stretching techniques, when applied individually, can be completed in 10-minute segments. These techniques include the following stretches: head, combination head/neck, neck, downward neck, shoulder extension, shoulder flexion, back, hind leg adductors, hind leg abductors, and rotational hind leg. These techniques can be applied in combination to create 20-minute and 30-minute sessions.

20-Minute Therapy Session

EQUINE MASSAGE THERAPY

Shoulder

Posterior Pectoral

Serratus

Rib Cage

Hip

Hamstring

Tensor Fascia Latae

EQUINE STRETCHING TECHNIQUE (same as 10-minute session)

30-Minute Therapy Session

EQUINE MASSAGE THERAPY

Neck

Back

Gluteus

EQUINE ACUPRESSURE THERAPY

Arthritis (cold/hot temperature management)

Cold/Cough

Cribbing

Immune System

Shoulder Discomfort

Stress Management

Swollen Joint

EQUINE STRETCHING TECHNIQUES (same as 10-minute session)

EQUINE HERBAL THERAPY

Infusion

Inhalant

Poultice

60-Minute Therapy Session

EQUINE MASSAGE THERAPY

All massage techniques combined into one 60-minute session.

EQUINE ACUPRESSURE THERAPY

Azoturia

Back Pain

Colic

Heaves/Heaving

Hock Joint Issue

Neck Issue

Stifle Joint Issue

5

Equine Massage Therapy

Most horse owners share a common goal, regardless of discipline: to maximize their horses' physical potential and ability. Massage therapy is an ancient healing modality in which a person moves, kneads, and stimulates the body's muscles. A variety of massage strokes alleviate knots, spasms, and entanglements in muscle groups. The results include increased blood flow through the muscles and decreased discomfort from the muscle spasms and entanglements. Moreover, equine massage is a wonderful way for horses and their owners to bond.

Nearly every horse is a candidate for massage therapy. Work and sport horses, especially, benefit from this therapy, as it alleviates pain and prevents future injury. Also, horses recovering from illness or injury benefit from massage, as it prevents muscle atrophy while the horse is inactive during the healing process.

BENEFITS OF EXERCISE

Massage balances a horse's entire body and its systems, allowing the horse to move, work, and perform at full capacity. The increased flow of nutrient-rich blood to the muscle tissue flushes out toxins and excessive fluid, promoting healing. This therapy enhances a horse's total health, physical and emotional. Even mental acuity and learning benefit from the increased blood flow and restored balance.

▶ Massage improves the circulatory and lymphatic systems. It increases the number of red blood cells in the horse's system, in turn easing strain on the heart. Because massage increases blood supply and nutrition to muscles without increasing lactic acid, it helps prevent muscle fatigue during stressful work. Massage therapy also stimulates the lymphatic system, which supports the body's defenses against disease.

▶ Massage relieves muscle tension and pain, allowing muscles to function properly and at full capacity. It also decreases inflammation in the joints and releases endorphins, or hormones, both of which alleviate pain.

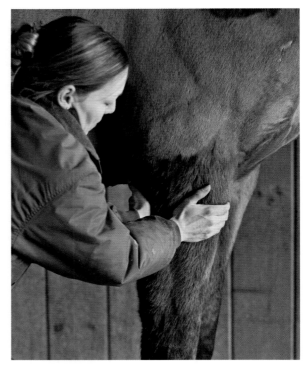
Separating the long digital extensor muscle

▶ Massage enhances muscle tone. It helps prevent and reduce atrophy (loss of muscle). It lengthens connective tissue, thereby increasing the horse's range of motion. This allows for longer strides; easier gait and lead changes; better jumping, turning, maneuvering, and overall physical performance; and increased speed and endurance. In short, massage assists in balancing the horse's entire body, allowing the horse to move at its own maximum capabilities.

▶ Massage improves the general demeanor and disposition of a horse. For example, it can relax a horse that is anxious and easily spooked. It can present a welcome change of routine for a horse; variety improves a horse's emotional health and mental abilities.

Did You Know?

Equine massage therapy has origins that date back thousands of years. The ancient Greeks often massaged their horses before battle and during the Olympic Games. They believed massage enhanced an animal's performance. The Egyptians also documented this practice in their picture writings.

An Ounce of Prevention

For massage therapy to be effective and lasting, the root of the muscle pain must be recognized and addressed. For example, if a horse's back is sore because his saddle doesn't fit properly, massage will temporarily alleviate the pain, but until the saddle itself is replaced or reflocked, the pain will return. The services of equine professionals, including veterinarians, dentists, farriers, and saddle fitters, should always be employed in conjunction with massage therapy.

▸ Massage enhances learning and training. Increased emotional and mental relaxation and blood flow to the brain lay the groundwork for mental clarity and, thus, improved learning and training.

▸ Massage is a noninvasive preventive treatment. If the horse's muscular system is free of problems and functioning properly, the horse's chance of future injury decreases significantly. It is much easier to work toward preventing an injury than resolving one.

▸ Massage may serve as an alternative to drug therapy. Pharmaceuticals often mask a problem rather than resolve it. A horse owner can use massage frequently and effectively as an economical way to restore and maintain a horse's health, reducing other professional or veterinary expenses. Rather than mask a sore muscle with steroids, for example, massage can often resolve the problem.

▸ Massage is a wonderful way to bond and strengthen the relationship between horse and owner. Time spent in a relaxing, hands-on fashion also provides conversation and social time with your companion.

▸ Aging and elderly horses better maintain their muscle condition and strength through massage. Competition horses enjoy reduced stress levels and relief from the physical rigors of competition with regular massage. Horses for sale should be massaged frequently to show them at their best.

Note: As with all complementary and alternative treatments, massage therapy is never a substitute for veterinary care. If your horse appears ill or injured, contact your veterinarian immediately.

Symptoms Indicating Muscular Problems

Outward Signs	Description	Muscles to Treat
Your horse has difficulty bending his body and appears generally stiff.	This is most noticeable when you are riding or driving your horse and ask him to bend left or right. The horse may bend easily in one direction but minimally in the other.	Neck, shoulder, serratus, back, rib cage, hip, latae, tensor fascia
The horse has short strides, moves with tight, restricted shoulder movement, and resists when asked to lengthen stride.	These signs imply tangled muscle groups. Your horse will be able to open, lengthen, or loosen her step when the affected muscles and compensatory muscles are treated.	Chest, shoulder, posterior pectorals, extensor carpi radialis, back, hips, gluteus, hamstring, tensor fascia latae, long digital extensor
The horse experiences cantering problems such as bucking into the canter or landing incorrectly after jumping.	These may be signs of muscular problems rather than behavioral or training issues. A horse's balance is greatly affected by restricted muscles. After massage, cantering may improve.	Shoulder, back, hip, extensor carpi radialis, gluteus, hamstring, tensor fascia latae, long digital extensor
The horse forges or travels unevenly.	Forging (hitting the sole of the front foot with the hind foot) results from tight shoulders that do not move the front feet out of the way quickly enough. Traveling unevenly is often a sign of a muscle issue. Sore, locked muscles cannot perform, so other muscles compensate and become overworked, resulting in uneven movement, motion, and travel.	Wither, shoulder, chest, posterior pectoral, serratus, extensor carpi radialis
The horse is agitated and appears girthy when being saddled.	A horse's body changes shape and form over a year, even months. To address the problem, monitor and adjust tack fit consistently, and treat affected muscle groups. If ill-fitting tack is used, the horse's aggressive behavior may increase, and the behavioral damage may be permanent.	Cheek, wither, shoulder, chest, serratus, rib cage, back

Symptoms Indicating Muscular Problems *(continued)*

Outward Signs	Description	Muscles to Treat
The horse is a flat jumper.	Horses may jump flat when they develop hardened muscle tissues that inhibit completion of the task.	Neck, wither, shoulder, chest, posterior pectoral, serratus, rib cage, hip, extensor carpi radialis, back, gluteus, hamstring, tensor fascia latae, long digital extensor
The horse has sticky hind leg motion, resists picking up his feet for the farrier, or has difficulty engaging his hind end.	Hind end problems may derive from soft tissue or skeletal issues. The horse's source of power is the hind end. If this is compromised, he will have limited power.	Back, rib cage, hip, gluteus, hamstring, tensor fascia latae, long digital extensor
The horse has trouble with lateral movements.	If muscle groups are entangled or muscles are sore from overwork, the horse will have trouble bending, balancing, and moving his frame to complete sideways movements..	Neck, wither, shoulder, chest, serratus, posterior pectoral, extensor carpi radialis, back, rib cage, hip, gluteus, hamstring, tensor fascia latae, long digital extensor
The horse is sensitive when groomed or becomes angry when blanketed.	These may be behavioral problems or the horse's way of saying he has painful muscles that need attention. Palpate to locate areas of sensitivity. You may find areas of hardened tissue or knots.	Full body treatment (all sequences) is appropriate
The horse has difficulty stretching his head and neck downward or tosses his head incessantly.	Horses use their heads and necks to balance their bodies, so their neck muscles often carry tension, knots, pain, and sensitivity.	Cheek, neck, wither, back, gluteus
The horse travels with his tail off to one side.	This may indicate a sore back. The back muscles may be sore, spasmodic, or tight, causing discomfort and inhibiting the ability to move.	Wither, serratus, back, gluteus, rib cage

SIGNS OF MUSCULAR PROBLEMS

This chart lists outward signs of muscular problems and identifies the muscles involved. Some of the signs mentioned may seem to be behavioral in nature. However, behavioral problems are often organic in nature—that is, manifestations of underlying physical imbalances or disease.

Note: As always, when in doubt, consult a veterinarian.

CONTRAINDICATIONS OF MASSAGE

Massage can be harmful in certain circumstances. Certain conditions may be exacerbated by the increased rate of metabolism triggered by massage. In addition, injuries, such as torn tissue or broken blood vessels, often need several days to heal before massage is possible.

▸ *Fever*—Massage increases the rate of metabolism, exacerbating the fever.

▸ *Shock*—Massage therapy lowers blood pressure, worsening the shock.

▸ *Cancer*—Do not massage unless the horse is under the care of a veterinarian and written permission is granted. Massage may encourage cancer growth as it increases the body's metabolism rate.

TIP

Muscles and Vices

Horses with stereotypies (repetitve movements cribbing, weaving, wall kicking) overexert their muscles due to the repetitive nature of these behaviors. Such movements often lead to problems within the muscle groups.

▸ *Severe injury or torn tissue*—Massage should not be performed for at least 7 days after an injury, and should be performed only lightly for up to 14 days after therapy is implemented, depending on the severity of the tear or injury. This window allows the horse's blood vessels to heal. Premature treatment may cause muscle bleeding and thence muscle hardening, which inhibits the healing process.

▸ *Pregnancy*—Pregnant mares should be massaged only after consulting a veterinarian. A pregnant mare should not be massaged around the genitalia or abdominal region in order to protect the developing fetus.

▸ *Open wound*—Wounds need time to close and heal properly. Massaging a wounded area increases the risk of reopening the wound.

PRE-TREATMENT SETUP

Before the start of a treatment, address these environmental elements:

Secure the Horse

You will need a halter and a lead or a set of crossties to safely tie and secure the horse for the massage session. If using a lead, secure your horse with a quick-release safety knot. This particular knot secures the horse but releases easily and quickly if he pulls back on it forcefully.

Owner (or Masseuse)

Dress appropriately for the season so you are comfortable and able to focus on the session. In colder temperatures, wearing layers is advised, as massaging the horse warms both the horse and owner, and removing layers may be necessary. Similarly, in warmer temperatures, dress to avoid overheating. Bring along drinking water so you stay hydrated as you perform the treatment. As always, dress in a manner that is safe and appropriate for working with horses, including proper footwear.

Work Environment

Choose a time of day that is quieter than most so both horse and owner can focus with minimal distraction or interruption. Do not massage during feeding or turn-out time. Work in a location that is neither too warm nor too chilly, and stay properly attired and adequately sheltered in frigid temperatures.

Workspace

Massage in a location that is spacious and allows free movement. Tie the horse properly in a safe area, preferably an aisle instead of a stall, as the aisle is bigger. If a stall is the only option, be sure you can get out quickly. (If the horse becomes agitated or begins to bite and kick, a swift exit is advised.) Also, the owner (or masseuse) should never work between a wall and a horse. There is always a risk of being kicked or pressed up against a wall. Even a good-natured horse may kick or bite if a particularly sensitive spot is touched.

Additional Materials

A stool is helpful for reaching your horse's neck, spine, and hindquarters; chalk or stickers for marking sensitive body areas that require additional treatment; and an audio recorder or pen and paper to record treatment notes.

BEGINNING THE TREATMENT

Always approach your horse in a slow, quiet manner on his left side. General horsemanship teaches handling a horse on the left; therefore, most horses are comfortable with being approached on that side. Because treatment may be a new experience for your horse, begin with short sessions.

You may find your horse wants to move around when certain areas are touched. That is acceptable as long as he does so safely. It is unlikely the horse will stand perfectly still for a treatment. Soothing words of encouragement quiet a horse and help him make the connection that massage is a positive experience.

As you move from one part of the body to another, alert your horse first by merely placing your hand on the horse's body so he knows which area you will work on next. This gives him a chance to feel and acclimate to your touch before the actual manipulations begin.

When massaging your horse, do not focus on any one area too long, especially if it is highly sensitive. Work lightly and move on, leaving a very sore area for later on in the same session—or another session entirely.

If you will revisit an area later in the same session, mark it lightly with chalk or a small sticker. You can also keep your fingertips or palm resting on an area, continuing the treatment with the free hand. (If any area proves a concern, contact your veterinarian.) You may want to take notes or record your findings on an audio recorder. As you work on your horse over time, note areas of improvement, new areas of reactivity, and any significant changes.

Horses should be massaged regularly for best results. If single treatments or random treatments are applied infrequently, the therapy will be less effective. Several sessions may be required to resolve an issue. The more consistently a muscle is treated, the more it will release and the longer the beneficial effects will last.

Observing Behavior During Treatment

Observe how your horse moves away from or into you, and try not to confuse your horse's muscle movements with actual spasms. If your horse is moving his body, you will see muscles move; if your horse is standing still and you see ripples along the muscle tissue, that is a spasm.

Avoid being kicked or bitten. Horses that generally do not kick or bite may do so during a session. It is their way of saying you have found a sensitive area. Always keep a watchful eye on your horse's teeth, legs, and feet.

Major Equine Muscles

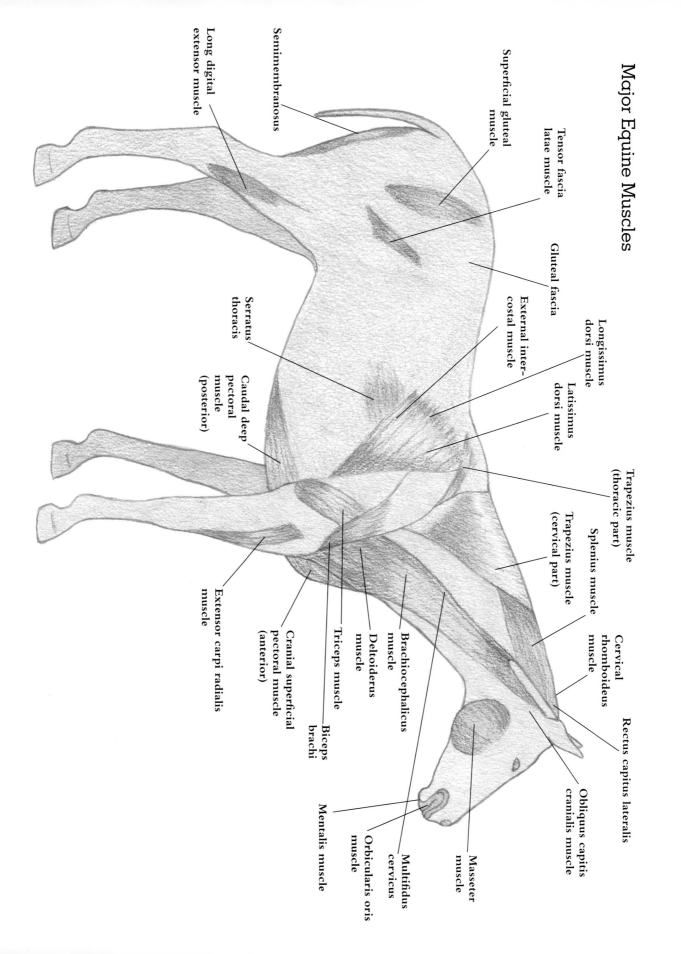

Long digital
extensor muscle

Semimembranosus

Superficial gluteal
muscle

Tensor fascia
latae muscle

Gluteal fascia

Serratus
thoracis

External inter-
costal muscle

Longissimus
dorsi muscle

Latissimus
dorsi muscle

Caudal deep
pectoral
muscle
(posterior)

Trapezius muscle
(thoracic part)

Splenius muscle

Trapezius muscle
(cervical part)

Cervical
rhomboideus
muscle

Rectus capitus lateralis

Extensor carpi radialis
muscle

Cranial superficial
pectoral muscle
(anterior)

Triceps muscle

Biceps
brachi

Deltoiderus
muscle

Brachiocephalicus
muscle

Mentalis muscle

Orbicularis oris
muscle

Multifidus
cervicus

Masseter
muscle

Obliquus capitis
cranialis muscle

General Massage Sequence

Begin the massage sequence with clear mental focus and the intention of helping your horse to the best of your ability. Adjust your breathing pattern so it is deep and slow, transmitting a sense of relaxation. Horses are intuitive, sensitive creatures and respond to your body language and energy.

DURING MASSAGE

Work each side equally, moving from top to bottom, front to back, one area or muscle group at a time. Begin each stroke with light pressure and observe your horse's reaction. Complete one technique and then complete the same technique on the opposite side. Compare the sides to establish a sense of the horse's physical balance. Always treat both sides, as one of the goals of massage is to establish symmetry to ensure the animal uses his body evenly, discouraging compensation.

Every series of strokes is completed in four main steps. First, prepare or *open* the area. Next, feel the area to *locate* any problems. Once you locate a problem, you can *treat* it. Finally, complete the treatment by *closing* the area.

While palpating, feel for knots, spasm, adhesions, and areas that trigger a reaction. A knot is an entanglement of muscle tissue, forming a hardened lump. A spasm is an involuntary muscular contraction, causing a rippling effect. An adhesion is muscle tissue abnormally bonded together, usually from inflammation.

Common reactions a horse may exhibit are flinching, pulling away, leaning into your hand, stomping, sighing, or tilting the head. These are all ways of saying you have touched a sensitive area.

AFTER MASSAGE

Your horse may be uncomfortable post-treatment. The manipulated tissue may never have been worked so acutely. The muscles may have been tight

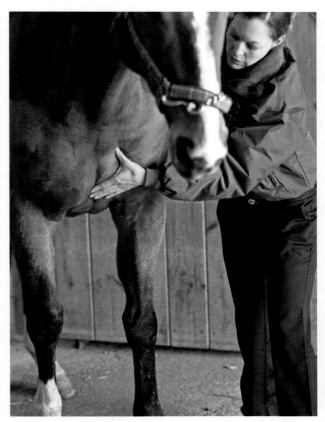

Separating the long digital extensor muscle

for some time, and your horse has been compensating for the imbalance.

After a treatment, a horse may seem unsound, sore, or agitated—maybe even worse than before. Initially, he may be reluctant to move, but his muscles will warm and loosen as the post-massage stiffness goes away. As always, if you have concerns about a horse's appearance after a treatment, contact a veterinarian.

Massage Strokes

Several types of massage strokes are used in equine therapy. During each session, each stroke is applied in three rounds, each with increased pressure—(1) light, (2) medium, (3) heavy)—and each firmer than the one before.

Effleurage is a stroke used to prepare the horse for a massage session. It is applied by opening your hand, turning your palm to face downward, and running it smoothly along your horse's body.

Step 1: Opening

Compression is applied with either an open hand (with the palm facing downward in the heel-of-the-hand position) or with a fist (back-of-the-hand position). Both positions are applied by turning the hand in a twisting motion. The right hand twists clockwise and the left hand turns counterclockwise. Compression presses muscle against bone, releasing entanglements and increasing circulation. Do not overuse this stroke; one rotation is sufficient.

Percussion helps soften the tissue, making it more pliable. The chopping motion is performed by lightly bouncing the side of a fist off the muscle or the side of an open hand off the tissue. It is essential to keep the wrist and elbow loose, allowing the hand to literally bounce. *Caution: Never apply this stroke over the kidneys or any bony area of the body.*

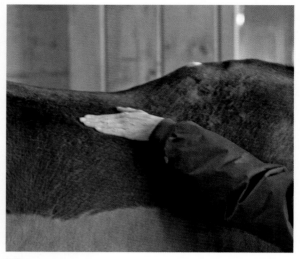

Effleurage

Heel-of-the-hand compression

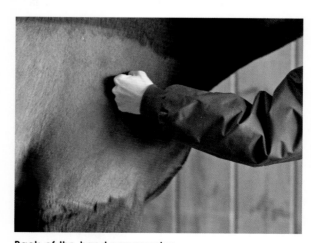

Back-of-the-hand compression

Percussion with a closed fist, working muscle

Slapping (a)

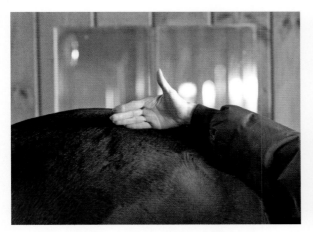

Percussion with the side of the hand, working tissue

Slapping (b)

Slapping is similar to percussion in technique and force; however, the hand is positioned with the palm downward instead.

Jostling is used to soften tissue, thereby promoting ease of movement. This stroke is primarily used along the top of the horse's neck. Place your hands over the top of your horse's neck, as if grasping the top ridge, and move the tissue toward and away from you, attempting to release the neck muscle.

Jostling

Step 2: Locating

Palpation

The locating step of the massage treatment is achieved through palpation. Palpation is performed by using the pad of the thumb or fingertip to press and run along the muscle tissue to feel for knots, congestion, or spasms and to assess the horse's possible reaction to deeper massage strokes.

Step 3: Treating

Direct pressure

The treating step involves two strokes. The first stroke is called *direct pressure*. Direct pressure increases nutrient, oxygen, and blood flow to a deficient area. Use the thumb pad or finger pad to press downward, directly into an area. Apply light downward pressure for several seconds, then ease the pressure (without losing contact). Repeat with moderate pressure, then slowly ease the pressure (without losing contact). Apply heavy downward pressure, and slowly release. (Respect whatever pressure your horse will allow, as he may not be able to tolerate heavy pressure during the first few treatments.)

Cross-fiber friction treats an issue by releasing entangled fibers. With the finger pad or thumb pad, move the finger or thumb in a sideways motion, left to right. If the pressure is too heavy or too rapid, the stroke may be painful. Begin slowly and lightly. The length of the stroke is 1 to 2 inches (2.5 to 5.1 cm).

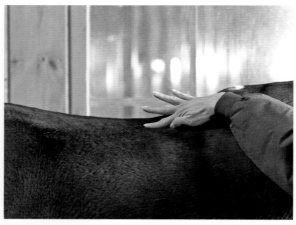
Palpation

Direct pressure

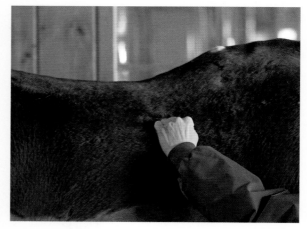
Cross-fiber friction

Step 4: Closing

Sweating is a stroke in which the open hand, palm facing downward, is placed on the massage area. Applying light pressure, the hand is held steadily in place for 25 seconds. It is useful for horses that cannot tolerate other strokes. It is effective because it transmits heat and energy to the area, helping soothe any discomfort.

The closing step can also be achieved with compression or percussion.

Massage Pressure

All massage strokes are applied in three cycles (or three applications) using three levels of pressure. The first round of a stroke is applied with gentle, light pressure for 5 to 10 seconds. The second round is applied with moderate pressure, maintained for 10 to 15 seconds. For the last round of a stroke, apply firm, even, heavy pressure for 15 to 20 seconds.

The amount of pressure applied can be adjusted according to your horse's reaction. A horse will always send a clear signal about the level of pressure he can tolerate. If your horse appears highly sensitive and reactive during the initial light-pressure phase, that degree of stroke might be adequate for the treatment session. If your horse is leaning into the strokes, enjoying the pressure, he is indicating that a heavier pressure would be appreciated. As both horse and owner become more comfortable with massage, the pressure (and duration) of the individual strokes can gradually increase.

Equine Massage Techniques

The following is a series of classic, professional equine massage techniques you can easily apply to your horse. You can use each technique on its own or in combination, depending on how much time you allot for the massage session or which muscle groups require treatment. Always begin massage on the left side of your horse. Once you have completed a technique, repeat it immediately on the right side.

Separating the intercostal muscles

CHEEK TECHNIQUE

This technique is especially effective for any horse that carries a mouth bit. Imagine holding a lollipop in your mouth for long periods. Eventually your mouth muscles would become sore from the exertion. This is the way the horse's mouth feels as he maintains bit carriage. The two muscles treated are the *masseter,* which enables chewing, and the *mentalis,* which raises and wrinkles the skin on the chin, lifting the lower lip.

The Masseter Muscle

1. Stand on the left side of your horse, at the head, facing in the same direction. Slowly place your open palms flat on each side of your horse's cheek, in the sweating stroke position.

2. Move your hands in a circular motion, working away from you for a few minutes; then reverse direction to work toward you for several more minutes. This circular motion loosens the masseter muscle.

Cheek technique, step 2

The Mentalis Muscle

3. Stand in front of your horse, facing the head. Gently place a hand on each side of the top of the head, at the base of the ears, in the sweating stroke position.

4. With flat, extended fingertips, gently pull the facial tissue down along the sides of the face toward the lower lip, the mentalis muscle. This pulling motion helps release skin and muscle tissue. For working horses, loosening this tissue may help to promote acceptance of the bit, as the muscles will become soft and pliable.

Cheek technique, step 4

WITHER TECHNIQUE

The trapezius and rhomboid muscles are found in the wither area. These muscles pull the scapula up, forward, and backward, elevating the shoulder. Excessive saddle pressure is often a problem for these muscles. The trapezius and rhomboid muscles are vital to shoulder movement; if these muscles are tight, shoulder movement is restricted. Shoulder spasms can be triggered from the wither area as well. During treatment, most horses have a strong, visible reaction, usually tilting the head, stretching the head and neck forward, and wriggling the lips.

1. Begin by percussing the area with a chopping motion. Work back and forth (a and b) along the muscle, varying the amount of pressure applied.

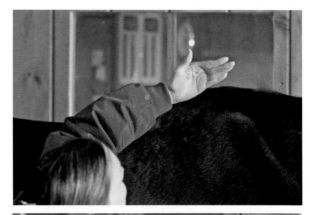

Wither technique, step 1 (a) and 1 (b)

2. Compress the soft tissue up into the bony area of the wither. Pressing the tissue into the bone helps release entanglements.

3. Palpate this section with the pad of your index finger or thumb. Treat knots or reactive areas with direct pressure and cross-fiber friction.

4. Close the sequence with compression.

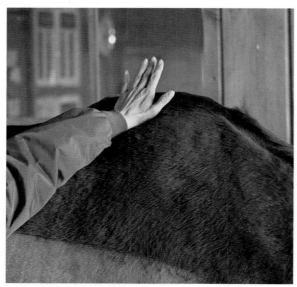
Wither technique, step 2

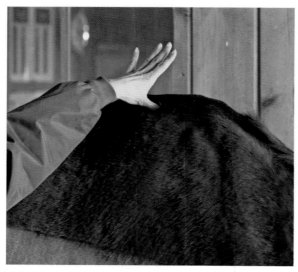
Wither technique, step 3

NECK TECHNIQUE

This neck technique treats two muscle groups: the top of the neck, where the rectus capitus lateralis and the splenius are located, and the lower neck, where the multifidus cervicus and the brachiocephalicus are. The rectus capitus lateralis muscle enables the horse to flex his head from side to side, and the splenius muscle bends the neck forward. The multifidus cervicus muscle allows the horse to rotate his head. The brachiocephalicus allows him to move his head and neck to the side and also aids in front leg movement (when the head and neck are stabilized).

Neck technique, step 1

1. Place the pad of the thumb about 1 inch (2.5 cm) behind the ear (on the obliquus capitis cranialis muscle; see page 104) and apply direct pressure. This encourages the horse to lower his head to the floor, releasing stress in the poll. If your horse does not drop his head to the floor, move on to step 2. (See tip box below.)

2. To loosen your horse's head and neck, stand on the horse's left side, facing the same direction. Hold the halter tightly on each side and gently swing your horse's head from side to side (a and b).

> ▽ **TIP**
>
> ## Monitoring Stress Release
>
> Sometimes a horse may seem agitated, reluctant, or uncooperative during a massage treatment. He may achieve only a limited amount of relaxation, especially if massage is still new. He may not understand why he is being physically manipulated, and he may be uneasy. Always monitor your horse's reactions to initial gestures. Does the horse respond by relaxing down to the floor, or does he react by raising his head and looking alarmed? Observe the response. Praise and talk calmly to your horse. If he does not relax, repeat the process two more times. Generally, as the session continues, the horse will begin to relax. However, if he is having trouble accepting and settling into the treatment, it is okay to move on—either to the next step or to another activity.

Neck technique, step 2 (a) and 2 (b)

▶ The Upper Neck

This portion of the massage addresses the rectus capitus lateralis and splenius muscles. See pages 110–111 for more on individual muscles.

3. Stand on the left side of your horse, facing him. Place both hands over the crest and jostle the top of the neck. (a) Slowly move your hands down the entire length of the neck, continuing to jostle (b and c). Repeat this for several minutes, increasing the rate of jostling. The neck muscles release and become loose and pliable.

The upper neck technique, step 3 (a)

The upper neck technique, step 3 (b) and 3 (c)

4. Starting at the top of the neck, just behind the ear, lightly compress up and down along the crest, increasing the amount of pressure with each pass along the neck. If your horse is agitated—that is, pinning ears or nipping—lighten the pressure.

The upper neck technique, step 4

5. Palpate the entire length of your horse's neck, working from the bottom to the top, feeling for hard, knotty areas or places that trigger a negative reaction. If you locate a reactive spot, treat it with direct pressure. The horse may lean into your hand, wanting more pressure, or move away because the area is sensitive. Both responses indicate the area requires attention.

6. Apply cross-fiber friction for about 20 seconds. This stroke usually elicits an obvious reaction from the horse; he stretches his head and neck forward, tilts his heads to one side, or wriggles his lips.

7. Close this area by using the compression stroke (see page 106).

Work the neck from top to bottom several times. Finish by jostling the entire length of neck. Notice your horse's neck is much more flexible when jostled at this phase of treatment.

▼ The Lower Neck

This portion of the massage addresses the multifidus cervicus and brachiocephalicus muscles. See pages 110–111 for more on individual muscles.

8. Work the muscles of the lower neck by compressing up and down the entire length.

9. Palpate the lower neck using your thumb pad or index finger pad. As you feel for knots, watch your horse's reaction. If you locate sensitive or hard areas, treat with direct pressure and cross-fiber friction.

10. Close this area by using the compression stroke (see page 106).

The lower neck technique, step 9

SHOULDER TECHNIQUE

The deltoid and triceps muscles are located in the shoulders. The deltoid is responsible for shoulder joint extension, while the triceps is responsible for shoulder joint flexion and elbow joint extension.

1. Face your horse's shoulder. Begin by percussing the shoulder from top to bottom, front to back, using a chopping motion.

2. Compress the shoulder to soften the tissue. Bend your knees so you can freely move up and down the shoulder muscles. Your horse may be sensitive and tight in this area and may try to move away. Just follow your horse wherever he steps, varying the pressure. The muscle tissue will soften and become pliable.

3. Palpate the groove between the deltoid and triceps muscles. Place the pad of your thumb or index finger at the bottom of this groove. This spot is located at the base of your horse's arm. Palpate upward, following the line of the groove. Treat reactive areas with direct pressure and cross-fiber friction.

4. Close the shoulder with back-hand compression.

5. Encourage additional movement in the shoulder by placing the palms of your hands, facing downward, on the shoulder muscles and moving them in a circular pattern.

You will see the shoulder muscles move much more freely after applying this technique.

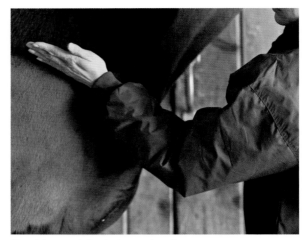
Shoulder neck technique, step 1

Shoulder technique, step 2

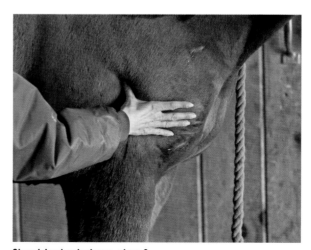
Shoulder technique, step 3

CHEST TECHNIQUE

The biceps and anterior pectoral muscles are located in the chest region. These muscles are responsible for the extension of your horse's front legs.

1. Stand facing your horse's left shoulder. Reach around to the front of his chest with your left hand and open the chest with slapping (a and b). As you work back and forth across the chest, be watchful of nipping. On the last pass, close the hand a bit, grasp the tissue, and wiggle each section back and forth to loosen the area (c).

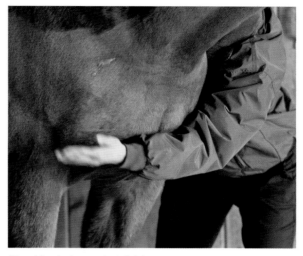

Chest technique, step 1 (c)

2. Palpate up the biceps. This muscle can be quite fleshy, so press in firmly. Treat any findings with direct pressure.

3. Move your hand over to the anterior pectoral and palpate. Treat hardness or sensitivity with direct pressure.

4. Close the chest off with slapping strokes.

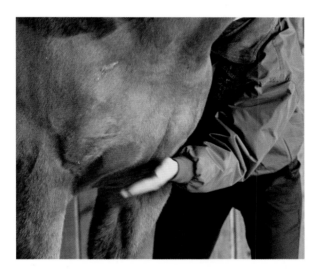

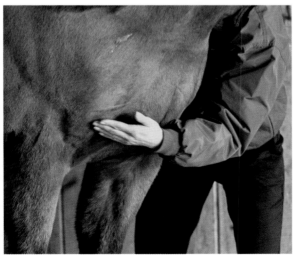

Chest technique, step 1 (a) and 1 (b)

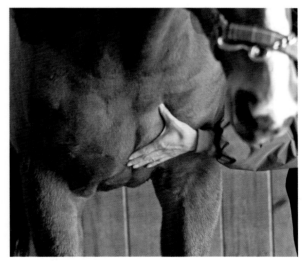

Chest technique, step 2

POSTERIOR PECTORAL TECHNIQUE

The posterior pectoral muscle enables your horse to pull the front legs backward. This muscle is often highly sensitive. Pay close attention to your horse's feet so you are not stepped on accidentally if he moves around while you are working on the posterior pectoral. This muscle is responsible for shortening your horse's step and correct leads when cantering.

1. Face your horse's left shoulder. Bend your knees and reach underneath him to find the posterior pectoral muscle.

2. Open with slapping.

3. Palpate the entire length of the muscle. Treat issues with direct pressure and cross-fiber friction.

4. Close the area with slapping.

SERRATUS THORACIS TECHNIQUE

The serratus thoracis muscle is highly reactive in most horses and often experiences overexertion, especially in jumping, racing, and dressage horses. It is responsible for stabilizing the horse's trunk when his legs are fixed. If your horse travels unevenly, or your saddle moves over to one side, resting unevenly, this muscle may be the cause. If you observe your horse moving stiffly in the front legs, this muscle may need treatment. Also, if your horse experiences shoulder or hoof problems, check the serratus thoracis, as those problems may be referred to this muscle.

1. Open the muscle cautiously with compression. Work the muscle tissue from top to bottom, moving from the front of the muscle toward the back.

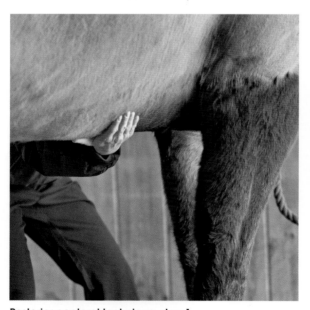

Posterior pectoral technique, step 1

Serratus thoracis technique, step 1

2. Palpate down the area, using the pads of the pointing, middle, and ring finger together. Palpate down the muscle in 3- to 4-inch (7.6 to 10.2 cm) increments, dividing the muscle into front, middle, and back sections. If any discomfort presents, treat with direct pressure and cross-fiber friction.

3. Close the muscle using compression.

4. Check on post-treatment looseness by cupping your hands, palms downward, on the muscle (a). Lightly make circular motions throughout the entire muscle (b). Observe the movement the tissue now exhibits.

Serratus thoracis technique, step 2

Serratus thoracis technique, step 4 (a) and 4 (b)

EXTENSOR CARPI RADIALIS TECHNIQUE

These muscles help maintain healthy tendons. If they are supple and functioning properly, the tendons receive less strain and injury to them is less likely. The extensor carpi radialis muscles enable your horse to flex his front legs.

1. Stand facing your horse's left shoulder. Bend your knees in a semi-squat position. Place your right hand around the top of your horse's leg to stabilize it.

2. Open the muscle by compressing with your left hand, working from the top toward the bottom.

3. Trace the lining of the muscle tissue with the pad of your thumb or fingertip. Follow the grooves of the muscle tissue (a, b, and c). It is now time to separate the muscle tissue. Place the palm of each hand on the outer edge of the muscle and gently pull the tissue away from the center, literally separating the muscle (d).

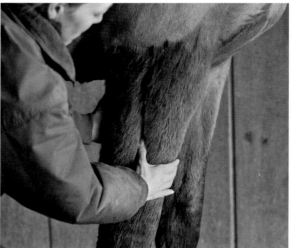

4. Close the area, percussing it with a chopping motion.

Extensor carpi radialis technique, step 1

Extensor carpi radialis technique, step 3 (a), 3 (b), and 3 (c)

Extensor carpi radialis technique, step 3 (d)

BACK TECHNIQUE

The back is a source of discomfort for many horses. Ill-fitting tack, poor riding, the aging process, exertion from work, and conformation all contribute to back problems. When your horse has a sore back, he will have a difficult time when asked to bend to either side, and his coordination and power will be affected. The longissimus dorsi and the latissimus dorsi muscles are located in your horse's back. These muscles enable your horse to extend his back and bend his spine laterally.

1. Face your horse's spine. Begin by sweating the entire length of the spine. While doing this, breathe deeply and slowly, transmitting calmness to your horse. This will help him settle, as many horses are concerned when their backs are touched because of underlying areas of sensitivity.

2. Cautiously percuss along the back muscles using a chopping motion (a and b). Do not percuss over the kidneys. The kidneys are located on each side, underneath the backbone, level with the last rib.

3. Sweat the kidney area.

Back technique, step 2 (a) and 2 (b)

4. Compression is the next stroke. Starting at the front of the spine and working your way back, compress the tissue up into the backbone. This will help break up any adhesions. Do this lightly, only once, as you do not want to agitate your horse. Keep in mind that your horse's back, like the human spine, is a tender area.

5. Palpate along the backbone, feeling for knots, watching for spasms, and observing your horse's reaction. If you feel a hard area, see a rippling spasm, or your horse ducks away from your hand, stop and treat the area with direct pressure, followed by cross-fiber friction.

6. Once the treatment phase is complete, give your horse a back rub. Place the palm of your hand horizontally along the front of the backbone, fingers facing the hind end. Slowly and lightly push the heel of your hand down and press it along the backbone toward the hind end. Repeat this with a bit more pressure, eventually working up to heavier pressure, if your horse allows. If your horse does not react positively to the increase in pressure, use only light pressure.

7. Finish the back muscle technique by closing with percussion, using a chopping motion.

Back technique, step 4

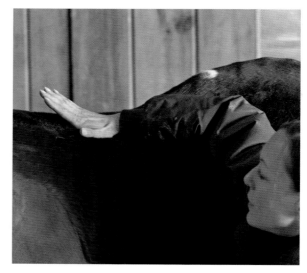
Back technique, step 6

RIB CAGE TECHNIQUE

The supporting muscles that lie within the ribs are the intercostals. These muscles help your horse's breathing process. The intercostals are often quite sensitive. Typically, if your horse has back problems he will also have problems in the intercostals. Saddles sit on top of this area, and riders kick these muscles when signaling their horses. Your horse may be highly reactive and agitated when you try to work on this region. Always use caution, moving slowly and lightly, speaking words of encouragement to your horse when manipulating these tissues. Beware of kicking and biting.

Divide the rib cage into three sections visually, working the front, middle, and rear sections individually.

1. Face your horse's left rib cage. Begin by placing both of your palms flat on the top front portion of the rib cage. Gently spread the rib cage apart with the palms of your hands, working the tissue to separate the ribs. Manipulate each section from top to bottom.

2. Repeat the separation step in all three sections of the rib cage (a and b).

3. Palpate down each individual section (a, b, and c). Treat findings or areas of discomfort with direct pressure and cross-fiber friction. If your horse does not tolerate any work in the rib cage, sweat the area. It may take a few sessions before you can apply the other strokes to the intercostals. (See page 124.)

4. Close the muscle by repeating the separation step, pulling the ribs apart, in all three sections.

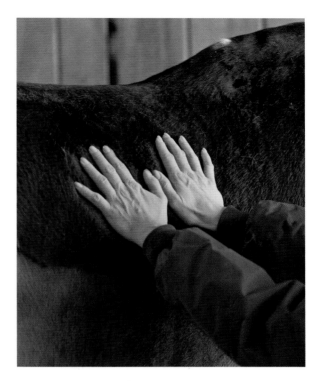

Rib cage technique, step 2 (a) and 2 (b)

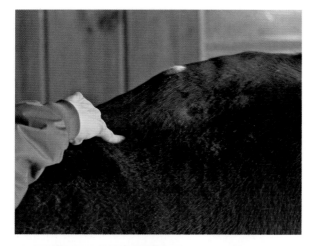

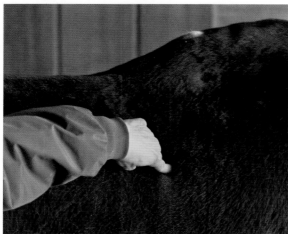

Rib cage technique, step 3 (a) and 3 (b)

HIP TECHNIQUE

The hips are highly sensitive and should be treated with care and caution.

1. Stand facing your horse's left hip. Begin by sweating the hip with both of your palms. This will give you a moment to observe your horse's reaction to the hip being touched. Does he move away? Does he offer a hoof? Does he pin his ears flat back? Be careful, as he may try to kick out to the side.

2. Proceed with caution. Begin working directly in front of the hip (a). Starting at the top, compress downward, following the curve of the hip (b).

3. Percuss, using a chopping motion directly behind the hip. Follow the contour of the hip downward (a, b, and c).

4. Palpate down the front and back of the hip, using your finger or thumb pad. If you locate knots, spasms, or reactive areas, treat them with direct pressure. You will often see spasms in the front lower portion of the hip area. If you do, apply direct pressure and sweat the area.

5. Close the hip with compression in the front and percussion behind the hip, as in the opening step.

Rib cage technique, step 3 (c)

Hip technique, step 2 (a) and 2 (b)

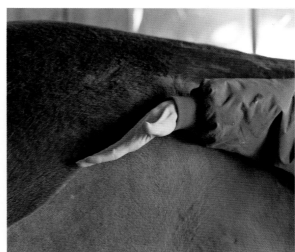

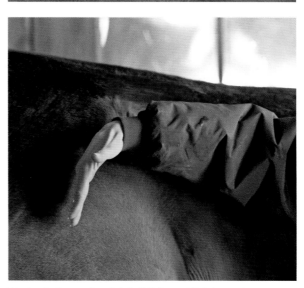

Hip technique, step 3 (a), 3 (b), and 3 (c)

GLUTEUS TECHNIQUE

The gluteus muscles are usually highly stressed because they are responsible for a horse's power. They work in conjunction with the back muscles and are a major source of back problems.

1. Face your horse's hind end. Begin by percussing the area, using a chopping motion. Work the muscle from top to bottom, front to back (a and b). Notice the muscle becomes quite pliable after several minutes of percussion.

2. Palpate. Place your finger or thumb pad in a horizontal position, 2 to 3 inches (5.1 to 7.6 cm) away from the spine (a). Press down and trace a line in the direction of the hind end (b and c). If you observe any reactions or find entanglements, treat them with direct pressure and cross–fiber friction.

3. Repeat the palpation line every 2 to 3 inches (5.1 to 7.6 cm), working toward the floor. Treat all the problems you locate on each palpation line along the entire muscle. Complete three or four lines of palpation.

4. Close the gluteus muscle by percussing, using a chopping motion. Take a moment to observe the bounciness the muscle now displays.

Gluteus technique, step 1 (a) and 1 (b)

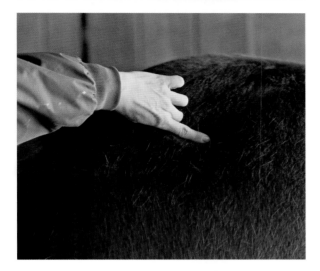

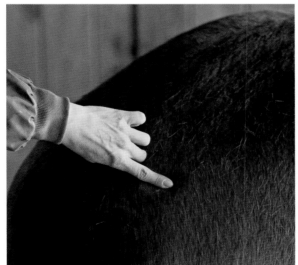

HAMSTRING TECHNIQUE

The semimembranosus muscle, or hamstring, is highly sensitive. It enables the hip joint to extend. If your horse takes tiny steps, appears sticky in his lateral motion, or is sensitive in the stifle, this muscle is involved. If your horse carries his tail off to one side when traveling, suspect hamstring trouble.

1. Face your horse's left hind leg. Do not stand behind your horse. Stand to the side and place your free hand gently on the outside of his lower leg to help prevent him from kicking.

2. Reach between your horse's hind legs. Gently slap the area to open it. Observe if one hamstring is larger than the other. This indicates your horse is overcompensating with the hind leg that has the larger hamstring.

3. Palpate the muscle lightly with your thumb or finger pad, avoiding the large, protrusive vein that runs through the area. If you locate knots or reactive spots, apply direct pressure. Be careful when applying direct pressure to this muscle. Your horse may stand quietly during the opening and locating steps of this sequence but may react strongly when direct pressure is applied. If your horse has difficulty with direct pressure in this muscle, sweat the area instead.

4. Close the hamstring with slapping strokes.

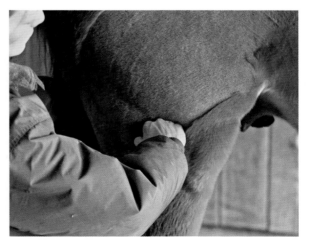

Gluteus technique, step 2 (a), 2 (b), and 2 (c)

Hamstring technique, step 1

TENSOR FASCIA LATAE TECHNIQUE

This muscle allows the hip to extend and the stifle to flex. If your horse has difficulty with lateral movements, he may be tight in this area.

1. Face your horse's left hind leg. Open the muscle using compression (a and b). Work lightly and slowly, as many horses are not fond of being touched in this region.

2. Using your finger or thumb pad, palpate the center of the muscle. If you locate a knot or reactive area, treat it with direct pressure and cross-fiber friction.

3. Close this muscle with compression.

Tensor fascia latae technique, step 1 (a), 1 (b)

LONG DIGITAL EXTENSOR TECHNIQUE

Work these muscles in the same manner as the extensor carpi radialis technique (page 120). These muscles enable your horse's hind legs to flex. You may find his horse's hind extensors are tight. This is quite common, as tremendous exertion is placed on them because your horse's main source of power is his hind end.

Tensor fascia latae technique, step 2

POST-MASSAGE

Once you have completed a massage session, offer your horse water. Massage therapy increases circulation and flushes toxins out through the skin. Your horse may be thirsty. He may drink heavily for several days following a session.

Hand-walk your horse for 10 to 15 minutes after a massage. This helps reduce post-massage soreness. Ask him to move forward, using his freshly loosened muscle tissue. Massage stimulates bodily functions; therefore, your horse may need to relieve himself. Return your horse to the stall or paddock for a few minutes fairly soon after the massage.

You may work or ride your horse after a treatment. However, if time allows, let him rest and relax in the stall or paddock for a while after the treatment. This allows the body to settle after the muscles have been manipulated. If it is a cold day and your horse is usually blanketed, blanket your horse after the session to prevent chill.

6

Equine Stretching

Stretching is an act or motion in which body parts spread, reach out, or flex to offer release. Release may be from physical restriction or emotional tension. Stretching, which has both physical and emotional benefits, is an important part of maintaining a happy, healthy horse. Stretching prevents injuries, reinforces strength, alleviates pain, enhances performance, reduces stress, and restores balance naturally.

PHYSICAL BENEFITS OF EQUINE STRETCHING

Stretching is an excellent preventive care measure. It promotes muscular flexibility, elasticity, and suppleness, thereby allowing the muscle to function properly. When muscles are loose and free from entanglements, spasms, and rigidity, they function at their optimum level, lessening the risk of injury.

Muscle can become tight and knotted through exertion, tension, or trauma. If the tightness or knots are not released, problems worsen. Tendon, ligament, and additional muscle groups become involved.

Stretching allows muscle to either maintain the shape of or lengthen the muscle fiber, increasing suppleness. Proper functioning eases the strain placed on tendons and ligaments. If muscles are functioning and tendons and ligaments are less stressed, injury is less likely to occur.

Stretching helps relieve pain. Think about awakening in the morning—your body is stiff and uncomfortable. You get out of bed and stretch, and you generally feel better. Why? You have released tension from your muscles, alleviating the discomfort.

This is true for your horse as well. Stretching releases muscular spasms triggered by pain. These occur when the muscle tissue is deprived of oxygen. Oxygen deprivation occurs when muscle fibers are knotted, restricting circulation.

Stretching is a natural performance enhancer for your horse. People generally recognize that muscles must be strong to increase performance, but they rarely consider that muscle must also be pliable to achieve and maintain strength. Pliable muscle tissue not only means better function but also optimum joint mobility.

Stretching develops and maintains overall balance and coordination. Keen balance is achieved through responsive coordination skills. Coordination is improved through stretching exercises. Stretching exercises promote circulation of blood, oxygen, and nutrients throughout your horse's system. They also flush out toxins. Toxin removal and muscle nourishment increase your horse's ability to contract his muscles and relax the opposing muscles.

Equine stretching visually demonstrates areas of flexibility or restricted motion. It heightens awareness of his body—both your awareness and his. Stretching stimulates cells located at the ends of muscles. These cells transmit changes in muscular tissue to the central nervous system, where the changes are processed. If the action is repetitive, the nervous system acclimates to the motion, recalling and improving muscle response and thereby enhancing coordination and balance.

Horses in general are aware of their body functions. For example, your horse can step over a ground rail without actually seeing the obstacle the moment he steps over it because his brain recognizes his body placement through its sensory capabilities and responds accordingly. It is similar to your walking down a flight of stairs carrying a large box. Your mind and body coordinate and judge the distances appropriately without the use of your eyes. The more your horse is aware of, able to use, and reminded to use his body, the more coordination and balance he will develop.

EMOTIONAL BENEFITS OF EQUINE STRETCHING

Equine stretching promotes relaxation, improves energy circulation, and releases tension, just as it does in humans. A relaxed horse is able to focus, bond, learn, and perform much better than one full of anxiety, fear, worry, panic, or tension. Horses are generally on alert, as they are animals of prey ready at any moment to flee danger. When this alert mechanism is heightened by such stressors as unkind treatment, poor riding, ill-fitting tack, social dominance by other horses, isolation, illness, or injury, your horse's emotional well-being deteriorates. This triggers poor physical performance and impaired learning ability. Whatever the root cause, horses often harbor emotional anxiety in their necks and backs, just like their owners do. Stretching these muscles releases tension, eliminating discomfort and, in turn, emotional anxiety. Emotional and physical balance are restored. The result is a happier, more peaceful horse.

Equine stretching increases the flow of energy throughout your horse's system. In complementary/alternative therapy, energy that flows freely throughout the body is responsible for maintaining whole health. Energy that is stagnant or blocked can lead to health problems. Your positive healing energy interacts with and stimulates your horse's energy as you touch and stretch each part of his body. Your own energy, positive intention, and physical manipulation encourage your horse's energy to flow unimpeded. These factors promote a positive cellular response in your horse's system, negating the effects of pain or trauma.

Balance is the ultimate goal of equine stretching. You are seeking to restore and maintain physical balance—front to back and side to side—and to remove compensatory mechanisms your horse has developed.

Emotionally, you are seeking to remove fear, anxiety, and worry by soothing your horse through bonding, emotional support, pain alleviation, and energy flow. The combination of the emotional and physical benefits of equine stretching is invaluable.

SAFETY PRECAUTIONS

Please read these safety precautions carefully and thoroughly *before* attempting any of the stretching techniques presented in this book.

As with all treatments, consult your veterinarian before using stretching techniques on your horse.

Never stretch a cold muscle. Always warm up your horse thoroughly before stretching.

Do not force any stretching technique on your horse. Stretching should not inflict pain on or agitate your horse. If you suspect the horse is in pain or agitated, stop *immediately*.

All stretching techniques should be performed slowly and smoothly. Abrupt, rushed, jarring motions can result in injury.

Always begin stretching by holding the stretch for a minimal amount of time. Increase the time gradually as your horse becomes more flexible. Never hold a stretch longer than 20 seconds.

Do not allow children to perform equine stretching techniques.

Set limbs down gently and carefully. Dropping a limb could lead to injury. Also, your horse may come to distrust you if you are careless in this way.

Consider weather conditions when stretching your horse. It is not appropriate to exercise and stretch a horse in extreme temperatures (cold or hot).

If you choose to wear a glove when applying stretching techniques, be sure it is well-fitted, thin, and offers gripping capability. Bulky, ill-fitting, or slippery gloves can be hazardous.

Stretch your horse on areas of safe footing. Slippery, untidy, wet, deep, or rocky footing is dangerous. Do not perform stretches on these or other unsafe surfaces.

Use extreme caution and care not to get kicked or bitten when working around your horse's front and back areas.

WHEN NOT TO STRETCH

Below is a list of circumstances in which horses should not be stretched. Again, consult with your veterinarian before beginning an equine stretching program.

Do not stretch your horse if...

▶ your horse recently had surgery. Complete healing, as well as your veterinarian's permission, must be attained before you apply any sort of stretching technique.

▶ your horse is ill or injured and/or undergoing medical treatment.

▶ your mare is pregnant. Her body is already imbalanced and taxed from the pregnancy. Stretching is not appropriate, as her body is continuously undergoing changes to support the fetus. You do not want to risk injury.

▶ your horse is on stall rest. As mentioned, muscles must be warmed up through exercise before stretching to prevent injury. A horse on stall rest cannot be exercised.

▶ your horse is young (under the age of 5) or old (15 or more). Consult your veterinarian. Discuss whether or not your horse can undergo stretching and how the techniques should be altered according to his age.

TYPES OF EQUINE STRETCHES

Equine stretching techniques can be grouped into two main categories: mounted and unmounted. All mounted stretches should be implemented *after* you have spent about 20 minutes warming up your horse. (Riding, lunging, and brisk hand-walking are all suitable.) Stretching a cold muscle can result in injury. A cold muscle has less elasticity and therefore tears more easily.

Mounted Stretches

These stretches are performed when your horse is under tack. You, the rider, initiate the stretching techniques, encouraging muscle fibers to lengthen and emotions to release. Monitor mounted stretching, as you should not repeat any one stretch too often during a session. Additionally, do not make your horse stretch in a way he physically can't.

Unmounted Stretches

Unmounted stretches are performed from the ground. You manipulate your horse's body parts in ways that lengthen muscle fibers.

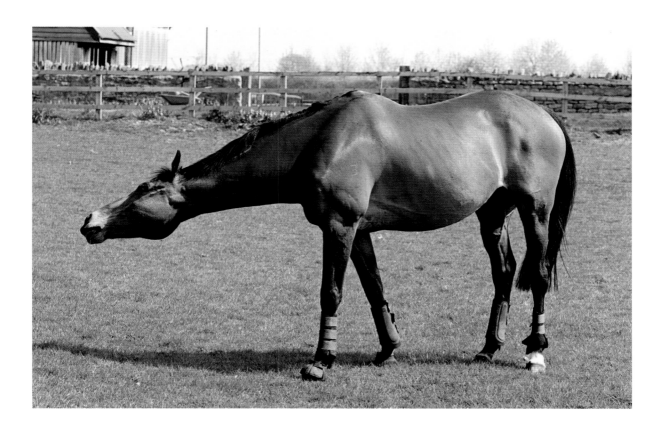

GENERAL GUIDELINES

These guidelines may be adjusted according to your horse's age and health. Consult with your veterinarian before beginning any type of stretching program with your horse.

Begin daily unmounted stretching with 10-minute sessions. Ask for each stretch three times on each side of your horse. Hold the stretch for 5 to 15 seconds. It is important to hold the stretch to establish lengthening of the muscle fibers.

Expect your horse to hold the stretches for several seconds only in the beginning phases of your stretching program. As his body adapts to the stretching, he will be able to hold the stretches for 5 to 15 seconds. After 14 days of consistent stretching, increase the sessions to 15 minutes. Allow two more weeks of stretching to pass before increasing to 20 minutes. You may then combine all of the stretching techniques into one session lasting 25 to 30 minutes.

Most horses are stronger and more flexible on one side of their body than the other. Stretch both sides equally to strengthen the weaker side and to maintain the stronger side. All stretching techniques must be performed slowly, with continuous fluid motion. Never rush or force any stretching technique, as this can injure your horse.

Before You Begin

Stretching must be done carefully. Before you attempt to perform these techniques, consult your veterinarian. Thoroughly review the safety precautions listed in this chapter. It would be wise to find a professional equine therapist to demonstrate the stretching techniques to you. If this is not possible, work slowly, carefully, and incrementally.

Choose the stretching technique you are most comfortable with and ask for just 1 minute's effort from your horse. He may not be open to stretching and balancing at first. Minimal range of motion should be expected until you become more proficient at asking for the stretch and your horse becomes emotionally willing and physically able to perform the technique.

It is important to vary techniques so you stretch all the horse's body parts consistently. It is best to limit the number of times you ask for a stretch, as continuous drilling overextends and strains the muscle fibers, causing harm rather than benefit. As you continue in your stretching program, your horse's body will develop better flexibility, increased range of motion, and better balance, resulting in a more noticeable stretch. Listen to your horse. If he shows signs of agitation (pinned ears, biting, kicking, loss of balance, pulling away), stop the technique immediately. Stretching should not cause pain to your horse. Move on to another technique or another therapy entirely.

Equine muscle tissue stretches more rapidly than human muscle tissue. Equine muscles begin to stretch after a mere 5 seconds. Human muscles do not begin to stretch for 25 to 30 seconds. Work slowly. If you are unsure if you have stretched a particular body part long enough, err on the side of caution and release the stretch. Never hold a stretch for longer than 20 seconds, as this could lead to cramping from insufficient blood supply to nerve tissue in the area.

As for all other therapies discussed in this book, document your equine stretching program thoroughly. This allows you to track your horse's reactions and progression. It will also keep track of the stretching techniques you have completed, the techniques you are currently working on, and the techniques you will introduce next. Record dates, times, techniques, durations, and reactions. Be sure to distinguish which side of your horse you are writing about. Don't trust anything to memory. Distinguishing right side from left in your notes avoids any confusion.

You Will Need...

Human: Appropriate barn wear, including proper footwear, and (optionally) a well-fitted, thin glove. Remove all jewelry before beginning. Be sure to bring along a writing tablet and pen or pencil for recording the stretching session.

Horse: A well-fitted halter and lead. Insect repellent if needed.

Workspace: A clean, organized space that has safe footing, shelter from the elements, and designated areas to safely fasten your horse either by cross-tie or tying (using a safety square knot). This space should be secure because some stretching techniques require working with your horse while he is untied. If you are working in a stall, never lock yourself in. Always have a way to escape quickly.

Human Stretching Safety

Consider your own safety when implementing a stretching program with your horse. First, do not wear any jewelry while applying stretches. Necklaces, rings, and bracelets can become entangled in your horse's limbs or caught on his shoes.

Be aware of your own posture. Always bend your knees when lifting limbs so you do not strain your own back. Use your entire body weight to conduct stretching techniques from the ground. Do not rely on your hands or arms; engage your abdominal muscles for added strength. Stand with your legs separated, one foot in front of the other. This stance allows you to balance and provides additional power when needed.

Use slow, thoughtful, fluid motions. Do not force any of the movements, as you could harm your own body as well as your horse's. Also, when placing your horse's feet back on the ground, look first, so you do not accidentally release the hoof onto your own foot.

Use extreme caution when working behind your horse. All horses can kick and may do so if unsure of the process, uncomfortable with a stretching exercise, or spooked by something out of your control.

Basic Stretching Terminology

Several common terms are used when discussing stretching exercises, whether for humans or animals.

- *Abduction*—A motion in which a limb is drawn away from the body.
- *Adduction*—A motion in which a limb is drawn into the body.
- *Extension*—A motion in which a body part is stretched outward from the body in a reaching movement that elongates and thus straightens the part.
- *Flexion*—A motion in which body parts bend.
- *Hyperextension*—A motion in which the limbs are stretched outward, reaching away from the body beyond their physical capabilities. If the limbs are hyperextended, injury occurs. Muscle tissue, ligaments, and tendons can tear or sprain if forced beyond their range of motion.
- *Hyperflexion*—A motion in which the limbs are bent inward, closing into the body beyond its physical capability. If a limb is hyperflexed, injury occurs. Muscle tissue, ligaments, and tendons can tear or sprain if forced beyond their range of motion.
- *Range of motion*—The degree to which a joint can move or position itself.

EQUINE STRETCHING TECHNIQUES

Each unmounted stretching technique works one part of your horse's body, including the head, neck, shoulders, spine, and hind legs. Make sure to stretch all parts of your horse's body to promote balance, flexibility, and relaxation. Each technique promotes suppleness, flexibility, range of motion, elasticity, and muscle tone. If you are interested in performing mounted stretching techniques with your horse, see Chapter 3.

Head Stretching Technique

1. Place a halter and lead on your horse and lead him to your workspace.

2. Halt and gently toss the lead over the base of your horse's neck so you have access to it if needed. Make sure it is not hanging low enough for the horse to step on it or for either of you to become entangled in it. Do not cross-tie or otherwise tie your horse when working the head.

3. Stand on your horse's left side, facing the same direction, directly next to his head.

4. Place your right palm, open and flat, underneath your horse's right ear so your fingers are stretching toward the ceiling. Your palm is just below the ear, while your extended fingers touch the outer edge of the ear.

5. Place the open flat palm of your left hand on your horse's muzzle. Your palm is close to the nostril while your fingers extend upward toward your horse's cheek.

6. Gently, slowly, and simultaneously push your right palm toward the left and the left palm toward the right. This causes the top of your horse's head to fall to the left and his muzzle to press up toward the right. Continue this motion until your horse offers resistance.

7. Hold the stretch for 5 to 20 seconds.

8. Gently and slowly release both of your hands, allowing your horse to have his head and neck free for a few moments.

9. Repeat the stretch twice more on the left side.

10. Perform the stretch three times on the right side.

11. Release your hands and praise your horse vocally and with reassuring pats along the neck.

Head stretching technique, step 5

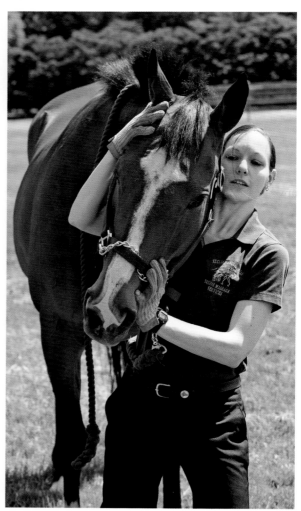

Head stretching technique, step 6

▶ Combination Head/Neck Extension Stretching Technique (Upward Stretch)

1. Place a halter and lead on your horse and lead him to your workspace.

2. Halt and gently toss the lead over the base of your horse's neck so you will have access to it if needed, but it is not hanging low enough for your horse to step on or for either of you to become entangled in it. Do not cross-tie or otherwise tie your horse when working the head and neck.

3. On your horse's left side, face the same direction as your horse, next to his head.

4. Place one open, flat palm on each of your horse's cheeks, allowing your thumbs to gently close underneath his cheekbones for holding purposes while bending your elbows.

5. Keeping your hands in place and elbows bent, slowly bend your knees.

6. Gently straighten your legs while pressing upward with your hands and straightening your elbows, causing your horse's head and neck to stretch toward the ceiling. Continue this motion until your horse offers resistance.

7. Hold the upward stretch for 5 to 20 seconds.

8. Gently release your horse's head and neck to its usual position by slowly lowering your hands, bending your elbows, and bending downward into your knees.

9. Repeat the stretch twice more on the left side.

10. Perform the stretch three times on the right side.

11. Release your hands and praise your horse vocally and with reassuring pats along the neck.

Combination head/neck extension stretching technique, step 6

▼ Neck Stretching Technique

1. Place a halter and lead on your horse and lead him to your workspace.

2. Halt and gently toss the lead over the base of your horse's neck so you will have access to it if needed, but it is not hanging low enough for your horse to step on or for either of you to become entangled in it. Do not cross-tie or otherwise tie your horse when working the neck.

3. Stand on your horse's left side, facing his neck.

4. Place your flat, open right palm in the center of the neck.

5. Hold your horse's halter with your left hand, just below his ear.

6. Stand so your right leg is slightly in front of your left leg and bend both knees.

Neck stretching technique, step 7

7. Gently pull the halter toward you while pressing into the neck with your right hand. Be sure to keep all motions slow and all pressure even. Continue this motion until your horse offers resistance.

8. Hold the stretch for 5 to 20 seconds.

9. Gradually reverse the motion in your hands so you are pressing the halter away from you and releasing your right hand away from the neck, returning it to its usual position.

10. Repeat the stretch twice more on the left side.

11. Perform the stretch three times on the right side.

12. Release your hands and praise your horse vocally and with reassuring pats along the neck.

▶ Downward Neck Stretching Technique

1. Place a halter and lead on your horse and lead him to your workspace.

2. Halt and gently toss the lead over the base of your horse's neck so you have access to it if needed, but it is not hanging low enough for your horse to step on or for either of you to become entangled in it. Do not cross-tie or otherwise tie your horse when working the neck

3. Standing on your horse's left side, facing his neck.

4. Place the pad of your thumb 1 inch (2.5 cm) behind your horse's ear. Apply your thumb pad vertically so your hand is positioned perpendicular to the horse's neck.

5. Gently apply pressure with your thumb pad while placing your open, flat left palm just below the horse's mouth.

6. As you press into the neck with the thumb pad, slowly bend your knees, allowing your left hand to gradually drift toward the floor and encouraging your horse to follow your left open palm downward. The combination of your thumb pressure and

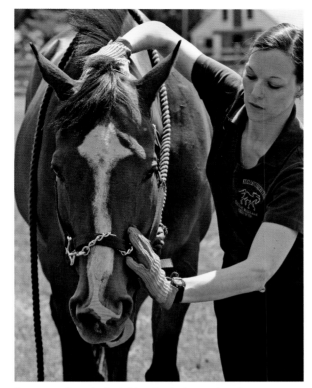

Downward neck stretching technique, step 5

Downward neck stretching technique, step 6

your lowering left palm draws your horse's head and neck toward the ground, similar to his natural grazing posture.

7. Hold the stretch for 5 to 20 seconds.

8. Gently release your thumb and return your left hand to your side, straightening your knees and allowing your horse to raise his head and neck to his usual position.

9. Repeat the stretch twice more on the left side.

10. Perform the stretch three times on the right side.

11. Release your hands and praise your horse vocally and with reassuring pats along the neck.

▼Shoulder Stretching Technique (Extension)

1. Place a halter and lead on your horse and lead him to your workspace.

2. Halt and secure your horse safely by attaching to cross-ties or tying with a safety square knot.

3. Stand on your horse's left side, facing his chest.

Shoulder stretching technique (extension), step 4

Be aware of your foot placement, as you do not want your horse accidentally stepping on you.

4. Bend forward, bending your knees, and grasp your horse's front left leg by holding just above the knee with your left hand and just above the hoof with your right hand.

5. Slowly and gently pull the front left leg off the ground about 3 inches (7.6 cm).

6. Hold the stretch for 5 seconds.

7. Bring the entire leg toward your body, extending the leg forward so it is reaching toward you. Your horse will offer just a bit of extension in the early phases of this technique. Do not expect the leg to completely extend forward. *Do not force the leg forward.*

8. When you feel the slightest resistance, stop and hold the stretch for 10 to 15 seconds.

9. Gently return the leg to the floor, allowing your horse to rest and balance for several minutes.

10. Repeat the stretch twice more on the left side.

11. Perform the stretch three times on the right side.

12. Release your hands and praise your horse vocally and with reassuring pats along the neck.

Shoulder stretching technique (extension), step 5

Shoulder stretching technique (extension), step 7

▼ Shoulder Stretching Technique (Flexion)

1. Place a halter and lead on your horse and lead him to your workspace.

2. Halt and secure your horse safely by attaching to cross-ties or tying with a safety square knot.

3. Stand on your horse's left side, facing the same direction, just behind his left front leg. Be aware of your foot placement, as you don't want your horse accidentally stepping on you.

4. Bend forward, bending both of your knees. Grasp your horse's front left leg by placing your right hand just above the knee and your left hand just above the hoof.

5. Slowly and gently pull the front left leg off the ground about 3 inches (7.6 cm).

6. Hold this stretch for 5 seconds.

7. Gently push the lower leg slightly upward by pressing up with your left hand. When you feel the slightest resistance, stop the motion and move to the next step.

8. Press the upper leg backward toward you slightly by gently pulling backward with your right hand. When you feel the slightest resistance, stop the motion and hold the position.

9. Hold this stretch for 10 to 15 seconds.

10. Gently return the leg to the floor, allowing your horse to rest and balance for several minutes.

11. Repeat the stretch twice more on the left side.

12. Perform the stretch three times on the right side.

13. Release your hands and praise your horse vocally and with reassuring pats along the neck.

Shoulder stretching technique (flexion), step 5

Shoulder stretching technique (flexion), step 8

▶ Back Stretching Technique

Note: Use extreme caution when performing this technique, as you will be standing directly behind your horse. If your horse is a kicker, do not attempt this stretch.

1. Place a halter and lead on your horse and lead him to your workspace.

2. Halt and secure your horse safely by attaching the halter to cross-ties or tying him with a safety square knot.

3. Slowly make your way toward your horse's hind end. Talk to him and keep your hands flat on his body, allowing them to gently glide along the body until you reach his hindquarters.

4. While standing on the left side of his body, facing his hip, gently grasp his tail just below the dock with your right hand. Keep your flat, open left palm resting on his left hindquarter.

5. Stand squarely behind your horse's hind end, facing the tail, and grasp the tail with both hands.

6. Slowly and gently pull the tail toward you while you bend your knees.

7. Hold the stretch for 15 to 20 seconds. You may feel your horse pull forward against you. This simply increases the stretch.

8. Gently release the tail and allow your horse to stand for several minutes before repeating the stretching technique twice more.

9. Release your hands and praise your horse vocally. Step away from your horse's hind end.

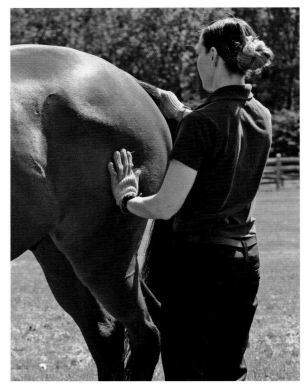

Back stretching technique, step 4

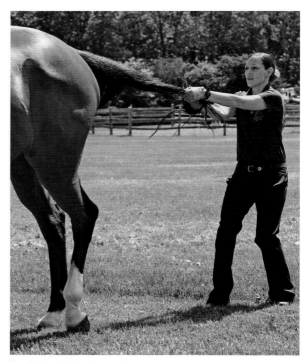

Back stretching technique, step 6

▼ Hind Leg Stretching Technique (Adductors)

Note: Use extreme caution when performing these two techniques, as you will be working near your horse's hind end. Be aware of kicking.

1. Place a halter and lead on your horse and lead him to your workspace.

2. Halt and secure your horse safely by attaching the halter to cross-ties or tying him with a safety square knot.

3. Stand on your horse's left side, next to his left hind leg, facing the opposite direction (he is facing forward and you are facing backward).

4. Bend your knees and reach down, asking him to raise his hind leg off the ground as he normally would when you clean his feet out.

5. Once he has raised his hoof, place your left hand just below the hock and your right hand just below the fetlock.

6. Gently pull the entire hind leg away from the horse's body toward yours, extending it outward until you feel the slightest resistance.

Hind leg stretching technique (adductors), step 6

7. Hold the stretch for 10 to 15 seconds.

8. Gently return the leg to the floor, allowing your horse to rest and balance for several minutes.

9. Repeat the stretch twice more on the left side.

10. Perform the stretch three times on the right side.

11. Release your hands and praise your horse vocally.

Hind Leg Stretching Technique (Abductors)

Note: Use extreme caution when performing this technique, as you will be working near your horse's hind end. Be aware of kicking (see page 146-147).

1. Place a halter and lead on your horse and lead him to your workspace.

2. Halt and secure your horse safely by attaching the halter to cross-ties or tying him with a safety square knot.

3. Stand on your horse's left side, next to his left hind leg, facing the opposite direction (he is facing forward and you are facing backward).

4. Squat and ask your horse to raise his right hind leg off the ground as he normally would when you clean out his feet. He may be a bit confused, as you are asking him to raise the "wrong" leg. In this case, simply grasp his tail and pull it toward you so he transfers his weight to the left hind leg. Ask him again to lift his right hind leg by squeezing the lower rear portion of the hind leg, where his tendon (the superficial digital flexor tendon) is accessible, between your thumb and pointing finger.

5. Place your left hand on the outside of the right hind leg, on the pastern, and place your right hand over the right hock.

6. Gently lift the entire leg slightly upward and pull it forward, moving toward and crossing in front of the left hind leg in a diagonal motion. When you feel resistance, stop and hold the stretch. Do not continue the motion.

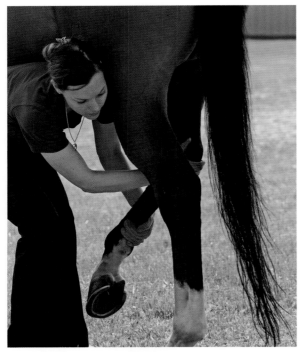

Hind leg stretching technique (abductors), step 5

Hind leg stretching technique (abductors), step 6

7. Hold the stretch for 5 to 10 seconds.

8. Gently return the leg to the floor, allowing your horse to rest and balance for several minutes.

9. Repeat the stretch twice more on the left side.

10. Perform the stretch three times on the right side.

11. Release your hands and praise your horse vocally.

▶ Rotational Hind Leg Stretching Technique

Note: Use extreme caution when performing this technique, as you will be working near your horse's hind end. Be aware of kicking.

1. Place a halter and lead on your horse and lead him to your workspace.

2. Halt and secure your horse safely by attaching the halter to cross-ties or tying him with a safety square knot.

3. Stand on your horse's left side, next to his left hind leg, facing the opposite direction (he is facing forward and you are facing backward).

4. Bend your knees, reach down, and ask your horse to raise his hind leg as he normally would when you clean out his feet.

5. Hold the hind leg with your right hand just above the hock and your left hand just above the fetlock.

6. Gently raise the leg 1 inch (2.5 cm) off the ground and slowly pull it forward and toward you. Hold the stretch for 5 seconds. If your horse is unable to raise his leg 1 inch (2.5 cm), raise it only as high as her leg allows. Do not raise the leg more than 1 inch (2.5 cm).

7. Raising the leg once again (1 inch [2.5 cm]), slowly move the entire leg to the left. Hold the stretch for 5 seconds.

Rotational hind leg stretching technique, step 6

Rotational hind leg stretching technique, step 7

8. Raising the leg once again (1 inch [2.5 cm]), gently press the entire leg backward, away from you. Hold the stretch for 5 seconds.

9. Finish by raising the leg 1 inch and gently pressing it inward, toward the right. Hold the stretch for 5 seconds.

10. Gently return the leg to the floor, allowing your horse to rest and balance for several minutes.

11. Repeat the stretch twice more on the left side.

12. Perform the stretch three times on the right side.

13. Release your hands and praise your horse vocally.

Rotational hind leg stretching technique, step 9

7

Equine Acupressure Therapy

In traditional Chinese medicine (TCM), energy circulation, just like blood circulation, is crucial to whole health. Acupressure therapy, a branch of TCM, is a healing modality that balances the body's energy flow. It is a noninvasive technique that uses a person's touch to stimulate energy points and restore proper energy circulation throughout the body. The treatment is performed in logical, sequential steps using various hand postures, practical applications, and breathing techniques. Keen observation, clarity of mind, and defined purpose are vital when offering an acupressure treatment.

Acupressure therapy distinguishes discrepancies that Western medicine does not, giving it a distinctive interpretation of an existing problem. For example, among many other considerations, factors such as time of day and season are considered when addressing health concerns, as these factors are related to organ function.

This therapy is not a magical cure for all illness or injury. It is used to encourage and enable the body to heal itself as well as that particular body can. Results vary according to the health problem and the horse's bodily function. Chronic issues are more difficult to resolve than acute problems.

Acupressure can often resolve or manage illnesses. It usually takes several sessions to note marked improvement. Each horse has his own system of energy and will have a different reaction to this therapy. Some become relaxed and tired, while others display increased symptoms post-treatment as the body's energy adjusts to the stimulation and cycles through the horse's system.

Western medicine admits that acupressure and acupuncture work, but it has yet to discover how. Studies have revealed that noninvasive touch can restore energy flow. Horses are especially responsive because they are open, accepting, intuitive, sensitive beings. Both applications are effective in resolving certain physical and even emotional problems.

BENEFITS OF ACUPRESSURE THERAPY

Acupressure's benefits are many and varied.

- ▶ It strengthens the body's immune system.

- ▶ It initiates the release of spasmodic muscle tissue.

- ▶ It assists in the production and distribution of endorphins, which alleviate pain.

- ▶ It releases the natural hormone cortisone, which reduces inflammation.

- ▶ It enables toxins to be dispersed from the equine system while increasing blood flow, both of which promote the healing process; improves mental focus; and offers emotional balance and rejuvenation.

ACUPRESSURE CONCEPTS

Chinese documents from 3,000 years ago and even earlier record the use of acupressure therapy. Many other ancient cultures used some form of acupressure or acupuncture. Both therapies are based on the same concepts. However, acupressure is noninvasive, while acupuncture requires the insertion of fine needles into the skin.

The essential underpinnings of acupressure entail the concepts of energy; the flow of that energy throughout the body along meridians or channels connecting the inner organs to the dermis, or external system, and to each other; the balance or imbalance of the bodily systems; and the points, along those meridians, that can be manipulated to restore balance and free the flow of energy throughout the body.

Energy

Living entities contain energy. In Western medicine, the energy is referred to as *electromagnetic energy.* Traditional Chinese medicine refers to this energy as *chi.* TCM teaches that chi (variously transcribed as ch'i and qi) must flow freely throughout the system to achieve balance. If there is balance, there is health. If the circulation of energy is interrupted, an imbalance occurs, leading to a health problem. The energy cycles through the body once every 24 hours. Chi is essentially the life force.

Chi moves through a network of invisible channels in the body called *meridians.* Along the meridians lie various points associated with health. These points are called *acupoints.*

Yin and Yang

Chi is separated into two forces, *yin* and *yang.* These energy forces are opposites. However, one cannot exist without the other. For example, you can never experience joy if you never experience sorrow. In this way, yin and yang are forever bonded. They circulate continuously, each increasing and decreasing proportionately so balance between them is maintained.

Yin energy is a supportive, nurturing force. It is associated with the interior and front region of the body. Conversely, yang energy is protective, positive. It is associated with the back and surface regions of the body. If either of these energy forces is excessive or deficient in your horse's system, the system becomes unbalanced. The imbalance manifests itself in physical and even emotional problems. Equine acupressure therapy seeks to locate imbalance and restore energy flow to promote healing and continued wellness.

Meridians

Energy is transported to all of the body's parts through the meridians. These are interconnected, forming one long energy highway. This interconnectedness is why working on one meridian influences the horse's entire system.

The energy that travels through the meridians is located near the surface of the skin, allowing access to the energy by hand (acupressure) or needle (acupuncture). Meridians connect the body's inner organs to the exterior system. The 12 major meridians are each connected to a major organ in the body. A network of smaller channels branches out from the major meridians.

Again, the yin meridians run up the front of your horse's body while the yang meridians run down the back. Yin and yang are interconnected as well. They are opposing and complementary. If too much of one or the other exists, the bodily system becomes unbalanced. Acupressure and acupuncture address this imbalance.

The 12 meridians are paired into yin and yang partners. (In TCM, organs are labeled by function, not anatomy.)

- *Yin meridians*—liver, lung, heart, kidney, pericardium, spleen

- *Yang meridians*—bladder, gall bladder, large intestine, small intestine, stomach, and triple heater

The 12 meridians are linked by eight channels called *extraordinary vessels.* These channels play a major role in energy exchange among the meridians. The vessels can sponge up excessive energy or move energy to various meridians as needed.

Two of the major extraordinary vessels are the *governing vessel,* which affects the yang meridians, and the *conception vessel,* which affects the yin meridians.

The governing vessel begins at the anal opening and flows across the top of your horse's body, traveling through the center and ending inside the mouth, between the gums and top lip. The conception vessel begins at the point directly underneath the anal opening and flows through the center of the body, on its underside, and ends at the lower lip. The meridians work in conjunction with one another. Therefore, if an organ, system, or meridian malfunctions, the complete energy network experiences imbalance.

Equine Acupressure Meridians and Acupoints

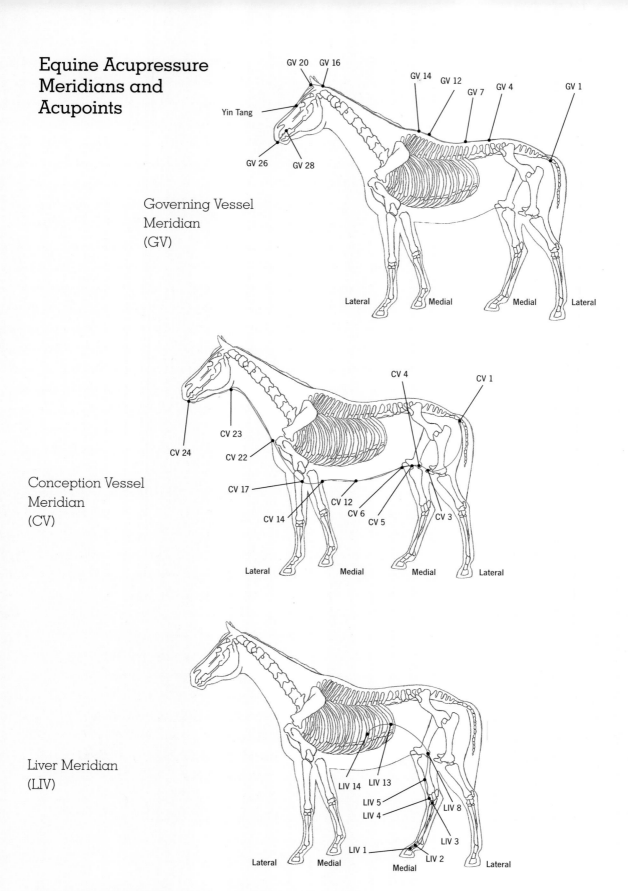

Governing Vessel Meridian (GV)

Conception Vessel Meridian (CV)

Liver Meridian (LIV)

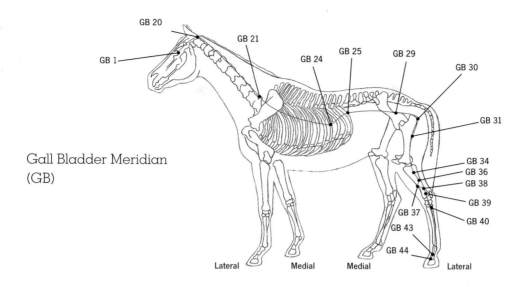

Gall Bladder Meridian
(GB)

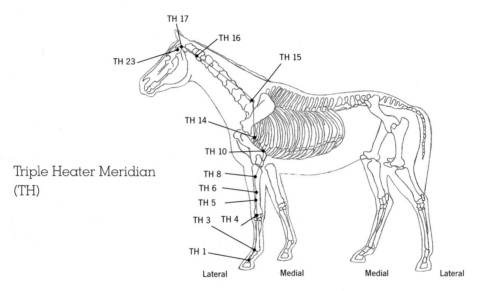

Triple Heater Meridian
(TH)

A Note on the Triple Heater Meridian

The triple heater meridian is not directly associated with an organ as the other meridians are. It correlates with many organs. The triple heater is a yang meridian responsible for the regulation of the body's temperature. Its name derives from the Chinese belief that the body possesses three regions:

- Head and chest, responsible for delivering bodily fluids
- The diaphragm and the area situated below the navel, responsible for digestion
- The navel and lower portions of the body, responsible for sorting nourishment into usable and waste elements

Each of these regions needs a way to communicate with one another. The triple heater meridian does this job by helping regulate the body's metabolic function.

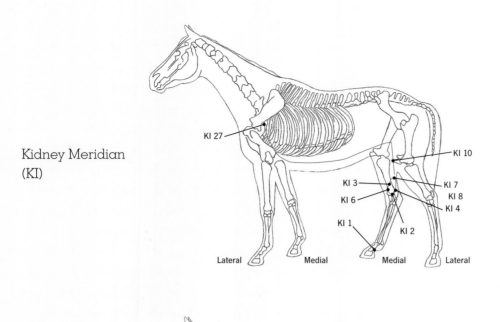

Kidney Meridian
(KI)

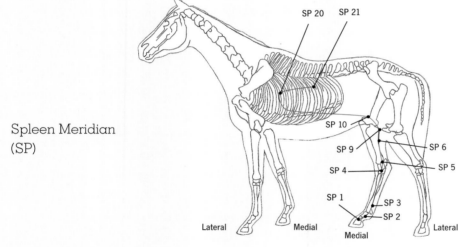

Spleen Meridian
(SP)

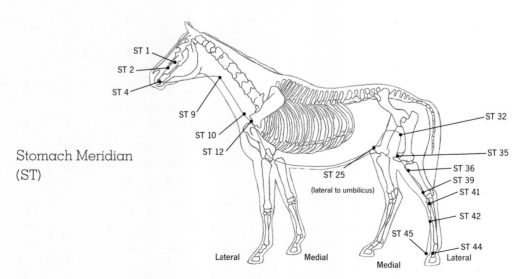

Stomach Meridian
(ST)

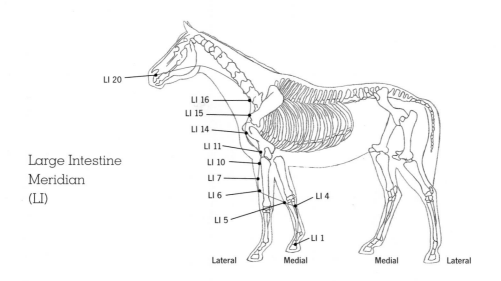

Large Intestine Meridian (LI)

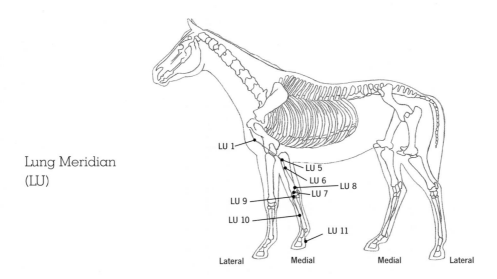

Lung Meridian (LU)

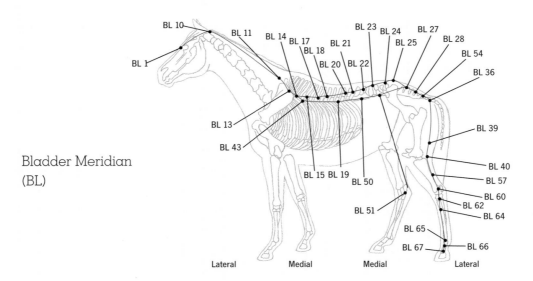

Bladder Meridian (BL)

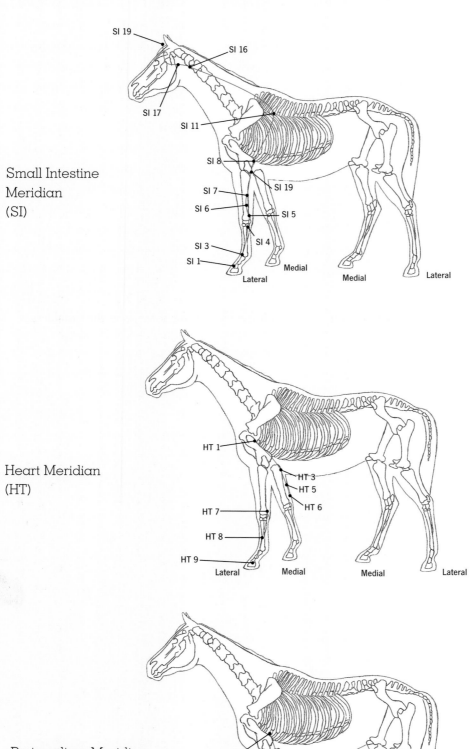

Small Intestine
Meridian
(SI)

SI 19
SI 16
SI 17
SI 11
SI 8
SI 7
SI 6
SI 19
SI 5
SI 3
SI 4
SI 1
Medial
Medial
Lateral
Lateral

Heart Meridian
(HT)

HT 1
HT 3
HT 5
HT 6
HT 7
HT 8
HT 9
Lateral
Medial
Medial
Lateral

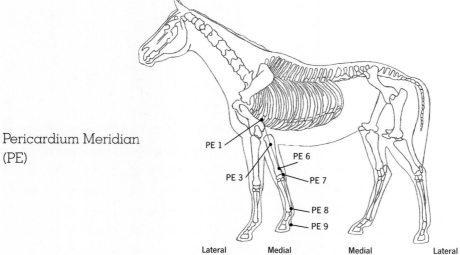

Pericardium Meridian
(PE)

PE 1
PE 6
PE 3
PE 7
PE 8
PE 9
Lateral
Medial
Medial
Lateral

Acupoints

Acupoints are located throughout the body and can be directly influenced by touch. Varying methods of touch aid in restoring energy balance in the body, thus promoting healing capabilities. Touch can increase (tonify) energy flow where it is lacking or decrease (sedate) energy flow where it is excessive or blocked.

Stimulating the acupoints influences the internal and external systems in the body. These points are located on or off the meridian channels. A horse has over 600 acupoints. Acupoints are identified by the meridian on which they are located, followed by a number. For example, the acupoint referred to as "ST1" is interpreted as Stomach 1. It is found on the stomach meridian.

Acupoints possess certain qualities. They have more electrical transmission in comparison to other areas of the body. The skin is usually thinner where acupoints lie; they are often located in the depressions of the body. Blood circulation is greater at these points, as more blood vessels and nerve fibers are present in an acupoint area.

Categories of Acupoints

Acupoints are grouped into categories according to their function. These groupings are ting, accumulation, command, influential, sedation, tonification, alarm, master, source, association, and connecting points.

▶ *Ting points*—Ting points begin or end each meridian. They are highly influential areas that correlate with one another. When checking ting points, compare them to one another,

observing differences in temperature and feel. These differences indicate imbalance.

▶ *Accumulation points*—As the name implies, these points are the areas in which energy collects. They are often associated with the sudden onset of an illness that presents with severe discomfort. These points are used to restore energy flow in a meridian.

▶ *Command points*—Command points correlate with the Five-Element Theory (see page 158). Each element is represented along each meridian.

▶ *Influential points*—Influential points are treated as adjuncts to assist in healing. For example, if a horse has chronic soreness in the shoulders, treating an influential point for muscle/tendon discomfort can help.

▶ *Sedation points*—Each meridian possesses a sedation point. These points are treated when energy must be quieted or disbanded.

▶ *Tonification points*—One tonification point is located on each meridian. This point correlates with the meridian and its associated organ. Tonification points are treated to increase energy flow in the meridian and, thus, to its associated organ.

▶ *Alarm points*—Each of these points correlates to a specific organ. Therefore, reaction to touch on these points may indicate a problem with the associated organ or the energy flow associated with it.

▶ *Master points*—These points affect defined parts of your horse's body. Use them for specific regions of your horse's body that are experiencing a problem. For example, if your horse's back is sore due to an ill-fitting saddle, treat the master point associated with the back and hips (BL 40).

TIP

Phantom Gall Bladder

Horses do not have gallbladders—the name of this meridian was adapted from its human counterpart.

▸ *Source points*—Each meridian has its own source point, which can increase or decrease energy flow along the associated organ's meridian. Source points are generally treated when working with yin organs. Use them to enhance organ energy or restore equilibrium within the organ's energy.

▸ *Association points*—These points partner with individual organ meridians—that is, they are palpated to see if an issue is present within a certain meridian and to help determine whether the problem is sudden or recurring. They are directly used to increase energy flow to an organ. Association points are also effective in restoring emotional equilibrium within your horse. It is wise to work these points during treatments to encourage emotional health in your horse.

Association points are palpated to determine whether the actual organ or its energy connection is affected. Reactivity to both alarm and association points is associated with issues specific to the organ. Reactivity to association points only relates to energy flow imbalance in the complete organ system.

Association points aid in identifying acute versus chronic conditions. If an association point is sensitive to light palpation, this indicates acute. If an association point is sensitive when palpated heavily, this indicates chronic. For example, if BL 18 (liver association point) and alarm point LIV 14 (liver alarm point) are sensitive when palpated deeply, this indicates chronic liver involvement.

▸ *Connecting points*—These points link the yin and yang energies of the partnered meridians. Energy from one meridian may be transported to its partnered meridian by working these points.

THE FIVE-ELEMENT THEORY OF BALANCE IN NATURE

The Five-Element Theory is a study of the balance that exists outside of the body—that is, the balance in nature. It is based on the concept that nature influences the body. It examines the relationship between the cycles in nature and those in the human body—the cycles of birth, life, and death. It is not a literal concept but rather a symbolic one that examines and compares the parallels between nature and the human body.

Each of the five elements that exist in nature is associated with an organ in the body. They are, however, symbols, or metaphors, correlating with organ function. Again, organs are labeled by function, not anatomy, in traditional Chinese medicine.

The five elements are water, fire, wood, metal, and earth.

▸ *Water* corresponds to the kidneys and bladder (responsible for the internal plumbing of the body).

▸ *Fire* corresponds to the small intestine and the heart (responsible for circulatory patterns in the body).

▸ *Wood* is linked to the gall bladder and liver (responsible for cleansing the body of toxicity).

▸ *Metal* is linked to the large intestine and lungs (responsible for ridding the body of waste).

▸ *Earth* corresponds to the stomach, spleen, and pancreas (responsible for the digestive function in the body).

Each of the five elements belongs to two cycles. These cycles explain the continuous change nature undergoes, just as the physical bodies of living creatures continuously change. These cycles are a form of production and regulation of the elements.

Creation Cycle

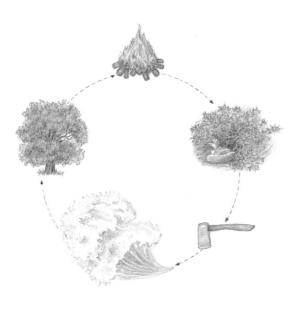

Control Cycle

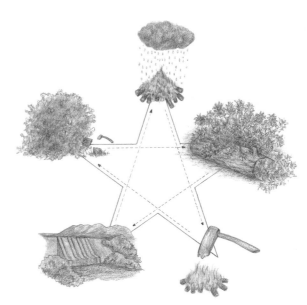

They are the creation cycle and the control cycle, both of which must exist for the five elements to exist, function, support, control, and regulate one another.

The Creation and Control Cycles

During the creation cycle, the elements produce one another. For example, beginning with the water element, water is essential for wood to grow; wood is burned by fire, which creates ashes, producing earth; earth creates metal through ore; and metal supports water by offering it minerals. Thus the cycle continues. Each element nurtures and supports each of the others.

If creation were the sole cycle, the five elements would overproduce, leading to imbalance; hence the need for the control cycle. This cycle regulates the elements. Water extinguishes fire; fire softens and melts metal; metal cuts wood; wood regulates earth through its root systems; and earth dams water flow.

If the five elements are functioning harmoniously, health is present. If any element is deficient or excessive, the imbalance leads to poor health. Each of the five elements corresponds with scent, taste, color, season, emotion, and time of day. If a health concern exists within an organ or bodily function, the theory of the five elements can be applied to determine which other organs, functions, or systems are affected so treatment can be planned accordingly. This theory has been used for thousands of years in TCM and is widely used today.

APPLYING ACUPRESSURE THERAPY

As you prepare to apply an equine acupressure treatment, remember that the visual guides in this book are for general reference. As you practice, you will become familiar with the feel and contour of your own horse's body and his reactions to your touch.

Before you begin an acupressure treatment, there are several preparations to make.

▸ *Human*—Choose a time of day that is quiet so neither you nor your horse will be disrupted during the treatment. Prepare yourself for the treatment by breathing deeply for a few moments, mentally reviewing the steps of the session, and vigorously rubbing the palms of your hands together to generate warmth and energy. Spend a few minutes mentally focusing on the outcome you are trying to achieve by performing the therapy. Clear your mind of the day's business so you are focusing solely on the treatment. Allow yourself plenty of time, especially when first offering acupressure therapy, so you can observe, perform, and record the session thoroughly. During the session, you may encounter new reactions or sensations that will lead you to work on other areas of your horse's body that day.

▸ *Horse*—Ready your horse for treatment by placing a well-fitted halter and lead on him. You can choose to have a helper hold your horse or to work on your horse while he is properly secured on cross-ties or tied off in a square knot to a safe and appropriate fixture. Groom your horse so no dirt, mud, or debris will interrupt your touch.

▸ *Workspace*—Do not expect your horse to stand perfectly still during the session. He will react to your touch and the sensation of the energy by moving around a bit. Be sure your work-space is open and large enough to allow your horse movement. Clear the area of objects or items that could be dangerous or simply in the way. It is best to choose an area familiar to your horse. If your horse feels secure, he will be more open to the session.

▸ *Tools*—Have a stool available so you can use it to reach difficult areas on your horse's body. Have a pen and writing tablet available, or some kind of recording device, so you can document the session accurately. Don't forget this journal. It will serve as a guide in locating the meridians and acupoints you will be working.

When Not to Apply Equine Acupressure Therapy

Equine acupressure therapy is not appropriate or suitable in all circumstances. Do not apply acupressure in the following situations.

▸ *Pregnancy*—If your mare is pregnant, her energy, emotions, and hormonal levels are imbalanced while her body supports the foal. This state of imbalance is natural and should not be disturbed. Once the foal is born, the mare can receive acupressure treatment.

▸ *Breeding*—If you own a stallion and he has recently bred, allow his body time to settle. Breeding stimulates energy and hormonal levels. These levels need time to settle and readjust after such activity. Do not perform acupressure until 12 hours have passed.

▸ *Fever*—Horses with an elevated temperature need the immediate care of a veterinarian. Fever is a sign of infection and can lead to extreme results if left untreated. Veterinary care is appropriate here.

▸ *After feeding*—Allow three to four hours after feeding your horse before performing a treatment. The body needs time to digest and release waste products after food consumption. This natural process is best left uninterrupted.

▸ *After exercise*—Cool your horse out thoroughly before offering an acupressure treatment. His muscle function, temperature, respiration, and pulse should be within normal limits and settled before you manipulate the energy.

▸ *Disease*—If your horse is presenting with an infection or disease, contact your veterinarian immediately. A professional must examine your horse to determine a diagnosis and the course of treatment. Veterinary care is needed here.

Pre-Treatment Information

As you prepare for an equine acupressure therapy treatment, consider that the visual guides provided in this publication are just that: guides. Each meridian and acupoint presented exists in the general area depicted. Each horse, however, has his own size, shape, frame, and matter. As you practice, you will become familiar with the feel, sensation, and contour of your horse's body. You will also learn your horse's reactions to your touch; his reactions will indicate what is happening in the palpated areas. In this way, you will learn to locate and work on your horse's energy system more effectively.

Observation is a key element when performing acupressure therapy. Observing your horse before a session, after a session, and between sessions allows you to note your horse's general condition. These observations help you determine change (or lack thereof), improvement, or regression. Each time you give a treatment, record the session thoroughly. Remember, TCM thinks about your horse as a whole entity; therefore, the observations should be all-inclusive. The questions below are meant to guide you in your observations and indicate the kinds of details you should record.

▸ What is your horse's overall condition? Bright, open, even eyes? Flat, shiny coat? Intact, symmetrical hooves? Pink, healthy gums?

▸ What is your horse's attitude and presence like? Curious, angry, frightened, distracted, happy, content?

▸ What is your horse's physical presentation? Bearing weight evenly on all four limbs? Any hairless patches in the coat? Any unusual odors from the ears or feet? Symmetrical muscling throughout? Any discomfort anywhere? Breathing easily and normally or labored and shallow?

▶How is your horse moving? Is movement loose, free, and even or tight, stilted, and uneven? Any stiffness or pain? Willing or unwilling to move? What is the ear posture in motion—upright and alert or pinned back and agitated?

These observations tell the story of how your horse is feeling emotionally and physically that day. Pay close attention and log your observations before and after each treatment.

Lastly, do not perform an acupressure treatment immediately before an event or competition. Your horse will need time to relax, the energy needs time to circulate, and your horse may need time to recover from the initial treatment before its effectiveness can be fully acknowledged. Plan accordingly when offering a treatment so you do not interfere with your horse's performance schedule.

Acupressure Illustration Terminology

Acupoints and meridians are located on the top and bottom, inner and outer regions of your horse's body. The following terms are used in the accompanying illustrations to indicate the locations of the meridians and acupoints.

Anterior—Toward the front of the body

Posterior—Toward the rear of the body

Dorsal—Near the top of the body

Ventral—Near the underside of the body

Lateral—Toward the outer side of the body

Medial—Toward the midline of the body

Performing an Equine Acupressure Treatment

Acupressure treatment consists of four stages: the opening stage, the acupoint stage, the closing stage, and the stretching stage.

Opening Stage

This stage allows your horse to become comfortable with the treatment; allows you to use your senses to feel, see, and smell your horse's reactions; and opens the longest meridian in your horse's system—the bladder meridian (see diagram, p. 155). You will begin all treatments in this manner:

1. Stand on the left side of your horse's body, facing his head.

2. Talk calmly and quietly to your horse as you slowly place the palm of your hand flat against your horse's face, resting it on acupoint BL 1, the beginning point of the bladder meridian (a and b). Slowly move your hand along the meridian, tracing its pathway throughout the horse's body (b and c). Use light to moderate pressure as you trace, similar to the pressure you use when pressing on your horse's body to make him move away from you.

3. Repeat this tracing twice more on the left side of the body, for a total of three tracings. Record any reactions from your horse and any observations you made during this stage.

4. Trace the bladder meridian three times on the right side of your horse's body and note any reactions and observations.

5. Document your observations.

Step 2 (c)

Step 2 (a) and (b)

Acupoint Stage

The acupoint stage is the essence of equine acupressure therapy. You will palpate and treat your horse by working on these points. Through your touch, you will attempt to free blocked energy and draw energy to areas lacking sufficient energy, thereby creating effective energy circulation and, ultimately, allowing the body to heal itself.

This stage is logical in its application as you usually work from front to back, top to bottom, as you would in equine massage. One hand palpates and treats the point while your other hand rests elsewhere on your horse's body to offer comfort.

Your breathing pattern is important during this stage. Exhale as you press into the point and inhale when releasing the point. When pressing and releasing the points, use light pressure. If your horse tolerates moderate pressure, you can gently increase the application by stepping one foot forward and slowly leaning into the acupoint. Use your own weight to increase the pressure.

You can apply several types of touch to the acupoints:

▶ Direct pressure application (using your thumb), as described in Chapter 5. Rest your thumb on the acupoint, forming a right angle with the meridian on which you are working.

▶ Rhythmical thumb beat application—Again, position your thumb so it creates a right angle with the meridian you are working on. Press in and out rhythmically on the point. The speed at which you perform this application depends on your intention. If you are trying to free an area of blocked energy, press in and out slowly. If you are trying to draw energy to an area that is lacking, press in and out quickly. Either way, press in and out consistently, evenly, and rhythmically.

Direct pressure application

Rhythmical thumb beat (a) Rhythmical thumb beat (b)

▶Rotational thumb application—As in the two other applications, place your thumb on the acupoint, creating a right angle with the meridian. If you are trying to draw energy to the area, move your thumb in a clockwise rotation until you feel the temperature warm. Conversely, if you are trying to disband an area of blocked energy, move your thumb in a counterclockwise rotation until you feel the temperature cool. The number of rotations will vary; as a general guide, use eight rotations.

Rotational thumb application (a)

> **TIP**
>
> ## Hand Posture
>
> If you have difficulty applying your thumb to an area of the body, change your hand posture by crossing your middle finger over your pointing finger. This will allow you to use your index finger without disturbing the energy patterns, as this finger placement creates a neutral polarity. It possesses neither negative nor positive energy.

Rotational thumb application (b)

1. Beginning on the left side of your horse's body, after you have opened the appropriate meridian, locate the correlating acupoints and palpate each using one of the above applications.

2. If the acupoint shows too much energy, the area will feel warm or even hot. In addition, your horse may be highly reactive, tender, and sensitive to your touch. If the acupoint shows blocked energy, it will usually be protrusive and dense. This is often the case for a condition that comes on suddenly. If the acupoint is lacking in energy, it will often feel cool or cold and soft and easily pressed down into a lower position. Increased pressure may reveal sensitivity. These responses are signs of chronic conditions.

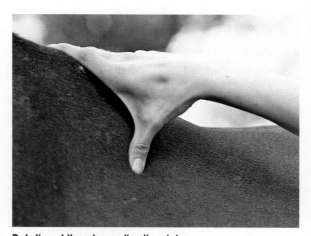

Rotational thumb application (c)

3. Repeat this on the right side of your horse's body.

4. Document your observations.

Closing Stage

The closing stage of a session reconnects the energy circulation throughout the system. It also helps the horse's cell response become positive, as cell response is negative when it has been afflicted with pain due to illness or injury. Therefore, helping the cell back to a positive memory is important in this closing stage so your horse receives the utmost benefit from the therapy.

1. Face the left side of your horse's body. Place your hand flat, palm facing downward, on your horse's body at the beginning of the appropriate meridian. This hand position is similar to the effleurage stroke discussed in Chapter 5.

Slide your palm gently along each meridian opened for this treatment three times. You will be closing each meridian three times during this stage.

2. Repeat the closing stage on the right side of your horse's body.

3. Document your observations.

Stretching Stage

The stretching stage of the treatment increases energy circulation throughout the body. Stretch your horse according to what you treated him for during the session. For example, if you performed acupressure therapy because he has a sore neck from receiving inoculations, complete the head and neck stretches listed in Chapter 6. Always stretch both sides of your horse to promote symmetry throughout.

Document your observations here as well so you can track your horse's progress with respect to his stretching capabilities. Again, consult Chapter 6 for details on stretching your horse.

Observations after Treatment

Once the four stages of the acupressure treatment are completed, record your horse's physical, emotional, and mental states. As mentioned earlier, energy circulates throughout your horse's system on a 24-hour cycle. Therefore, after you have performed an acupressure treatment, allow your horse to relax for 24 hours. You may not notice any changes in your horse's condition until the energy has fully cycled. Check your horse periodically after the session and record any new or different observations.

Equine Reactions to Acupressure

Each horse reacts differently during an acupressure treatment. Your horse may lower his head and neck, stretching down toward the floor, or tilt his head down to one side, or extend or wriggle his lips. He might chew or lap continuously. He might yawn or cough, or his eyes might appear glazed. Your horse may breathe deeply or sigh loudly. He may snort, pass gas, or shift his weight, pulling away from or leaning into your touch. Muscles may spasm or twitch, gut sounds may be stimulated, or limbs may buckle. Ears may fall sideways. These are all forms of releasing anxiety, concern, tension, pain, and discomfort. These are all reactions to the energy work you are performing.

EQUINE ACUPRESSURE THERAPY MAINTENANCE SCHEDULE

Several factors affect how often you should apply an equine acupressure technique to your horse. Scheduling and time availability varies from horse owner to horse owner. You want to have time to plan a technique, apply it, and allow your horse to rest for 24 hours post-treatment. Your travel or competition schedule must be considered. It is not wise to offer a session the day before an event, as your horse may need its entire 24-hour energy cycle to pass before the effects of the technique are felt. Frequency also depends on whether you are treating a chronic or acute condition. Chronic conditions usually require more frequent sessions than do acute conditions.

Taking all of these factors into account, you can create an acupressure therapy schedule suitable for your horse. However, all things being equal, a basic scheduling guide can include the following:

▸ two sessions per week in the beginning phase

▸ when marked improvement is noted, once per week

▸ when the issue has resolved or improved greatly, once a month for maintenance

If the problem begins to reemerge, go back to two times per week and restart the treatment schedule. Be sure to allow a rest period of at least 24 to 48 hours between sessions. If you are working a technique once a month and do not notice any changes, add another session to the schedule.

TIP
Time Management

Do not work on too many health issues during a single equine acupressure treatment. Focus on one issue at a time and plan a course of action for that issue. Working on numerous meridians and acupoints only leads to chaos in your horse's energy system and confusion for you when trying to measure progress and effectiveness.

If your horse has a number of health problems, choose the one you are most concerned about and feel most confident in treating. Work on that issue first. Spend several sessions addressing that problem only. If you note marked improvement after several sessions, then you may choose to move on and work on another issue. Keep in mind that chronic problems are more difficult to work with than acute issues. When observing changes in your horse, management and improvement are as positive as resolution.

EQUINE ACUPRESSURE TECHNIQUES

The following is a series of equine acupressure techniques used to encourage and promote the healing process. If your horse appears ill or injured, contact your veterinarian immediately. Equine acupressure therapy is not a substitute for veterinary care. If you have a complicated problem to address, consult with a certified equine acupressure therapist after seeing your veterinarian.

Each technique works on multiple meridians and acupoints. You may want to limit the initial session to a few meridians and acupoints. As you become more comfortable with the applications, you may choose to work with all of the meridians and acupoints listed in each sequence.

Always consider *all* elements of your horse's world when addressing his health. Consider the mental, emotional, physical, environmental, and social elements that make up his life. All of these variables affect his wellness.

Guide to Acupoint Abbreviations

BL = Bladder Meridian

GB = Gall Bladder Meridian

TH = Triple Heater Meridian

LI = Large Intestine Meridian

SI = Small intestine Meridian

ST = Stomach Meridian

LU = Lung Meridian

LIV = Liver Meridian

HT = Heart Meridian

PE = Pericardium Meridian

SP = Spleen Meridian

KI = Kidney Meridian

Begin each session on the left side of your horse's body. Once the technique is completed, repeat it on the right side of the body. All techniques begin with observation and opening the bladder meridian. The bladder meridian must be opened three times on each side of your horse's body. Remember to open and close all meridians you work three times each. Document your observations throughout each stage of the technique.

Arthritis/Cold Temperature Management

Arthritis is commonly affected by weather and temperature changes and conditions. Just as humans do, many arthritic horses feel the effects of cold in their joints and present with pain, stiffness, and limited mobility. This technique is tailored to those horses.

1. Open the following meridians as described in the opening stage: bladder meridian, stomach meridian, spleen meridian, small intestine meridian, and large intestine meridian.

2. Palpate and (if necessary) treat, as described in the acupoint stage, the following points: BL 23, ST 36, SP 21, SI 5, and LI 11.

3. Close all of the meridians appropriately.

4. Perform stretches that correlate with your horse's arthritic areas, as described in Chapter 6. For example, if your horse has arthritis in his hocks, perform hind leg stretches.

Acupoint Summary for Arthritis (cold)

BL 23—eases general arthritis
ST 36—releases cortisol and stimulates adrenals; builds immune system
SP 21—eases general pain
SI 5—lessens inflammation
LI 11—important anti-inflammatory point for upper body; regulates the immune system

Arthritis/Hot Temperature Management

This technique can be applied to arthritic horses affected by warmer temperatures. Warm or hot temperatures often cause swelling, increased pain levels, and general discomfort, inhibiting a horse's ability to move well.

1. Open the following meridians as described in the opening stage: bladder meridian, stomach meridian, spleen meridian, small intestine meridian, and large intestine meridian.

2. Palpate and (if necessary) treat, as described in the acupoint stage, the following points: BL 23, ST 44, SP 9, SP 10, SI 5, LI 4, and LI 11.

3. Close all of the meridians appropriately.

4. Perform stretches that correlate with your horse's arthritic areas, as described in Chapter 6. For example, if your horse has arthritis in his knees, perform front-leg stretches.

Acupoint Summary for Arthritis (hot)

BL 23—eases general arthritis
ST 44—relieves arthritis
SP 9—eases discomfort associated with arthritic knee joints and hind limbs
SP 10—relieves hind limb discomfort
SI 5—lessens inflammation
LI 4—balances the meridian; offers pain relief; eases muscle tension
LI 11—important anti-inflammatory point for upper body; regulates the immune system

Azoturia/Tying-Up Syndrome/Monday Morning Sickness

Note: If you suspect this condition in your horse, contact your veterinarian immediately. Apply acupressure only after veterinary care is established. However, this technique can be used as a preventive measure to hinder the recurrence.

Azoturia causes severe muscle spasms and tremors. Your horse will not be able to move forward. He may perspire, and his respiration and pulse rates will elevate excessively.

1. Open the following meridians as described in the opening stage: bladder meridian, gall bladder meridian, stomach meridian and liver meridian.

2. Palpate and (if necessary) treat, as described in the acupoint stage, the following acupoints: BL 19, BL 23, BL 50, GB 21, GB 24, GB 34, GB 44, ST 2, ST 32, LIV 1, and LIV 3.

3. Close all of the meridians appropriately.

4. Discuss with your veterinarian which, if any, stretching techniques you may use.

Acupoint Summary for Azoturia

BL 19—balances the gall bladder; alleviates muscle discomfort
BL 23—addresses arthritis, lower back, and knee discomfort or pain; strengthens bone
BL 50—alleviates back discomfort
GB 21—eases tightness in head, neck, shoulders, and back
GB 24—eases muscle pain; eases stomach distension and pain
GB 34—relaxes muscles, ligaments, and tendons
GB 44—eases emotional distress
ST 2—alleviates discomfort
ST 32—eases spasmodic muscle tissue
LIV 1—balances the meridian
LIV 3—eases muscular spasms; alleviates arthritis

Back Pain (Lumbar/Lower)

Back pain is common in horses as a result of ill-fitting saddles, poor riding, and general exertion. If your horse is highly sensitive or spasmodic throughout his back area, or if he is agitated when saddled, dips his back when the muscles are palpated, and does not want to travel forward, he may be experiencing discomfort in the back region.

1. Open the following meridians, as described in the opening stage: bladder meridian, governing vessel, gall bladder meridian, spleen meridian, and kidney meridian.

2. Palpate and (if necessary) treat, as described in the acupoint stage, the following acupoints: BL 11, BL 20, BL 23, BL 24, BL 27, BL 40, BL 50, BL 67, GV 4, GB 21, GB 30, GB 34, GB 44, SP 21, and KI 8.

3. Close all of the meridians appropriately.

4. Perform back and hind leg stretches as described in Chapter 6.

Acupoint Summary for Back Pain

BL 11—relieves back discomfort
BL 20—aids in digestion; balances the spleen and pancreas
BL 23—eases arthritis, lower back, and knee pain; strengthens bones
BL 24—promotes the flow of stuck energy in the body; resolves lower back pain
BL 27—eases lower back pain, indigestion, and sciatica
BL 40—relieves lower back pain
BL 50—relieves back discomfort
BL 67—balances the bladder meridian
GV 4—eases chronic lumbar pain; strengthens lumbar region
GB 21—eases tightness in head, neck, shoulders, and back
GB 30—alleviates arthritis
GB 34—relaxes muscles, ligaments, and tendons
GB 44—eases emotional distress; supports lumbar region
SP 21—relieves discomfort and weakness
KI 8—eases lumbar pain

Cold/Cough

If your horse presents with a cough, nasal discharge, and decreased energy, you may offer this treatment. It rids the lungs of congestion, allowing for optimum breathing.

1. Open the following meridians, as described in the opening stage: bladder meridian, large intestine meridian, conception vessel, pericardium meridian, and lung meridian.

2. Palpate and (if necessary) treat, as described in the acupoint stage, the following acupoints: CV 17, LI 4, LI 20, LU 1, LU 5, LU 6, LU 8, LU 9, and PE 1.

3. Close all of the meridians appropriately.

4. Perform head and neck stretches as described in Chapter 6.

Acupoint Summary for Cold/Cough

CV 17—drains chest congestion; relieves chronic coughing
LI 4—balances the meridian; offers pain relief; eases, alleviates chest clogging
LI 20—clears sinuses
LU 1—relieves chest issues
LU 5—eases cough and muscle tension
LU 6—quiets coughing
LU 8—alleviates labored breathing
LU 9—balances the meridian; clears the lungs
PE 1—drains lymphatic glands

Colic (Preventive)

Note: If you suspect this condition in your horse, contact your veterinarian immediately. Apply this technique only after veterinary care is established. However, this technique can be used as a preventive measure to hinder recurrence.

The following technique may be applied as a preventive therapy for horses that frequently have colic. It is not a substitute for veterinary care.

1. Open the following meridians, as described in the opening stage: bladder meridian, conception vessel, liver meridian, stomach meridian, spleen meridian, and pericardium meridian.

2. Palpate and (if necessary) treat, as described in the acupoint stage, the following acupoints: BL 20, BL 21, BL 25, BL 27, CV 4, CV 6, CV 12, LIV 13, ST 25, ST 36, ST 39, ST 45, SP 2, SP 6, SP 20, and PE 8.

3. Close all of the meridians appropriately.

4. Stretches do not accompany this technique.

Acupoint Summary for Colic

BL 20—aids in digestion; balances the spleen and pancreas
BL 21—aids with gastrointestinal discomfort
BL 25—addresses constipation or diarrhea
BL 27—relieves indigestion
CV 4—aids in resolving abdominal discomfort
CV 6—channels energy through the abdominal region and alleviates discomfort
CV 12—alleviates digestive troubles
LIV 13—eases abdominal discomfort
ST 25—loosens cramps; addresses flatulence
ST 36—releases cortisol; stimulates adrenals; builds immune system; relieves bloating, constipation, and stomach problems
ST 39—channels energy of the small intestine; resolves abdominal pain
ST 45—eases indigestion
SP 2—promotes regular bowel movements
SP 6—supports liver, kidney, and spleen; resolves gastrointestinal discomfort; strengthens the mind
SP 20—assists digestion
PE 8—alleviates stomach issues

Cribbing

Cribbing is a behavior that a horse develops when he is bored or sees other horses doing it. The horse continuously grasps a stationary object with his teeth, pulls back against the object, and sucks air down into his throat. It is destructive and can be harmful to the health of your horse. If you own a cribber, you may apply this technique.

1. Open the following meridians, as described in the opening stage: bladder meridian, triple heater meridian, small intestine meridian, and stomach meridian.

2. Palpate and (if necessary) treat, as described in the acupoint stage, the following acupoints: BL 17, BL 21, TH 8, TH 15, TH 16, SI 3, SI 6, SI 17, ST 4, ST 9, ST 12, and ST 45.

3. Close all of the meridians appropriately.

4. Perform head and neck stretches as described in Chapter 6.

Acupoint Summary for Cribbing

BL 17—settles the stomach; regulates energy flow
BL 21—aids gastrointestinal discomfort
TH 8—eases neck discomfort
TH 15—alleviates tight neck tissue
TH 16—relaxes neck muscles
SI 3—relieves tight neck tissue
SI 6—eases neck tension
SI 17—relaxes muscle tissue
ST 4—eases jaw tightness
ST 9—disperses gas; promotes proper stomach function
ST 12—settles stomach energy; relieves anxiety
ST 45—relieves stomach indigestion

Heaves/Heaving

Heaving is a condition that affects your horse's ability to breathe properly. The usual presentation is labored breathing; your horse's abdominal muscles will display tremendous motion or pumping as he exhales. His inhalations and exhalations become noisy, and he opens his nostrils wide. Heaving is usually accompanied by a cough. If your horse is heaving, contact your veterinarian immediately. Apply this technique only after veterinary care is rendered.

1. Open the following meridians, as described in the opening stage: bladder meridian, kidney meridian, large intestine meridian, lung meridian, pericardium meridian, liver meridian, and conception vessel.

2. Palpate and (if necessary) treat, as described in the acupoint stage, the following acupoints: BL 13, KI 27, LI 1, LU 1, LU 8, LU 9, PE 6, LIV 3, LIV 13, and CV 17.

3. Close all of the meridians appropriately.

4. Perform head, neck, and shoulder stretches as described in Chapter 6.

Acupoint Summary for Heaving

BL 13—aids in strengthening the lungs and lung meridian; addresses chronic respiratory infections, bronchitis, asthma
KI 27—relieves chest discomfort, cough, and asthma; stimulates energy
LI 1—eases throat inflammation
LU 1—relieves chest issues
LU 8—aids in relieving breathing difficulties
LU 9—balances the meridian; clears the lungs
PE 6—balances the spleen, kidneys and liver; calming properties; supports chest area
LIV 3—quiets allergic reactions
LIV 13—eases abdominal discomfort and expansion
CV 17—empties chest congestion; relieves chronic coughing

Hock Joint Issues

Hock issues are common in horses. Because the hocks are major joint formations in the hind legs, they are exposed to tremendous exertion. If your horse has arthritic changes in this joint; edema; sensitivity; and inability to bend this joint or bear weight on this area, you may apply this technique.

1. Open the following meridians, as described in the opening stage: bladder meridian, gall bladder meridian, spleen meridian, stomach meridian, liver meridian, and kidney meridian.

2. Palpate and (if necessary) treat, as described in the acupoint stage, the following acupoints: BL 39, BL 60, BL 62, GB 21, GB 29, GB 37, GB 38, SP 4, SP 5, ST 41, LIV 2, LIV 8, KI 3, and KI 7.

3. Close all of the meridians appropriately.

4. Perform hind leg stretches as described in Chapter 6.

Acupoint Summary for Hock Joint

BL 39—identifies hock issues; helps hind leg problems
BL 60—effective for general pain, often called the aspirin point; relieves hind leg and lower back pain
BL 62—soothes arthritic hocks; softens tendons and outer leg muscles
GB 21—eases arthritis pain
GB 29—relieves joint conditions
GB 37—eases discomfort in limbs; strengthens weak legs
GB 38—eases painful hock joints
SP 4—promotes leg circulation
SP 5—eases stifle and hock discomfort
ST 41—promotes strength in hind limbs; relieves joint discomfort
LIV 2—removes heat
LIV 8—alleviates muscular discomfort in limbs
KI 3—balances the meridian; resolves hock issues
KI 7—nourishes and supports weak legs

Immune System Strengthening

Your horse's body is exposed to many factors that tax the immune system. If he travels or competes, is recovering from an illness or injury, has been in the company of other ill horses, is under stress, is elderly, or has recently undergone a change in work program, environment, or living arrangement, his immune system may be compromised. Apply this technique when you feel it is important to build up your horse's immunity.

1. Open the following meridians, as described in the opening stage: bladder meridian, triple heater meridian, lung meridian, gall bladder meridian, stomach meridian, and large intestine meridian.

2. Palpate and (if necessary) treat, as described in the acupoint stage, the following acupoints: BL 14, BL 17, BL 23, TH 15, LU 11, GB 39, ST 36, LI 4, and LI 11.

3. Close all of the meridians appropriately.

4. Perform stretches you feel are most appropriate for your horse, as described in Chapter 6. Perhaps pick those that stretch the front, center, and rear portions of his body.

Acupoint Summary for Immune System

BL 14—governs the heart muscle
BL 17—strengthens all blood and energy in the system
BL 23—supports immunity; strengthens skeletal bones
TH 15—strengthens immunity
LU 11—strengthens immunity
GB 39—builds the immune system
ST 36—releases cortisol; stimulates adrenals; builds immune system; relieves bloating, constipation, and stomach problems
LI 4—balances the meridian; eases pain; softens muscle tissue
LI 11—governs the immune system; anti-inflammatory properties in the upper body

Neck Issues

Horses' necks are particularly susceptible, as the horse uses his head and neck to balance the body. Therefore, the neck is constantly in a state of exertion. It is also common for horses to carry stress and tension in the neck. If your horse has difficulty bending or stretching his neck; carries his head tilted or unevenly; or has a sensitive neck, you may apply this technique.

1. Open the following meridians, as described in the opening stage: bladder meridian, gall bladder meridian, small intestine meridian, triple heater meridian, and lung meridian.

2. Palpate and (if necessary) treat, as described in the acupoint stage, the following acupoints: BL 10, BL 11, GB 20, GB 21, GB 39, SI 3, SI 6, SI 7, TH 8, TH 15, and LU 7.

3. Close all of the meridians appropriately.

4. Perform head, neck, and shoulder stretches as described in Chapter 6.

Acupoint Summary for Neck Issues

BL 10—resolves neck and shoulder tightness
BL 11—alleviates neck discomfort and tightness
GB 20—eases tension in neck and shoulders
GB 21—resolves arthritic pain; eases tension in head, neck, shoulders, and back
GB 39—restores neck flexibility
SI 3—releases neck tissue
SI 6—alleviates tightness in neck
SI 7—settles spasmodic neck tissue
TH 8—eases neck and shoulder discomfort
TH 15—releases neck stiffness
LU 7—relieves neck stiffness

Shoulder Discomfort

Discomfort or restricted movement in the shoulder is a common problem for horses. Causes include ill-fitting saddles, general unsoundness, and overexertion of the muscle groups. Ex-race horses are particularly susceptible, as they spent many years bearing tremendous weight on the shoulders. If your horse appears to have difficulties in the shoulder region, you may apply this technique.

1. Open the following meridians, as described in the opening stage: bladder meridian, gall bladder meridian, small intestine meridian, large intestine meridian, and triple heater meridian.

2. Palpate and (if necessary) treat, as described in the acupoint stage, the following acupoints: GB 21, SI 3, SI 6, SI 9, SI 11, LI 4, LI 14, LI 15, TH 8, TH 14, and TH 15.

3. Close all of the meridians appropriately.

4. Perform neck and shoulder stretches as described in Chapter 6.

Acupoint Summary for Shoulder Discomfort

GB 21—eases arthritic pain, and tension in head, neck, shoulders, and back
SI 3—eases stiff neck, back, and shoulders
SI 6—releases tight shoulders
SI 9—relieves shoulder discomfort
SI 11—promotes shoulder motion
LI 4—balances the meridian; eases pain; softens muscle tissue
LI 14—eases shoulder tightness
LI 15—relieves arthritis, shoulder, and elbow discomfort
TH 8—alleviates shoulder distress
TH 14—eases shoulder discomfort
TH 15—relieves shoulder pain

Stifle Joint Issues

The stifle joint in your horse's hind leg can be thought of as his knee. Just as human knee joints can be afflicted with pain and arthritis, so too can your horse's stifle joint. If your horse appears to be lame, has a shortened stride, or is unwilling to push off his hind leg when in motion, he may have a problem in the stifle joint.

1. Open the following meridians, as described in the opening stage: bladder meridian, gall bladder meridian, spleen meridian, liver meridian, kidney meridian, and stomach meridian.

2. Palpate and (if necessary) treat, as described in the acupoint stage, the following acupoints: BL 11, BL 20, BL 21, GB 34, GB 36, GB 37, SP 1, SP 9, LIV 8, KI 10, ST 35, and ST 36.

3. Close all of the meridians appropriately.

4. Perform hind leg stretches as described in Chapter 6.

Acupoint Summary for Joint Issues

BL 11—eases arthritis discomfort
BL 20—balances the spleen and pancreas
BL 21—alleviates hind limb discomfort
GB 34—relaxation point for muscles, tendons, and ligaments; promotes hind limb circulation
GB 36—resolves stifle joint discomfort; eases stiffness of hind legs; supports weak hind legs
GB 37—eases discomfort in hind legs; supports weak hind limbs
SP 1—eases joint discomfort
SP 9—resolves arthritic pain involving stifle and lower leg joints
LIV 8—eases muscle discomfort and tightness in the legs
KI 10—alleviates knee discomfort and promotes strength
ST 35—eases hind limb discomfort and arthritic pain
ST 36—releases cortisol, easing stifle discomfort

Swollen Joints

If your horse has joints that become warm, tender, and swollen with fluid, you may apply this technique. The symptoms may indicate injury/trauma, infection, or arthritis. Contact your veterinarian for an examination.

1. Open the following meridians, as described in the opening stage: bladder meridian, large intestine meridian, triple heater meridian, and stomach meridian.

2. Palpate and (if necessary) treat, as described in the acupoint stage, the following acupoints: BL 20, BL 60, BL 66, LI 5, TH 4, ST 2, and ST 41.

3. Close all of the meridians appropriately.

4. Discuss stretching applications with your veterinarian.

Acupoint Summary for Swollen Joints

BL 20—reduces swelling in the hind limbs
BL 60—eases general discomfort; "aspirin point"
BL 66—removes heat
LI 5—alleviates fluid retention in the front legs
TH 4—reduces swelling in the front limbs
ST 2—eases overall discomfort
ST 41—alleviates joint discomfort

Stress Management Technique

You can apply this technique to a horse that is generally worried and concerned about his surroundings. A horse that exhibits a hot personality is a valid candidate. It may be applied to a horse about to experience or who recently experienced a significant change—as, for example, a horse that was recently moved to a new boarding facility. You may want to use this technique prior to an upcoming event, such as a competition, that may provoke anxiety in your horse. This technique is also appropriate for a horse that has experienced a difficult and abusive past.

1. Open the following meridians, as described in the opening stage: bladder meridian, governing vessel, gall bladder meridian, stomach meridian, and spleen meridian.

2. Palpate and (if necessary) treat, as described in the acupoint stage, the following acupoints: BL 15, GV 24, GB 25, GB 44, ST 2, SP 3, and SP 6.

3. Close all of the meridians appropriately.

4. Perform head, neck, and back stretches as described in Chapter 6.

Acupoint Summary for Stress Management

BL 15—calms
GV 24—release anxiety; dissolves fear; quiets the mind
GB 25—reduces fear
GB 44—eases grief
ST 2—stimulates relaxation; alleviates general pain
SP 3—balances the meridian; calming properties
SP 6—eliminates nervousness

8

Herbs and Essential Oils

Herbal and essential oil therapies can stand alone as treatments or complement other modalities. When considering complementary therapies, assess your horse's condition thoroughly so each therapy you use works together with the others. For example, if you are applying acupressure or massage to relieve muscle discomfort, consider herbal or essential oil therapies, which provide relief from muscular pain, as complementary therapies. In this way, all of the modalities address the same health concern, combating it on multiple levels.

Always consult your veterinarian before using any herb in any manner on any horse. Some herbal therapies have potentially harmful side effects as well as adverse interactions with medications. Herbs should be thought of and treated with the same caution and respect as conventional medications. Further, herbal therapy is not a means of diagnosis.

HERBAL THERAPY

Herbal therapy is a natural way to encourage healing and restore balance within the whole horse. An herb is a plant or plant part valued for its medicinal benefit. Such herbs can be easily grown or purchased. They can be bought in mixtures to address specific issues or purchased individually and combined to produce various healing mixtures.

Herbs can be used for tissue rejuvenation, pain relief, digestive disorders, antibacterial properties, antioxidants, respiratory issues, wound healing, calming properties, and organ cleansing, to name a few. They are also used as anti-inflammatories, diuretics, and antiparasitics.

Herbal therapy does not diagnose conditions, nor is it a substitute for veterinary care. It must be studied and applied carefully and thoughtfully. Herbs must be given the same respect prescription medications are given. Consult your veterinarian and a professional equine herbalist before administering any herbal therapy to your horse.

Effective Components of Herbs

Herbs contain biochemical compounds that possess medicinal or toxic properties. This is why all herbs should be administered with care and caution after consultation with a veterinarian and professional equine herbalist. Dosages, duration, and constituents must all be considered when choosing the appropriate herb or herbal combination.

Herbal components include alkaloids, bitters, flavonoids, glycosides, mucilage, saponins, and tannins.

▸ *Alkaloids*—Organic compounds found in plants. They can function as analgesics, stimulants, depressives, or narcotics. Low doses of these compounds can be found in many herbs. Alkaloids often trigger healing properties in other plants. Many of today's synthetic drugs are based on alkaloid compounds.

Herbal remedies: (a) honey; (b) peppermint; (c) chamomile; (d) lavender; (e) garlic; (f) oatmeal; (g) essential oils

▸ *Bitters*—Plant components that affect the digestive system. They can alleviate stomach problems and encourage appetite in a poor eater. Bitters stimulate the nerves in the digestive tract and promote the streaming of gastric fluids within the horse's gut.

▸ *Flavonoids*—Water-soluble plant pigments. They possess anti-inflammatory and antispasmodic properties. They can also be used as diuretics.

▸ *Glycosides*—Organic compounds formed from simple sugar. *Caution:* Glycosides can be toxic when combined with water.

▶ *Mucilage*—Any of the gummy secretions or gelatinous substances present in plants. It is used to sedate tissue inflammation and irritation, as it forms a gel when dissolved in bodily fluids.

▶ *Saponins*—Plant glucosides that form soapy lathers when mixed with water. They are used in detergents, foaming agents, and emulsifiers. *Caution:* Most saponins are toxic. Do not apply to irritated or open skin. Administer with extreme caution only under the supervision of a veterinarian.

▶ *Tannins*—Compounds that occur naturally in the bark and fruit of various plants, especially nutgalls and oak bark. Tannins are polyphenols and form yellowish to light brown powdery, flaky, or spongy masses. They are used as astringents. They can prevent the loss of bodily fluids such as blood and can protect the skin.

History of Herbal Medicine

Nearly every civilization throughout history has used herbs for medicinal purposes. India is often credited with the development of herbal therapy, dating back several thousand years. The Egyptians and the Greeks were known for their use of herbs in healing and treatment. The texts authored by ancient Romans and Greeks discussing herbal therapy served as catalysts for much of modern-day medicine. Works published in the seventeenth century discussing herbal therapy are still available today. On the North American continent, Native Americans, as well as many generations of farmers, have used herbal therapies on themselves and their horses.

Precautions

As with all complementary/alternative therapies, safety issues are important. Take these precautions:

▶ Buy certified organically grown herbs only. If you are cultivating herbs yourself, you will obviously be aware of the quality of the plant. However, when buying from an outside source, make sure you are receiving a healthy, clean plant. If you are purchasing dried herbs, a label stating the herbs are "natural" does not mean they are certified organic. To ensure quality and authenticity, read all labels and packaging thoroughly to be certain you are receiving valid, pure product that does not contain harmful plant matter, pesticides, or fillers.

▶ Be sure to discuss all herbal therapy with your veterinarian regarding equine competition rules and regulations. You do not want to inadvertently violate any rules that affect your sport horse's eligibility or status as a participant. Each region and governing agency has its own set of regulations.

▶ Never use a plant you cannot identify. If you are unsure what a certain plant is or what the plant you need looks like, seek professional help.

▶ Ingesting or otherwise coming into contact with certain herbs can lead to negative reactions, harmful side effects, or toxicity. Know how to handle your herbs.

▶ Do not exceed the supplier's recommended dosage. Overdosing herbal remedies can harm your horse. Consult an equine professional (C/A veterinarian and equine herbalist) if you are unsure of proper dosage.

▶ All herbs should be clean, dry, fragrant, vibrant in color, and free of contamination. If herb plants have poor color, minimal fragrance, or obvious disease, mold, or insect infestation, do not use them. Discard them immediately.

▶ Proper preservation and storage of herbs is necessary to ensure potency and safety. When preserving herbs for future use, be sure the plants are thoroughly dry before placing into storage. If plants are wet or moist, mold can grow, contaminating the herb. If this happens, immediately discard the herb, as the mold may be toxic to your horse. Store homemade herbal remedies in your refrigerator and label each clearly. Indicate the contents and the date prepared. Discard remedies after seven days.

Benefits of Herbal Therapy

Herbal therapy offers several benefits. First, it can be quite cost-effective. Over-the-counter and prescription medications and salves are expensive compared to their herbal counterparts. Second, herbal therapy, used properly, can be as effective as synthetic medications for health problems such as burns, inflammation, immunity, digestive issues, respiratory problems, muscle discomfort, and cuts. Herbs provide a natural way to maintain your horse's health without introducing man-made chemicals into his system. Medicines may have long-term effects; herbs do not.

Next, herbal therapy is restorative. This therapy seeks to treat the cause of the problem rather than mask a presenting symptom. Also, herbal therapy can accelerate the healing process. As the herbs interact with and support one another, the body can be stimulated in its healing process, leading to more rapid healing. Lastly, most horses are receptive and open to herbal therapy, as they usually find herbs both appealing and palatable.

Precautions of Herbal Therapy

Do not use herbal therapy...

▸ if your mare is pregnant. Certain herbs can affect the uterus. Avoid this type of therapy during pregnancy.

▸ before consulting with your veterinarian if your horse is being treated for any sort of medical condition or illness. You do not want to complicate his treatment.

▸ f you are unsure about an herb's uses, dosage, or application. Thoroughly educate yourself on the uses of each herb. Some possess toxic elements and should not be given to your horse. Consult your veterinarian and equine herbalist.

▸ if your horse has a history of allergic reactions until consulting with your veterinarian. Once an herb is given, it cannot be retrieved. This therapy may not be the best option for a sensitive horse.

Herbal Dosages

Herbal dosages are not as precise as those for conventional allopathic medications. The core concept of herbal therapy is to consider the whole horse— his health, general demeanor, living environment, work program, medical history, diet, age, overall condition, and the current season. This consideration will help you choose herbs with healing properties that are effective for your particular horse. Whether you are seeking general wellness or addressing a chronic or acute condition, consider the multiple facets that make up your horse and his world so you can include herbs that possess the most appropriate elements.

That being said, this chapter offers general guidelines for herbal dosages. These are provided as a starting point; however, each horse's body reacts differently to herbal therapy. Therefore, the dosages listed may need to be altered in response to your horse's reactions.

Caution: Herbs should not be given in large doses. Small amounts work better. In fact, excessive dosing can cause harm and should be avoided. If you give your horse too large a dose, you may see an effect *opposite* from the one you are trying to achieve. For example, castor oil is generally given to resolve constipation, but administering too much castor oil can result in diarrhea. Always follow the supplier's recommended dosages.

Dried Herbs

Always read and follow the suppliers' dosing instructions. Dried herbs are more potent than fresh. In general, when using dried herbs, measure one-third the amount you would if using fresh herbs.

If no dosage instructions are given for dried herbs, a general guideline is to administer 1 cup (32 g) dried herbs twice per day until healing occurs. Once healing is noted, reduce the dosage to ½ cup (16 g) dried herbs twice per day. Continue this amount for 8 to 10 weeks after healing is complete.

Fresh Herbs

Administer fresh herbs to your horse in amounts your horse would naturally eat in the wild—that is, small amounts. Consult your veterinarian and equine herbalist first, as some herbs may be beneficial long-term for a specific horse while others should be given only to address specific issues for specified lengths of time.

Possible Negative Reactions

Although it is not common, your horse may present with a reaction after being given herbs. If your horse's body needs some but not all of the elements present in the herbs, you may see a reaction. Stop the therapy, wait 12 to 14 days, and then begin the therapy again at a lower dose. Usually, the reaction will not reoccur.

Reactions may include worsening symptoms, diarrhea, or change of hair coat color. If any of these symptoms present with intensity, immediately stop the herbal therapy and contact your veterinarian.

If your horse displays symptoms such as change in appetite, inability to urinate or pass manure, or any behavior unusual for him, stop the therapy and contact your veterinarian.

If, after receiving an herbal remedy or essential oil, your horse develops a skin irritation such as hives, itchiness, hair loss, or swelling, or if he displays breathing difficulties such as labored breathing, heaving, or coughing, stop the therapy and contact your veterinarian immediately.

TIP

Herbal Patch Test

Always test herbal remedies on your horse *before* offering them in full application, whether internal or external. Place a small amount of the remedy on a small patch of your horse's skin and monitor it for 24 hours. Check the area for reaction (hives, swelling, irritation, itching). If any reaction presents, do not use that herbal remedy. Seek alternative herbs or another form of therapy such as equine massage.

Before You Begin

Consult your veterinarian before beginning any herbal therapy on your horse. It is also wise to consult an equine herbalist to learn more before offering the therapy. A clear understanding of herbs and their effects is essential for using them safely.

Be sure to document all herbal preparations you administer to your horse. Record which herbs you use and in what proportions; how often you administer the remedy; the duration of the therapy; the intention of the therapy; and your horse's condition and reactions each day of the treatment. Documenting these details allows you to re-create and fine-tune an herbal therapy for future use.

Gather the following items to make the herbal recipes (remedies) below:

- Herbs
- Water
- Heat source
- Cooking pot
- Clean towels
- Wooden stirring spoon
- Carrier substance (honey, molasses, vinegar)
- Food-safe/heat-safe storage containers
- Writing utensil, such as a pen or fine-tipped marker
- Labels
- Writing tablet or notebook

When preparing herbal remedies, make sure to always work in a clean, organized space. Keep all ingredients and items sanitized and labeled to avoid contamination and confusion.

Continuously monitor your workspace while making these recipes:

▸ Cooking materials left unattended can pose a fire hazard.

▸ Insects, debris, or rodents can contaminate the remedy.

▸ Interruption can cause you to forget which step you are on or which ingredients you have or have not added.

▸ Children and pets could eat or be burned by utensils and ingredients or ingest the remedy.

Herbal Applications

Herbal remedies may be applied in several ways: as a compress, poultice, infusion, or inhalant. The way you choose to apply a particular remedy will depend on a discussion with your veterinarian, the history of your horse, and the health concern you are addressing.

Choose the most appropriate mix of herbs for the condition you are treating. Herbs interact to provide healing stimulation for your horse's system. Keep your remedies simple and use the proper amounts. Numerous herbs and excessive amounts can lead to harmful side effects. In addition, if you are using a wide variety of herbs simultaneously, you will not be able to distinguish which herbs are effective and which are not. Four to six herbs should be sufficient in any given remedy.

Sometimes a carrier substance is used as a means to deliver the herbs. Examples of carrier substances include castor oil, honey, water, and vinegar. The herbs contain the healing properties while the carrier substance is the vehicle for administering them. Sometimes honey or molasses is added to a remedy to make it more appealing to the horse.

Herbal Infusion

An herbal infusion consists of herbs steeped in boiling water. Begin by heating water. When the water comes to a full boil, shut off the heat source and add the herbs to the water. Allow the herbs to steep for 12 to 14 minutes. The longer the herbs steep, the more potent the infusion will be. Allow the liquid to cool completely before adding it, herbs and all, to your horse's feed. Divide the solution between your horse's morning feed and evening feed. You may also add the solution to your horse's water. However, you must closely monitor his water intake to ensure he is ingesting the herbal infusion and staying well hydrated. Make a fresh solution each day.

Basic Herbal Infusion
1 liter water + ¼ cup *dried* herb OR ¾ cup *fresh* herb = herbal infusion solution

Herbal Compress

A compress is made from an herbal infusion (see above). A clean cloth is submerged in the infusion to absorb the solution. The cloth is removed, wrung out, and then gently applied to the horse's affected area. You can hold the compress on the area for 7 to 9 minutes, or, if feasible, wrap the compress around the area, allowing it extended time to saturate the tissue.

If you choose to wrap the area, be sure to remove the compress after several hours or, at most, the next morning. Do not leave a compress on for longer than that, as the area should be cleaned and aired out according to your veterinarian's recommendations. Be sure to make a fresh herbal solution for each application to ensure sanitation and potency.

Caution: To prevent burns, allow the herbal infusion to cool thoroughly before applying it via a compress. You can refrigerate the infusion to speed the cooling process. The solution may also be used to bathe an injury or simply as a bracer for your horse after he has been exercised. If using as a bathing solution, be sure to strain the herb from the liquid.

Herbal Ingestion

An ingestion consists of herbs your horse eats. Herbs may be offered in fresh or dried form. They can be added to feed or water. They can be offered in their natural state, as an herbal infusion, or combined with just a bit of an appealing substance such as molasses or honey to encourage your horse to eat them.

Caution: Always follow the dosing instructions on the supplier's packaging. Do not exceed the recommended dose. The dosages listed in this book are suggestions only. Discuss all dosages with your veterinarian and equine herbalist before administering.

Basic Herbal Ingestion Remedy
1 cup (340 g) honey + 1 tablespoon (2 g) dried herbs OR 3 tablespoons (6 g) fresh herbs = herbal ingestion remedy

Herbal Inhalation

Herbal inhalation uses the vapors from an herbal infusion. Your horse inhales the vapors for 10 to 12 minutes to aid in clearing the respiratory system so the infusion can function more efficiently.

When preparing an inhalation, do not use a hot plate in the stable. Prepare the inhalation in a separate cooking area and transport it to the stable. Offer the mixture to your horse in a bucket or other heat-safe, sanitized container. Stay with your horse while offering the remedy. Allow the vapors to saturate your horse's living space for 10 to 12 minutes, and allow your horse to inhale it. Offer this remedy in an area away from other horses, such as a separate stall, barn aisle, or paddock. If you have no choice but to offer it in the company of other horses, know it is an organic herbal mixture that does not contain toxic chemicals, so it is harmless. If your horse does not want to inhale the vapors, do not force him. Try another herbal mixture and see what his reaction is to a different aroma.

Caution: Do not allow your horse to touch the hot solution with his face, as burns may result. To prevent injury, monitor the distance of the solution from your horse and the amount of time he inhales it. Do not leave your horse unattended with a hot liquid.

Herbal Poultice

A poultice is a combination of herbs and a carrier substance such as castor oil, honey, water, or vinegar. Poultices are used to decrease inflammation, draw out infection, promote circulation, and prevent infection. They aid in overall healing. Poultices are external treatments only and are held in place through bandaging. They are usually applied for 24 hours. They are then removed so the area can be cleaned and aired out for approximately 10 hours before a fresh poultice is applied. This application process is continued until there are signs of healing.

Many different poultices can be made by varying ingredients and amounts according to purpose. A simple poultice consists of combining boiling water with herbs. Allow the herbs to soak just until the point of softening. Once the solution has cooled thoroughly, remove the softened herbs from the water, mix them with the carrier substance, and place them on the affected area, securing them with bandaging.

Basic Poultice Formula
½ cup (120 ml) carrier substance + ½ ounce (15 g) *dried* herbs OR 1½ (42 g) ounces *fresh* herbs. Discuss the use of a poultice with your veterinarian prior to use. Some poultices may not be applied to open wounds or irritated skin. Some require a protective barrier to be placed on the area before the poultice is applied.

EQUINE HERBAL TREATMENTS

The herbs listed in this publication are generally available in fresh and dried forms and as ingredients in various medicinal products. Familiarize yourself with their healing properties, as well as the precautions, so you can choose the most appropriate herbal treatment for your horse's needs. Always consult with your veterinarian before implementing any type of herbal therapy.

Eucalyptus (*Eucalyptus globulus*)

Aloe vera (*Aloe Barbadensis*)

Fenugreek (*Trigonella foenum-graecum*)

Chamomile (*Matricaria Chamomilla*)

Garlic (*Allium sativum*)

Devil's claw (*Harpogophytum procumbens*)

Kelp (*Ascophyllum nodosum*)

Marigold (*Calendula officinalis*)

Witch hazel (*Hamamelis Virginiana*)

Mint (*Mentha*)

Rosehips (*Rosa carnina*)

Valerian (*Centranthus ruber*)

Common Herbs for Treatment

A complete list of herbs and their properties is beyond the scope of this book. The Chinese herbal pharmacopoeia alone lists 6,000 herbs. If you are interested in learning more about herbal therapy, refer to the "Further Reading" section.

Here is a list of common herbs and their uses in equine herbal therapy. Note that some herbs are limited to either external or internal use, while others can be used both externally and internally. Herbs have a number of properties: analgesic, antibiotic, antihistamine, anti-inflammatory, antifungal, antihistamine, antiparasitic, antiseptic, antispasmodic, astringent, expectorant, and styptic.

Aloe Vera (*Aloe Barbadensis*): External

The fluid and gel secreted from the aloe vera plant act as sealing agents for skin damaged by burns or irritation. They stimulate the healing process and soothe the affected area. Apply the aloe vera juice or gel directly on the affected area immediately after the damage occurs.

Chamomile (*Matricaria Chamomilla*): External/Internal

This herb is used for its general calming properties. It is effective in balancing the nervous system and settling the digestive system. It is administered orally in fresh or dried form. It can also be used to make an herbal infusion to place on skin irritations.

General ingestion dosage: 1 ounce (14 g)/day

Devil's Claw (*Harpogophytum procumbens*): Internal

This herb is an anti-inflammatory and analgesic. It is administered orally, usually in dried form.

General ingestion dosage: 1/10 ounce/day

Caution: Do not use devil's claw on pregnant mares. This herb can affect the uterus.

Eucalyptus (*Eucalyptus globulus*): External

This herb is an antiseptic, antispasmodic, and expectorant. It can be used for respiratory problems as an inhalant.

Fenugreek (*Trigonella foenum-graecum*): Internal/External

The seeds of this herb are the most potent part of the plant. They are used for overall body conditioning or, combined with garlic, for respiratory dysfunction. This herb can be administered orally or made into a poultice for muscular or joint discomfort.

General ingestion dosage: ½ ounce (14 g)/day

Caution: Do not use fenugreek on pregnant mares. This herb stimulates the uterus.

Garlic (*Allium sativum*): Internal/External

Garlic has multiple properties including antibiotic, antihistamine, expectorant, and antiparasitic. This herb can be administered orally in clove or powder form. The cloves can also be crushed and applied to wounds.

General ingestion dosage: 1 ounce (28 g)/day

Kelp (*Ascophyllum nodosum*): Internal/External

Kelp is an excellent source of minerals, including calcium and potassium. It can improve overall skin and coat condition and ease arthritic discomfort. Kelp can also be made into an herbal compress and applied to sore joints. It can be administered orally in fresh or dried form.

General ingestion dosage: ½ ounce (14 g)/day

Marigold (*Calendula officinalis*): External only

Marigold has many properties, including anti-inflammatory, antifungal, antiseptic, and astringent. It can be used in poultices and braces as an all-purpose antiseptic.

Mint (Peppermint) (*Mentha*): Internal/External

Mint is anti-inflammatory and antispasmodic. It can be used to relax the muscles of the digestive system. It can be applied to swollen joints and insect bites, as it cools and soothes. It can be administered orally in fresh or dried form or used as an herbal infusion.

General ingestion dosage: 3 to 5 ounces (85 to 142 g)/day

Rosehips (*Rosa carnina*): Internal/External

This herb supports the immune system, supplies iron and vitamin C, and supports liver, kidney, and adrenal gland function. It can also be used to make an herbal infusion to bathe spasmodic muscles. It can be administered orally, usually in dried form.

General ingestion dosage: 1 ounce/day

Valerian (*Centranthus ruber*): Internal

This herb's natural sedative properties make it a calming agent.

General ingestion dosage: ¼ ounce/day

Witch Hazel (*Hamamelis Virginiana*): External

This herb is anti-inflammatory and styptic. It can be used in an herbal compress to treat bruises, stop bleeding, and soothe insect bites.

ESSENTIAL OILS THERAPY

Essential oils are obtained from plants. They maintain the odor and other characteristic qualities of the plant and evaporate on contact with air. They are used to improve physical and emotional well-being.

Essential oils are collected through the distillation of herbs and flowering plants. The distillation process produces highly potent oil because it concentrates the substance. One essential oil may contain several hundred chemical components. Each possesses certain properties that can heal or balance disorders within the mind and body.

An Equine-Friendly Therapy

This healing modality works well with horses because they are highly sensitive, refined in their ability to smell and in their instinctive ability to self-medicate using healing plants.

Horses rely on their sense of smell for survival in the wild. They need to be able to detect predators, other horses, watering areas, and weather changes. Domesticated horses have the same olfactory gift, making them ideal candidates for essential oil therapy.

In the wild, a horse instinctively chooses the appropriate plants his body needs at any given time. Domesticated horses have, for the most part, retained that ability and, therefore, are capable of determining which oil is acceptable and which is not based on their bodies' needs.

Functions of Essential Oils

Each essential oil has its own function in addressing emotional and physical concerns. Essential oils have innumerable uses: addressing respiratory issues, removing toxins, fighting inflammation, promoting circulation, cooling and soothing, easing muscle discomfort, warming, resolving skin issues, strength-

> **TIP**
> ## History of Essential Oils
>
> Essential oil therapy has been practiced for thousands of years. Ancient documentation from the Middle East to Egypt, India, and China describes the use of plant-derived oils for medicinal purposes. Essential oils are referred to in the Bible, perhaps the most familiar being frankincense and myrrh.
>
> Essential oils had a resurgence in the twentieth century when Rene Gattefosse, a French chemist, wrote a publication in 1937 discussing the healing properties of essential oils based on his own personal experience with lavender oil. He used the oil to heal his burned hand and found the results remarkable. He is credited with coining the term *aromatherapy*. As years passed, synthetic drug production grew in popularity, decreasing the use of essential oils. What many people do not know is that many synthetic drugs are based on the molecular structure of essential oils.

ening the immune system, eliminating fatigue, and alleviating arthritic conditions. They can be used as analgesics, sedatives, antiseptics, diuretics, and styptics.

Essential oils promote health through regulating, stimulating, or sedating the physical and emotional systems in the horse's body. These actions encourage the healing process by restoring balance within the systems. The oils can be taken into the horse's system through the skin, mouth (oral ingestion), and nose (inhalation).

Benefits of Essential Oils

Essential oils help your horse without the addition of synthetic chemicals that can cause serious side effects. They are composed of natural material that your horse's system is designed to utilize. Essential oil therapy can be combined with many other complementary or alternative therapies. The oils can also be used in conjunction with one another to promote health.

Essential oils address the horse on an emotional and physical level, resulting in harmony within the system and, in turn, healing and prolonging health. Essential oils therapy can be cost-effective in comparison to synthetic drug therapy. True, pure organic oil can be expensive; however, it lasts much longer than a traditional seven-day course of drug therapy.

Essential oils are not a substitute for veterinary care or treatment. They are meant to complement traditional veterinary care. If your horse appears ill or injured, contact your veterinarian immediately.

A holistic veterinarian is a wonderful resource when implementing herbal and essential oil therapies. This professional has the benefit of a dual education that encompasses both Eastern and Western medicine.

Counterindications for Essential Oil Therapy

Do not use essential oil therapy if...

▶ your mare is pregnant. Some oils that can affect the uterus. Avoid this therapy during pregnancy.

▶ your horse is currently being treated by your veterinarian for any medical condition or illness. Consult your veterinarian before administering oils. You do not want to complicate your horse's treatment.

▶ your horse is currently receiving homeopathic care from a holistic veterinarian. Consult this professional before using essential oil therapy, as some essential oils can negate the effects of homeopathic treatment.

▶ you are unfamiliar with essential oils. Educate yourself thoroughly before using this therapy. Some oils possess toxic elements and should not be given to your horse. If you are unsure about the dosage or application of an essential oil, do not use it. Once oil has been administered, it cannot be retrieved. Consult your holistic veterinarian.

▶ your horse has a history of allergic reactions. Speak to your veterinarian before applying essential oil therapy. This may not be the best option for a sensitive horse.

Safety Precautions

Here is a list of precautions that support working with essential oils. Please read the list carefully and thoroughly before attempting essential oil therapy.

- Purchase, handle, transport, and apply essential oils with the same care as any other medicine.

- Keep essential oils out of the reach of children.

- Do not apply essential oils longer than 14 days.

- Discontinue therapy immediately if your horse appears to have an allergic reaction to the substance. Contact your veterinarian.

- Essential oils are highly flammable. Keep them away from all heat sources.

- Oils are stored in glass bottles. Be careful when transporting and using the oils so as not to break the glass.

- Use the suggested dose when offering essential oils. Do not exceed the recommended amounts. These oils are highly concentrated and highly potent.

- Essential oils should not be used in high doses. Use the minimum amount possible to achieve results.

- Pure essential oils should not be applied directly to the skin. Dilute essential oils with a base oil before applying them.

- If your horse appears highly agitated when a specific body area is touched, do not apply oil to that region.

- Avoid contacting the eyes, genitals, rectum, and linings of the ears and nose with essential oils. Skin damage and severe reactions (burning) could occur if essential oils reach these areas.

Flush with cool water and wash the area with a mild, natural soap, if possible, immediately after an essential oil accidentally touches any of these regions.

- Do not apply essential oil therapy to any horse you do not own. You do not want to be held liable for someone else's animal.

- Always use a dropper when measuring oils. Most oils come with an insert dropper, but some do not. Keep several new droppers on hand so you always have a clean one available should you purchase oil that does not come with one. Each oil must have its own dropper.

- Never pour oil from its bottle and estimate the measurement. You will not be able to obtain an accurate reading. Precision is essential.

- Do not apply essential oils to pregnant mares. Some oils may influence the uterus.

- Do not apply essential oils directly on an open wound or broken skin because they are highly potent and could irritate the tender area. Instead, apply oils in proximity to the wound or opening.

- Do not contaminate oils during application. Wash your hands before working with essential oils. Remove oils from the bottle with a clean instrument every time you use them. If you insert an instrument into the bottle after it has touched the area you are treating, the entire bottle of oil is contaminated. Use a clean cotton swab for this type of application; dip the clean end of the swab into the bottle and then dip the other clean end into the bottle when giving a second application.

Toxicities

Horses can have negative reactions to essential oils. Learn about these reactions so you recognize them if they occur. Some essential oils are toxic; never use these on your horse.

If you apply an essential oil to your horse's skin and note the skin becomes inflamed, raised (hives), swollen, or itchy (rash), your horse is having a reaction to the oil. This reaction may take place immediately or after several applications over time. Wash the area thoroughly and apply aloe vera gel. Monitor the reaction closely, and, if it does not dissipate shortly after the area is cleaned and treated, contact your veterinarian.

Essential oils can cause your horse's skin to burn if the treated area is exposed to direct sunlight. The sensitive skin of the muzzle and around the nostril is especially vulnerable. Light-colored horses, such as grays and palominos, are more susceptible to this reaction. The citric oils are one type that can cause the skin to burn when exposed to sunlight. Citric oils originate in citrus fruits, including grapefruit, lemon, lime, orange, and tangerine. The oils opoponax and verbena can also cause this reaction. These oils have valuable healing properties; however, they must be used with care. Do not apply them to the muzzle or nostril area. It is not advisable to use them on light-colored horses.

If your horse has trouble breathing or develops a cough, contact your veterinarian immediately. These are signs of an allergic reaction.

Typical Reactions to Essential Oils

Each horse prefers certain oils and responds better to them. Each horse's emotional and physical conditions and imbalances vary. Essential oil therapy may offer improvement immediately or over the course of several days. If your horse has a chronic condition, oils may take longer to work. If the condition is acute, you may notice a more rapid response.

This therapy must be dictated by your horse's responses. Observation is crucial. Watch your horse's reactions when an oil is used, as he will indicate whether he accepts or rejects it. Do not force an essential oil on your horse. Your horse will reject certain oils because his body does not need them at that particular time. If your horse's body is in need of the essential oil, he will clearly express interest in it.

Your horse will display one of the following responses to an essential oil:

▶ *Positive response*—If you offer an essential oil for your horse to smell and he is genuinely interested in it, he will show his curiosity by actively smelling the aroma, with ears upright and eyes bright. If this is the reaction, use the essential oil (but only as indicated; don't let him ingest it if it is meant for external use only). This oil should prove beneficial for your horse.

TIP

Toxic Oils

The following oils are toxic and should never be used in essential oil therapy:

- aniseed
- arnica
- bitter almond
- bitter fennel
- boldo
- camphor
- cassia
- costus
- cinnamon bark
- dwarf pine
- elecampane
- horseradish
- mugwort
- mustard
- origanum
- pennyroyal
- sage
- sassafras
- savin
- savory
- tansy
- thuja
- wormseed

▶ *Negative response*—If you offer an essential oil for your horse to smell, he may become obviously agitated—ears pinned back and head turned away or pulled back from the scent. These are signs your horse's body does not need the essential oil. Do not use the oil.

▶ *Moderate response*—If you offer your horse an essential oil to smell and he responds with some interest—nostrils opening while nipping at the bottle—use the oil in low doses with limited frequency. Perhaps use only 1 drop, once a day. (In the rare instance in which a horse does not react at all, do not use the oil. It could indicate the horse's body does not need the oil, or that the horse is too ill to respond.)

Choosing the Appropriate Essential Oils

The root cause of a health concern must be addressed, or the problem will return. For example, if you use an essential oil that assists with digestive disorders but continue to offer low-quality feed, your horse may experience little or no benefit from the therapy because the root of the problem still exists.

This is why you must evaluate your horse holistically when choosing suitable oils for therapy. Consider the chief complaint, your horse's age, physical health, past health issues (chronic and acute), emotional state, history, current living arrangement, exercise program, nutritional intake, and overall condition.

Your horse will let you know if you have chosen correctly by accepting or rejecting the oils. Numerous oils are available, each with multiple healing properties. Choose wisely, and test the oils on your horse. Perform essential oil trials and skin patch tests (see pages 194) prior to full application. If you apply essential oil therapy and do not notice any improvement, reevaluate the situation and offer the therapy with a different selection of oils.

TIP

Possible Side Effect

Note: Although essential oils contain healing qualities, you may notice your horse's condition actually worsens slightly for a day or two after essential oil therapy. This may be the body's initial response and a sign that your horse's system is cleansing. If your horse's condition appears serious or lasts longer than two days, stop the therapy and contact your veterinarian.

Purchasing Essential Oils

Purchase organic essential oils. Oils labeled "pure" or "natural" are not necessarily organic; they must be labeled as such. With essential oils, you get what you pay for—and they can be expensive. An inexpensive oil is most likely not a pure organic one. On the other hand, be sure costly oils are certified organic before you buy them.

Purchase from reputable companies. These label the exact contents of the oils and indicate they are 100 percent pure. Ask if the company will provide a certificate of authenticity. Talk to a representative rather than simply ordering online. Ask how long the company has been in business and from which countries their products come. Inquire if they perform quality control tests and back up their claims of purity, and, if so, how. Ask if they offer an analysis of their products.

High-quality organic oils are generally shipped immediately as production, storage, and time all contribute to potency. A supplier should be knowledgeable and willing to answer all of your questions, so don't hesitate to ask. Many oils are accompanied by a fact sheet about the oil. Request that a fact sheet be included in your order.

Storing Essential Oils

Store essential oils in a cool, dark place that does not undergo severe temperature changes, as hot and cold can alter the chemical properties of the oil. A dark bottle is preferable, as ultraviolet rays can damage an oil's effectiveness. Make sure the tops of the bottles are secure, as the oils can oxidize.

Clean the outer surface of the bottle after each use to maintain the oil's purity. Store bottles upright to prevent leakage and contamination.

Label and date all oils. Most can be kept for 12 months; citrus oils are the exception, with a shelf life of six months. Do not use oil that is not labeled. It is vitally important that you can identify the oil and ascertain its expiration date. Treat oils with the same respect as conventional medications.

Essential Oil Patch Test

Dilute essential oils with a base oil before applying them to the skin. Place 1 or 2 drops of the diluted oil on a small patch of your horse's skin, preferably behind the elbow, and monitor for 24 hours. Check the area for reaction (hives, swelling, irritation, itching). If any reaction presents, do not use those oils. Seek alternative oils or another form of therapy, such as equine acupressure therapy.

Before You Begin

Generally, use one to three oils in any given remedy. Using more than three can be confusing, especially when you are new to this therapy. Using more than three can alter the effect of the oils as well.

It is wise to perform skin patch tests when your horse is healthy so when your horse is unwell, you already know which herbs, oils, and essences your horse responds to positively. Keep a current list of these elements and update as needed.

For each oil, conduct a trial several days before the therapy application as well as on the day of application. The trials allow your horse time to acclimate to the oil.

To conduct a trial:

1. Slowly approach your horse and allow him to smell the closed bottle in your hand. Remove the lid and allow the aroma from the oil to saturate the air for a few moments.

2. Offer the opened bottle to your horse and allow him to smell it with each nostril. Hold the bottle securely, as your horse may nip at the bottle if he favors the scent. Do not allow the oil to contact the skin. Document your horse's reaction to each of the oils. This helps ensure you are using oils your horse is accepting of at this time. If you are going to apply oils to your horse's skin, conduct a skin patch test first before offering them in full application.

Plan when you will be using essential oil therapy. If you are using oils to stimulate, apply them in the morning. Conversely, if you are using oils for sedation, apply them in the evening. If you are addressing issues such as swollen joints, apply the oils as needed.

Blending Oils

Blending oils involves combining essential oils with base or carrier oils. Base oils do not contain essential oil components. Examples of base oils include apricot, grapeseed, hazelnut, jojoba, peach kernel, sweet almond, and walnut oils. Like essential oils, carrier oils should be of the highest organic quality. Blending a pure essential oil with a low-quality carrier oil dilutes the mixture and alter its healing properties, in a sense contaminating the blend. Pure organic essential oils should be combined with pure organic carrier oils to ensure the excellence of the blend.

Essential oils can also be combined with other substances such as gels, creams, and lotions. Again, all of these products should be pure, organic, and free of dyes and perfumes.

Essential oils are highly concentrated. A general guideline is not to blend more than three oils, as the healing properties of each will lessen if the oil is diluted too much.

Equipment and Materials

▸ *Workspace*—Your workspace should be clean and organized. It should be out of the sunlight, as sunlight can affect oil potency. The space should be located away from your horses and well ventilated. Neither you nor your horse want to be overexposed to the scent of lingering oils.

▸ *Utensils*—Glass is the best material for utensils used for blending oils because they do not retain or absorb the oils. Plastic and wood absorb oils, while metal can alter their chemical elements. (If you choose to use wooden or plastic items, discard them after one use.) Stock your workspace with glass bottles, a glass measuring cup, a glass funnel, and a glass stirrer.

▸ *Materials*—You will need organic essential oils; organic carrier oils; dark, sanitized glass bottles with droppers; tissues (to wipe off the bottles); and writing utensils and labels for clearly labeling each bottle by date, contents, and proportions of each oil in the mixture.

Instructions for Blending Oils

1. Consult your veterinarian before using essential oil therapy on your horse.

2. Document the oils you use, including names, amounts, and dates.

3. Gather your utensils and materials. Be sure all of your items have been sanitized to prevent cross-contamination from prior blends.

4. Using a funnel, fill your glass bottle halfway to capacity with the carrier oil.

5. Add your essential oils.

6. Add the remainder of the carrier oil to the glass bottle. Do not fill the bottle to capacity. Leave a ¼-inch (6.4 cm) gap at the top so the oil blend has room to breathe.

7. Gently blend the oils by stirring them with the glass stirrer for 1 or 2 minutes or by securing the top on the bottle and then tipping it over and then upright several times.

8. Label each blend and store appropriately. See "Storing Essential Oils" in this chapter.

9. Clean and sanitize all utensils, and securely and properly store all oils.

Essential Oil Dosages

Essential oils are highly concentrated substances. Therefore, little is needed to take effect. Bearing this in mind, the following equation is general in nature and may be adjusted to meet the needs of your horse on consultation with a holistic veterinarian. Always begin using the least amount of essential oil listed in the equation.

General External Dosage Equation

1 to 3 drops essential oil + ½ ounce (14 g) carrier oil = skin application blend

General Inhalant Dosage Equation

Essential oils may be offered for inhalation in their natural state, in combination with one another, or in a blend with a carrier oil.

When offering an essential oil in its natural state, do not allow your horse's nostrils to touch it because that skin is sensitive and may react to the oil.

When combining essential oils, a general guideline is to blend 1 or 2 drops of each to create your inhalant.

When blending essential oils and carrier oils to create an inhalant, a general guideline is 1 to 3 drops essential oil + ¼ ounce (7 g) carrier oil.

Internal Ingestion Equation

These amounts must be determined by your holistic veterinarian.

Essential Oil Techniques

Essential oils can be applied using several techniques, including skin application, aromatherapy, and oral ingestion.

Skin Application

Essential oils can be applied to the skin after dilution with base oil and after a skin patch test is completed. Never apply an undiluted essential oil directly to the skin, as it is much too potent and can irritate the area. When an oil mixture is applied to the skin, it is absorbed into the bloodstream and takes effect from there.

Here are general guidelines for skin application of essential oils:

▸ If your horse displays tremendous interest in the oils, apply twice per day, up to 14 days. If your horse shows a moderate interest in the oils, apply once per day, up to 14 days.

▸ If your horse rejects the oils, do not use them. Offer another choice in oils.

▸ Apply oils to the poll, around the ears (never inside the ear), along the neck, on the shoulders, on the back, over the major organs, and on the feet (on the frog and along the coronet band).

▸ When using essential oil therapy to address an emotional or behavioral issue, apply the oils on the poll and along the top of the neck, following the length of neck from the top to the base. Apply the oils twice each day, up to 14 days.

▸ Treat respiratory problems by applying oils to the throat area and along the jugular groove. Apply these oils twice per day, up to 14 days.

▸ Do not use essential oils more than 14 days at a time to avoid overabsorption in the body. If you do not see signs of improvement or resolution after 14 days, reevaluate your horse and try a different therapy. The health problem may have a different underlying cause than the one you are treating.

Steps for Skin Application

1. Consult your veterinarian.

2. Read all safety precautions listed in this chapter carefully and thoroughly.

3. Choose and purchase appropriate organic oils.

4. Combine oils (see page 195).

5. Conduct an essential oil trial (see page 194).

6. Conduct a skin patch test (see page 194).

7. Apply the oil blend once or twice a day. Drop it directly from the dropper onto your horse's skin or onto your fingertips, and then carefully rub it into the area. Do not allow the dropper to touch your horse's skin or your own skin; this will contaminate the entire bottle.

8. Document the session thoroughly. Record your horse's reactions throughout the treatment. Note the types of oils applied, the amount of each oil used, the date, the time, the intention of the treatment, and the duration of the course of the treatment.

9. If you do not see signs of improvement after 14 days of use, discontinue the therapy. If your horse's condition noticeably worsens, discontinue therapy and contact your veterinarian immediately.

Aromatherapy

Essential oils emit an odor when they make contact with air. This odor evaporates and can then be inhaled by your horse.

Aromas affect the mind and body because they travel to the limbic system of the brain. The limbic system is involved with memory, emotion, and smell. Most horses naturally smell oil properly, one nostril at a time. Each nostril leads to the opposite side of the brain.

Steps for an Aromatherapy Session

1. Consult your veterinarian.

2. Read all safety precautions listed in this chapter carefully and thoroughly.

3. Choose and purchase appropriate organic oils.

4. Conduct an essential oil trial.

5. Remove the bottle top and, holding the bottle securely, allow your horse to inhale the scent of the oil, one nostril at a time. Do not allow your horse's nostrils to touch the bottle, as the oil could irritate the sensitive nostril skin. If your horse rejects the scent by pulling away or displaying agitation (pinning ears back), immediately remove the bottle and replace the top. If your horse expresses interest in the oil, allow him to inhale it, ideally until he stops. Inhalants may be offered once or twice per day.

> **TIP**
> ## Aromatherapy Responses
>
> It is believed the vapors are received and transformed into communications that are sent to various parts of the brain where emotion and bodily function may be affected. Have you ever walked into a bakery and smelled the delicious aroma of cookies baking? The cookie scent may trigger a physical response of hunger and an emotional response of desire. It may also trigger a mental response of memory—perhaps your mother always baked cookies for special occasions and you were reminded of those events by the cookie smell. Aromatherapy correlates to all of these responses.

Essential Oil Remedies

Simple Topical Blend

This blend can be applied in compress form to minor cuts, abrasions, sore muscles and arthritic conditions.

> 8 ounces (235 ml) warm chamomile water
> 2 teaspoons (9 g) aloe vera gel
> 3 drops lavender oil
> 3 drops tea tree oil

Blend all ingredients in a glass bowl, stirring with a glass stirrer. Place a clean cloth in the solution until it absorbs the mixture. Wring out excess solution and apply to the area for 5 to 7 minutes twice daily for 5 days or until healing is noted. Do not apply this treatment for more than 14 days.

Antibacterial Spray

This blend is sprayed into the air to combat bacteria. It is an ideal solution for spraying inside a horse trailer. Trailers can be breeding grounds because their stale, warm air often harbors bacteria. Keep this solution away from human and horse eyes. There-fore, do not load horses immediately after spraying this application inside of the trailer.

> 16 ounces (475 ml) warm clary sage water
> 3 teaspoons (14 g) fragrance-free organic shampo (may be purchased from essential oil company)
> 4 drops garlic oil
> 6 drops bergamot oil
> 6 drops tea tree oil

Combine these ingredients in a spray bottle (prefer-ably a glass disperser). Spray throughout the area. Take care not to spray in or near eyes.

Equine Insect Repellent Remedy

> 16 ounces (475 ml) peppermint water
> 3 teaspoons (14 g) aloe vera gel
> 2 teaspoons (9 g) fragrance-free organic shampoo (may be purchased from essential oil company)
> 10 drops eucalyptus oil
> 10 drops garlic oil
> 10 drops lavender oil

Combine these ingredients in a spray bottle (prefer-ably a glass disperser). Spray as needed. Do not spray in or near eyes.

6. Document the session thoroughly. Record your horse's reactions throughout the treatment. Note the types of oils applied, the amount of each used, the date, the time, the intention of the treatment, and the duration of the course of treatment.

7. If you do not see signs of improvement after 14 days of use, discontinue the essential oil therapy. If your horse's condition noticeably worsens, dis-continue therapy and contact your veterinarian immediately.

Oral Ingestion

Do not allow your horse to ingest essential oils unless therapy is closely supervised and monitored by your veterinarian. The oils approved for internal consump-tion are regulated by your governing agency (in the United States, the Food and Drug Administration). This book does not endorse oral ingestion unless all guidelines are strictly followed. Create and imple-ment an oral ingestion therapy only under the close supervision of your veterinarian.

COMMON EQUINE ESSENTIAL OIL TREATMENTS

The following is a list of common oils that may be used for essential oil therapy. It is best to use only high quality, organic, pure essential oils. Read all precautions associated with the oils prior to using them, and use care when working with them. Always consult your veterinarian before implementation.

Eucalyptus (*Eucalyptus globulus*)

Bergamot (*Citrus bergamia*)

Garlic (*Allium sativum*)

Carrot seed (*Daucus Carota*)

Jasmine (*Jasminum sambac*)

Chamomile (*Matricaria Chamomilla*)

Lavender (*Lavendula*)

Lemon (*Leptospermum petersonii*)

Tea Tree (*Melaleuca alternifolia*)

Peppermint *(Mentha piperita)*

Violet Leaf *(Viola)*

Sandalwood *(Santalum album)*

TIP

Sanitize Before Treatment

Carry a fresh supply of antibacterial wipes with you at all times so you will always be able to apply your essential oils with clean hands. The wipes also aid in cleansing your hands after applying oils.

Common Essential Oils

Bergamot (*Citrus bergamia*): **Internal/External**
This citric oil is derived from the rind of the bergamot. When exposed to sunlight, citric oils undergo changes that can burn the skin. Therefore, do not expose your horse to sunlight while applying this oil nor immediately after application. This oil is not recommended for use in light-colored horses(grays and palominos).

Bergamot oil is antiseptic, anti-itch, antiparasitic, and diuretic. It relieves anxiety, stimulates digestion, and strengthens the immune system. It is useful in treating minor cuts, insect bites, worm infestation, stress relief, stomach disorders, and infection.

Reminder: Citric oils have a shorter shelf life than others. Replace them every six months.

Carrot Seed (*Daucus Carota*): **Internal/External**
Carrot seed oil is antiparasitic. It promotes circulation, flushes toxins from the body, and restores health to the cells. It is useful in treating arthritis, joint pain, muscular discomfort, worm infestation, and general liver function.

Chamomile (German) (*Matricaria recutica*) **(Roman)** (*Chamaemelum nobile*)
The chamomiles are oils commonly known for their soothing properties. They are also anti-inflammatory, and they support liver and stomach function and alleviate skin problems. They are useful in treating allergic skin reactions, anxiety, arthritis, insect bites, joint discomfort, minor cuts, muscle tension, and stress.

Clary Sage (*Salvia sclarea*): **External**
Clary sage (not shown) oil is antiseptic and calming. It is useful in treating emotions because it quiets, settles, and sedates. Its sedative properties are also helpful in releasing taut muscle tissue. Clary sage can be used for stress relief and muscle discomfort.

Caution: Do not use this oil on pregnant mares.

Eucalyptus (*Eucalyptus globules*): **External Use Only**
Eucalyptus oil is toxic to horses if ingested. It can be used as an inhalant or skin application (diluted). Healing properties include opening the respiratory tract to relieve breathing difficulties from colds, coughs, or allergies; strengthening the immune system, and repelling insects. Eucalyptus is an ingredient in insect repellent.

Frankincense (*Boswellia serrata*): **External**
The healing properties of Frankincense (not shown) include relieving feelings of sorrow and anguish, strengthening the immune system, and healing the skin. It can be used for horses that display depression, have dealt with a taxing illness, or have a skin problem.

Garlic (*Allium sativum*): **Internal**
Garlic oil is antibiotic, antifungal, and antiparasitic. It can be used as an inhalant to assist with breathing, as an ingredient in insect repellent, and for ingestion (under veterinary supervision) to build the immune system.

Jasmine (*Jasminum sambac*): **External**
Jasmine oil is analgesic, anti-inflammatory, antispasmodic, and calming. It is useful for treating joint discomfort, muscle tension, and anxiety.

Caution: Do not use this oil on pregnant mares. It may stimulate contractions.

Lavender (*Lavendula*): **External**
Lavender oil is analgesic, antiseptic, and anti-anxiety, and it stimulates healing. It is also beneficial as an expectorant and insect repellent. It can be used to relieve breathing difficulties, heal minor cuts, for general pain and stress relief, and as an ingredient in fly repellent.

Lemon (*Leptospermum petersonii*): External

This citric oil is derived from the rind of the lemon. Citric oils undergo changes when exposed to sunlight that can cause burning of the skin. Therefore, do not expose your horse to sunlight while applying this oil or immediately after application. This oil is not recommended for use in light-colored horses (grays and palominos).

Lemon oil is antioxidant, antiseptic, antispasmodic, and astringent. It is uniquely able to regulate internal temperature. It can lower an elevated temperature and raise a low temperature. Lemon oil is useful in treating arthritis, strengthening the immune system, and addressing minor cuts and muscle pain.

Reminder: Citric oils have a shorter shelf life than others; replace them every six months.

Peppermint (*Mentha piperita*): External

Peppermint oil is analgesic and anti-inflammatory. It stimulates circulation and rejuvenates emotions, and it has expectorant capabilities. It is useful for treating breathing difficulties, pain, joint discomfort, mental clarity, muscle tension, and stomach disorders, and for removing toxins.

Sandalwood (*Santalum album*): External

Sandalwood oil is antispasmodic, antifungal, and astringent. It is beneficial in relieving breathing difficulties as well as restoring emotional health and combating panic, alarm, and distrust. It is useful for arthritis, muscle discomfort, respiratory infections, minor cuts, and sedation.

Tea Tree (*Melaleuca alternifolia*): External

Tea tree oil is antiseptic, antibacterial, antifungal, and antiviral. It helps resolve minor cuts, respiratory infections, skin irritations, thrush, and wounds.

Keep tea tree oil away from canines, which can experience limited paralysis with its use.

Violet Leaf (*Viola*): External

The healing properties of violet leaf oil include increasing emotional health, calming, and encouraging toxin removal by supporting liver function. This oil quiets, settles, soothes, and relaxes the horse. It is useful for a nervous horse or one that will be undergoing or has undergone a lifestyle change (new owner, new living arrangement, loss of stable mate).

Be aware that violet leaf oil contains an aspirin base (salicylic acid). This may interfere with competition regulations. Research this with your governing agency before using this oil on competition horses.

Appendix A: Equine Communication

Horses communicate through action, stance, expression, behavior, and vocalization. If you familiarize yourself with the equine communication system, you will have a better understanding of your horse's mood or physical condition at any given time.

*A common eye presentation when a horse is weary, going to sleep, being massaged, and sometimes being groomed or receiving acupressure
**Flehmen face: upper lip lifted and curled back, showing teeth and gums
***Often exhibited by a horse that is afraid of his rider to show he is surrendering or yielding to the human

Emotional State: Relaxed/tired
Ears: held sideways, with openings pointing forward and outward
Eyes: generally dark, open, and relaxed, or partially closed with a glazed effect*
Mouth: lower lip drooping, yawning
Nose: low carriage
Head/Neck: lowered
Tail: low
Vocalization: quiet

Emotional State: Greeting
Ears: stiffly upright, facing toward the sound of approaching human or horse
Eyes: open wide, alert
Mouth: may use tongue to lap human
Nose: large, open nostril
Head/Neck: raised upward, reaching toward horse or human
Tail: may raise tail slightly
Vocalization: nickering: a throaty sound that vibrates from deep within, carrying a deep pitch

Emotional State: Interested in/curious about sound, scent, objects
Ears: stiffly upright, facing toward the sound
Eyes: opened wide, focused on source of interest
Mouth: upper lip lifted and curled back, showing teeth and gums—referred to as the flehmen face**
Nose: open nostril, actively sniffing
Head/Neck: head and neck raised and pointed in the direction of source, head extended and neck downward to sniff object
Tail: tail may elevate, raising away from the body
Vocalization: blowing

Emotional State: Positive reaction to touch
Ears: upright, facing forward
Eyes: soft, may be partially closed
Mouth: lips extended, may wriggle lips
Nose: open nostril, deep breathing
Head/Neck: may lean head and neck into other horse or human
Tail: low tail carriage
Vocalization: quiet

Emotional State: Playful/happy
Ears: loose, forward, and upright
Eyes: soft, relaxed eye
Mouth: may wriggle lips
Nose: low posture
Head/Neck: may be low in position, or arched in posture
Tail: tail may be relaxed or slightly elevated
Vocalization: nickering

Emotional State: Frustrated/impatient
Ears: turned backward, pinned downward, close to the head
Eyes: dark eyes, watchful of other horse or human
Mouth: may wrinkle lips
Nose: may crinkle nostrils
Head/Neck: may elevate head and neck, may toss or wring head and neck
Tail: may elevate tail
Vocalization: may snort or squeal

Emotional State: Surrendering/yielding★★★
Ears: held sideways with openings turned back toward the hind end★★★
Eyes: eyes opened wide with concern, or whites may be displayed
Mouth: closed mouth
Nose: low nose carriage
Head/Neck: dropped, low head posture
Tail: lowered closely to the body
Vocalization: quiet

Emotional State: Fearful
Ears: upright, stiff rotational ears
Eyes: widening, exposing the whites of the eye; protruding
Mouth: may make flehmen face
Nose: nose positioned toward origin of fear
Head/Neck: raised, may be arched
Tail: tail carriage elevated
Vocalization: may whinny or snort

Emotional State: Angry
Ears: pointed backward and pinned down flat against the head
Eyes: dark, watchful
Mouth: may pull lips back, exposing teeth
Nose: may be crinkled or wrinkled
Head/Neck: head and neck may be stretched forward, reaching toward object, horse, or human; head and neck may be elevated; may wring or toss head and neck
Tail: may wring tail
Vocalization: may squeal

Emotional State: Dominating/aggressive/defensive
Ears: turned back, pinned down close to the head
Eyes: dark and focused on origin of aggression
Mouth: may wrinkle lips, may pull lips back and expose teeth
Nose: may be crinkled or wrinkled
Head/Neck: may toss head and neck up and down, may wring head and neck in circles
Tail: may wring tail, may turn hind end toward object, human, or horse that is the source of aggression
Vocalization: may squeal

Emotional State: Threatening/biting/kicking
Ears: turned back, pinned down close to head
Mouth: intently focused
Nose: may be wrinkled, pulled back to expose teeth
Head/Neck: may be crinkled
Tail: may be extended forward toward object, human, or horse, may turn hind end toward object, human or horse
Vocalization: may squeal

Emotional State: Alert/concerned
Ears: stiffly upright and pointed in the direction of concern
Eyes: opened wide, may show the whites of the eyes
Mouth: may extend lips
Nose: large, open, sniffing nostrils
Head/Neck: raised, arched head and neck
Tail: flagged tail posture
Vocalization: may snort or whinny

Emotional State: Alerting others to danger
Ears: facing forward, stiff
Eyes: opened wide, white may be showing
Mouth: may be extended or vocalizing
Nose: open, wide, sniffing nostrils
Head/Neck: may be arched or raised upward
Tail: may be elevated or fully flagged
Vocalization: whinny or neigh, snort

Emotional State: Negative reaction to touch
Ears: may turn backward, may pin down against head
Eyes: may open wide
Mouth: may pull lips back to expose teeth
Nose: may wrinkle nostrils
Head/Neck: may turn head and neck to look at source of touch, may toss head and neck up and down
Tail: may tuck tail under, close to body
Vocalization: may squeal

Emotional State: Unwell
Ears: may be loosely facing downward, flopping out to the side
Eyes: appear dull, and may be partially closed
Mouth: may be loose and hanging
Nose: may present with labored breathing
Head/Neck: low head and neck posture
Tail: low and close to the body
Vocalization: quiet

Appendix B: Quick Reference Charts: Herbs and Essential Oils

HERBS: CAUTION

Any herbs in the chart indicated for external use only can be toxic if ingested. Do not administer these herbs orally. Use only as directed.

ESSENTIAL OILS: CAUTION

Do not allow your horse to ingest essential oils unless the treatment program is closely supervised and monitored by your veterinarian. The oils are approved for internal consumption by your governing agency (in the United States, the Food and Drug Administration is responsible for this), and the dosages given are minimal and recorded.

This book does not endorse the practice of ingestion by a horse unless all guidelines are strictly followed and actively met. You must create and implement a plan for any sort of oral ingestion only under the supervision of your veterinarian.

HERBAL KEY

IG = Ingestion
IF = Infusion
IH = Inhalant
C = Compress

ESSENTIAL OILS KEY

I = Internal Use (Ingestion, Inhalant)
E = External Use (Compress)

Herbs and Essential Oil Treatment Chart

Ailment	Herbs	Essential Oils
Anxiety	Chamomile/IG, Valerian/IG	Chamomile (I/E), Clary Sage(E), Frankincense (E), Jasmine (E), Violet Leaf (E)
Arthritis	Devil's Claw/IG, Garlic/IG, Goldenrod/IG	Carrot Seed (I/E), Jasmine (E), Peppermint (E), Sandalwood (E)
Azoturia	Peppermint/IG and C; Kelp/IG; Rosehips/IF(for bathing)	Carrot Seed (I/E), Chamomile (I/E), Clary Sage (E), Jasmine (E), Lemon (E), Peppermint (E), Sandalwood (E)
Back Pain	Peppermint/IG	Carrot Seed (I/E), Clary Sage (E), Jasmine (E), Peppermint (E), Sandalwood (E)
Cold/Cough	Eucalyptus/IH, Garlic/IG	Eucalyptus (E), Garlic (I/E), Lavender (E), Peppermint (E), Sandalwood (E)
Colic	Chamomile/IG, Fenugreek/IG, Peppermint/IG	Bergamot (I/E), Chamomile (I/E), Jasmine (E), Peppermint (E), Violet Leaf (E)
Cribbing	Chamomile/IG, Valerian/IG	Bergamot (I/E), Chamomile (I/E), Clary Sage (E), Jasmine (E), Lavender (E), Sandalwood (E), Violet Leaf (E)
Heaving	Eucalyptus/IH, Garlic/IG	Eucalyptus (E), Garlic (I), Lavender (E), Peppermint (E)
Hock Joint Issues	Devil's Claw/IG, Witch Hazel/C	Carrot Seed (I/E), Chamomile (I/E), Jasmine (E), Lavender (E), Peppermint (E)
Immune System	Kelp/IG, Fenugreek/IG, Rosehips/IG	Bergamot (I/E), Eucalyptus (E), Frankincense (E), Garlic (I), Lemon (E)
Neck Issues	Garlic/IG, Goldenrod/IG	Carrot Seed (I/E), Clary Sage (E), Jasmine (E), Peppermint (E), Sandalwood (E)
Shoulder Problems	Garlic/IG, Devil's Claw/IG	Carrot Seed (I/E), Clary Sage (E), Jasmine (E), Peppermint (E), Sandalwood (E)
Stifle Joint Issues	Goldenrod/IG	Carrot Seed (I/E), Chamomile (I/E), Jasmine (E), Lavender (E), Lemon (E), Peppermint (E)
Swollen Joints	Kelp/IG, Witch Hazel/C	Carrot Seed (I/E), Chamomile (I/E), Jasmine (E), Lavender (E), Lemon (E), Peppermint (E)

Common Herbs and Their Uses

Herb	Properties	Uses	Suggested Dosage for Internal/Oral Use
Aloe vera	sealing agent (skin)	External: helps heal burns, skin irritations	
Chamomile	calming agent (digestive or nervous system or skin irritations)	Internal: balances nervous system External: calms skin irritations	1 oz/day (IG)
Devil's claw	anti-inflammatory, analgesic		⅒ oz/day (IG)
Eucalyptus	Antiseptic, antispasmodic, expectorant		
Fenugreek	overall body conditioning, respiratory dysfunction, muscular and joint discomfort	Internal: mix with garlic for respiratory dysfunction, general health External: poultice for muscular, joint discomfort	½ oz/day (IG
Garlic	antibiotic, antihistamine, expectorant, antiparasitic	Internal: clove or powder form External: crushed and applied to wounds	1 oz/day (IG)
Goldenrod	anti-inflammatory, analgesic		½ oz/day (IG)
Kelp	mineral source (especially calcium and potassium)	Internal: conditions skin coat, relieves arthritis External: compress applied to sore joints	½ oz/day (IG)
Marigold	anti-inflammatory, antifungal, antiseptic, astringent		3-5 oz/day (IG)
Mint/peppermint	anti-inflammatory, antispasmodic	Internal: aids digestion External: soothes swollen joints, insect bites	1 oz/day (IG)
Rosehips	antioxidant	Internal: supports liver, kidney, adrenal gland function; supports immune system; source of iron & vitamin C External: relieve muscle spasms	
Valerian	calming agent, sedative		¼ oz/day (IG)
Witch hazel	anti-inflammatory, styptic	External: helps bruising, stops bleeding, soothes insect bites	

Key: Compress (C), Poultice (P), Infusion (IF), Ingestion (IG), Inhalant (IH)

Appendix C: Therapies for Common Ailments

Always consult with your veterinarian before using any of the therapies listed.

AZOTURIA

▸ *Acupressure*—Equine acupressure is an effective complementary therapy. Refer to "Equine Acupressure Techniques/Azoturia" in Chapter 8 for a complete guide to this treatment.

BACTERIAL INFECTION IN A JOINT

▸ *Acupressure*—Equine acupressure can be a complementary therapy for this condition. Refer to "Equine Acupressure Techniques/Immune System" in Chapter 8 for a complete guide to this treatment.

▸ *Herbal remedy*—An herbal blend that strengthens the immune system can not only help a horse recuperate from a bacterial infection but also keep him from being susceptible to infection in the first place. Two immune strengthening herbal blends:

- *Rosehip blend:* 6 cups (1.4L) boiling water + 1½ tablespoons rosehip granules. Mix the granules into the boiling water and allow to cool. Incorporate ½ cup (120 ml) remedy twice a day into your horse's feed.

- *Garlic blend:* 1 pound (455 g) garlic cloves soaked in 1 gallon (93.8L) honey. Soak these ingredients for 15 days, and then combine the mixture (including the garlic cloves) into your horse's feed, using ½ cup (120 ml) daily.

BONE SPAVIN

▸ *Acupressure*—Refer to "Equine Acupressure Techniques/Arthritis" in Chapter 8 for a complete guide to this treatment.

BOWED TENDON

▸ *Herbal remedies*—An extract of white willow bark, which possesses anti-inflammatory and analgesic properties, can be incorporated into your horse's daily feed. General dosage is ⅓ ounce twice daily during the recovery period. Several poultices, one of which combines comfrey and linseed oil, can be applied directly to the tendon. Refer to "Equine Herbal Applications" in Chapter 9.

COLIC

▸ Massage therapy—If you suspect colic, you can implement massage techniques while you are waiting for your veterinarian to arrive. Refer to Chapter 6 for essential information before performing the following massage.

1. Working on the left side of your horse's body, place your thumb pad on the base of your horse's neck, above the multifidus cervicus muscle and in front of the deltoid muscle. Applying moderate, direct pressure, move your thumb pad in clockwise circular motions. The circular patterns will be about the size of a quarter. Complete 15-20 rotations.

2. Perform the Back Technique, as described in Chapter 5.

3. Perform the Rib Cage Technique, as described in Chapter 5.

4. Place your open flat palm just behind the posterior pectoral muscle and lightly slap it back and forth, so your hand moves toward your horse's genital area, back toward the rear portion of the posterior pectoral muscle. This is your horse's abdominal area.

Complete as many of these techniques as you can while waiting for the veterinarian.

HERBAL REMEDIES

▶ *Bach Flower Rescue Remedy*—This product is composed of five flower extracts—cherry plum, clematis, impatiens, rock rose, and star of Bethlehem—that promote emotional well-being in humans and animals. In times of emergency, administer the solution directly from the bottle and rub it into your horse's gums.

▶ If your horse is willing to ingest an herb, blend peppermint and warm water to create an herbal ingestion. See Chapter 9 to learn how to prepare an herbal ingestion.

DEGENERATIVE JOINT DISEASE

▶ *Acupressure*—Equine acupressure is the alternative therapy of choice for joint degeneration. Refer to "Equine Acupressure Techniques/ Arthritis" in Chapter 8 for a complete guide to this treatment.

EQUINE INFLUENZA

▶ *Herbal therapy*—Herbal therapy may be used in conjunction with traditional veterinary care. The concept is to rid the body of infection and strengthen the immune system. Garlic, rosehips, and eucalyptus are herbs and oils that support the immune system and aid in opening airways and clearing the nasal passages. Inhalants and ingestion are ways these herbs can be administered after consulting your veterinarian and herbalist.

▶ *Herbal remedy*—Add slices of fresh lemon to your horse's water. Lemon aids in regulating body temperature, possesses antioxidant properties, and promotes white blood cell production.

HIVES

▶ *Essential oil therapy*—After contacting your veterinarian and discussing this option, you may use the following essential oil remedy: Blend 1½ teaspoons organic honey + 4 teaspoons (10 g)/(27 g) aloe vera gel + 15 drops lavender oil + 15 drops chamomile oil + ½ cup (120 ml) peppermint water and apply to the affected areas.

▶ Herbal remedy—After contacting your veterinarian and discussing this option, apply 4 drops Bach Flower Rescue Remedy on the gums.

MALE GENITAL INFECTIONS

▶ *Natural soaps*—If your horse has particularly sensitive skin or reacts to soaps in general, choose an all-natural, organic cleaning solution for this task. Products are now available for sheath cleaning that do not contain chemicals. These products contain herbs, oils, and organic elements including aloe vera, soy, and essential oils such as chamomile and tea tree oil. These are gentle and effective.

NAVICULAR DISEASE

▶ *Herbal remedy*—An herbal ingestion remedy for this is millet. Millet is a plant rich in B vitamins, folic acid, calcium, iron, potassium, magnesium, and zinc. A general dosage guideline is ¼–½ cup (50-100 g) millet (ground fresh, or whole and soaked in water) combined with your horse's feed daily.

PASTURE-ASSOCIATED PULMONARY DISEASE

▶ *Essential oil therapy*—The following oils may be beneficial in managing this condition: Bergamot, peppermint, and eucalyptus. Refer to Chapter 9 to learn how to blend essential oils for skin applications.

▸ *Acupressure*—Refer to "Treatment for Heaving," Chapter 8.

RAIN SCALD

▸ *Herbal application*—Combine 2 drops eucalyptus oil + 5 ounces vinegar + 2–3 cloves garlic + 1–2 chamomile tea bags to make an effective remedy.

RINGWORM

▸ *Essential oils remedy*—An essential oil blend of ½ ounce aloe vera gel + 3 ounces chamomile water +¼ ounce linseed oil + 8 drops myrrh + 8 drops patchouli + 8 drops lavender + 8 drops yarrow can be applied to the affected area daily until healing occurs or the oil therapy has been followed for two weeks. Do not continue beyond 14 days. Refer to "Blending Oils" in Chapter 9.

▸ *Herbal remedy*—Combine 3 ounces vinegar (antifungal) + ¼ ounce eucalyptus oil (antiseptic) + 3 cloves peeled, crushed garlic (antibiotic). Apply this to your horse's skin. Caution: Ringworm is highly contagious to horses and people. Wear gloves when applying this remedy, and thoroughly sanitize your hands and clothing after applying it. Apply the remedy with clean, sanitized, disposable applicators, such as cotton swabs. Each time the remedy is applied to the skin, use a new, clean swab and discard it properly after use. Do not cross-contaminate the herbal blend by applying it to your horse's skin with an applicator such as a cotton swab and then touching the remaining remedy with your contaminated hands or reusing the swab.

SESAMOIDITIS

▸ *Acupressure*—Refer to "Equine Acupressure Techniques/Swollen Joints" in Chapter 8 for a complete guide to this treatment.

SPRAINS

▸ *Herbal remedy*—A professional equine herbalist can create an anti-inflammatory blend that may include apple cider vinegar, white willow bark, devil's claw, and arnica to reduce inflammation and ease discomfort.

STRINGHALT

▸ *Herbal remedy*—A professional herbal therapist can prepare a blend that includes comfrey, sage, and valerian to complement the conventional treatment. These herbs offer vitamin B12 and magnesium phosphate, both of which promote brain function and aid in repairing damaged nerve tissue.

STRONGYLES (DISTEMPER)

▸ *Acupressure*—Equine acupressure therapy for colds or coughs may be beneficial for this condition. Refer to "Equine Acupressure Techniques/Cough-Cold" in Chapter 8.

WOUNDS

▸ *Herbal therapy*—Bach Flower Rescue Remedy may be administered for wounds of any type. Put 4–6 drops on the tongue. Continue once daily until obvious signs of healing appear.

▸ *Herbal ingestion*—Strengthen your horse's immune system, thus promoting healing, by offering garlic and rosehips for ingestion. You may combine these herbs with honey, molasses, or warm water. See Chapter 8 to learn how to create an herbal ingestion.

▸ *Poultice*—Apply a poultice to drain puncture wounds. Refer to "Equine Herbal Applications" in Chapter 9 for additional information on and recipes for poultices.

Resources

EQUINE HEALTH

The following sites include holistic publications; holistic animal radio talk shows, some of which have call-in or email capabilities to answer your questions; equine health resource guides; and practitioners who offer phone consultations:

www.equinewellnessmagazine.com
wellness resource guide

www.rivasremedies.com
phone consultations available

www.naturalhorsetalk.com
phone and email consultations available

www.animaltalknaturally.com
holistic animal health radio show

www.iaamb.org
locate a practitioner in your area

www.holistichorse.com
equine holistic publication

www.petsynergy.com
phone consultations

RECOGNIZED HOLISTIC ORGANIZATIONS

The following are well-recognized organizations in the holistic veterinary healthcare field:

Academy of Veterinary Homeopathy,
www.theavh.org

American Academy of Veterinary Acupuncture
www.aava.org

American Holistic Veterinary Medical Association
www.ahvma.org and www.holisticvetlist.com

American Veterinary Chiropractic Associationm
www.avca.com

American Veterinary Medical Association
www.avma.org

Australian Holistic Veterinarians
www.ahv.com.au

British Association of Holistic Nutrition and Medicine, www.bahnm.org.uk

Complementary and Alternative Veterinary Medicine
www.altvetmed.org

International Association for Veterinary Homeopathy
www.iavh.org

International Veterinary Acupuncture Society
www.ivas.org

Veterinary Botanical Medical Association
www.vbma.org

American Holistic Veterinary Medical Association
www.ahvma.org

The Veterinary Institute of Integrative Medicine
www.viim.org

Dr. Edward Bach Centre
www.bachcentre.com

EQUINE DENTISTS

Academy of Equine Dentistry,
www.equinedentistry.com

International Association of Equine Dentistry
www.IAEQD.org

VETERINARY ACUPUNCTURE ASSOCIATIONS

American Academy of Veterinary Acupuncture
100 Roscommon Drive, Suite 320
Middletown, CT 06457 USA
(860) 635-6300
office@aava.org
www.aava.org

International Veterinary Acupuncture Society
I.V.A.S.
2625 Redwing Road
Suite 160
Fort Collins, CO 80526 USA
(970) 266-0666
www.ivas.org

FLORALS AND ESSENTIAL OILS

Bach Flower Essences
www.bachflower.com
www.bachcentre.com

Puritan & Genesta Natural Foods
2 Holmes Street
Mystic, CT 06355 USA
(860) 536-3537
www.puritan-genesta.com

Young Living Essential Oils and Aromatherapy
(609) 944-8819
Toll free: (888) 895-9668
www.essentialoilremedies.com

INTERNATIONAL INFORMATION ON TOXIC PLANTS

Association of Societies for Growing Australian Plants
www.usyd.edu.au

University of Sydney, Australia
http://asgap.org.au

Canadian Biodiversity Information Facility
www.cbif.gc.ca

UK-based equine resource
www.horseweb-uk.com

USDA/ARS Poisonous Plant Research Lab
www.ars.usda.gov

The American Society for the Prevention of Cruelty to Animals
www.aspca.org

Canadian Poisonous Plants Information
www.cbif.gc.ca/pls/pp

FDA Poisonous Plant Data
www.cfsan.fda.gov

MAGAZINES

Equine Wellness
8174 S. Holly Street
Centennial, CO 80122 USA
164 Hunter St. West
Peterborough, Ontario, Canada K9H 2L2
(866) 764-1212
www.equinewellnessmagazine.com

Holistic Horse
84 Irish Meetinghouse Road
Perkasie, PA 18944 USA
(215) 249-1965
www.holistichorse.com

Equus
P.O. Box 420235
Palm Coast, FL 32142 USA
(800) 829-5910 (U.S. and Canada)
www.equisearch.com/equus

HERBAL SUPPLIERS

Animal Herbery
P.O. Box 4836
Greenwich, CT 06831 USA
(203) 302-1991
animalherbery@optonline.net
www.animalherbery.com

Earth Angel Herbs for Horses
earthangelherbs@aol.com
www.earthangelherbs.com

Whole Horse Chinese Herbal Formulas
P.O. Box 544
Oakhurst, CA 93644-0544 USA
(559) 683-4434
G2@wholehorse.com
www.wholehorse.com

Silver Lining Herbal Equine Supplements Inc.
1208 Burley Avenue
Buhl, ID 83316 USA
Toll free: (866) 543-6956
www.silverliningherbs.com

EQUINE BODYWORK ASSOCIATIONS

International Association of Animal Massage
   & Bodywork
3347 McGregor Lane
Toledo, OH 43623 USA
(800) 903-9350
 info@iaamb.org
www.iaamb.org

International Federation of Registered Equine
   Massage Therapists
12 West Avenue
St. Thomas, Ontario N5R 3P5
Canada
(519) 660-8988

info@ifremt.org
www.ifremt.org

AROMATHERAPY AND NATURAL SUPPLIES

Abundant Health/Aromatherapy and Natural
   Health Accessories
1460 North Main Street Unit # 9
Spanish Fork, Utah 84660 USA
(800) 718-3068
orders@abundanthealth.us
www.abundanthealth.us

Birch Hill Happenings Aromatherapy Supply Shop
2898 County Road 103
Barnum, MN 55707-8808 USA
(218) 384-9294
bhhinfo@birchhillhappenings.com
www.birchhillhappenings.com

Wholistic Pet Organics
341 Route 101
Bedford, NH 03110 USA
(888) 452-7263
www.wholisticpet.com

SUGGESTED READING

Acupressure
Zidonis, Nancy; Snow, Amy; Soderberg, Marie.
Equine Acupressure: A Working Manual. Larkspur, CO:
Tallgrass Publishers, LLC, 1999.

Acupuncture
Rathgeber, Rhonda. *Understanding Equine Acupuncture.* Lexington, KY: The Blood-Horse, Inc., 2001.

Behavior
Morris, Desmond. *Horsewatching.* New York, NY:
Crown Publishers, Inc., 1988.

Essential Oils
Faith, Carole. *Essential Oils for Horses.* North Pomfret, VT: Trafalgar Square Publishing, 2002.

Rennels, Cheryl W. Equine *Essential Oils.* Livermore, CO: Beneficence, Inc., 2006.

Exercise

Benedik, Linda; Wirth, Veronica. *Yoga for Equestrians.* North Pomfret, VT: Trafalgar Square Publishing, 2000.

Hill, Cherry. *Intermediate English Exercises.* Pownal, VT: Storey Communications, Inc., 1998.

Hill, Cherry. *Advanced English Exercises.* Pownal, VT: Storey Communications, Inc., 1998.

Lilley, Claire. *Schooling with Ground Poles.* North Pomfret, VT: Trafalgar Square Publishing, 2003.

Swift, Sally. *Centered Riding.* North Pomfret, VT: Trafalgar Square Farm Publishing, 1985.

Swift, Sally. *Centered Riding 2:* Further Exploration. North Pomfret, VT: Trafalgar Square Farm Publishing, 2002.

Flower Essences

Devi, Lila. *Flower Essences for Animals.* Hillsboro, OR: Beyond Words Publishing, Inc., 2000.

Scott, Martin J. *Bach Flower Remedies for Horses and Riders.* Wykey House, Wykey, Shrewsbury, UK: Kenilworth Press, 2000.

General Care

Draper, Judith. *The Book of Horses and Horse Care.* London, England: Anness Publishing Limited, 2001.

Evans, J. Warren. *Horses.* New York, NY: W.H. Freeman and Company, 1996.

Harris, Susan E. *The USPC Guide to Conformation, Movement and Soundness.* New York, NY: Howell Book House, 1997.

McBane, Susan. *100 Ways to Improve Your Horse's Health.* Newton Abbot, UK: David & Charles Publishing, 2005.

Ramey, David W. *Concise Guide to Tendon & Ligament Injuries in the Horse.* New York, NY: Howell Book House, 1996.

Healing

Coates, Margrit. *Healing for Horses.* New York, NY: Sterling Publishing Co., Inc., 2001.

McBane, Susan. *100 Ways to Improve Your Horse's Health.* Newton Abbot, UK: David & Charles Publishing, 2005.

Herbs

Allison, Keith. *A Guide to Herbs for Horses.* Clerkenwell Green, London, England: J.A. Allen & Company Limited, 1995.

Cointreau, Maya; Kavasch, E. Barrie. *Equine Herbs & Healing.* Gaylordsville, CT: Earth Lodge Publishing, 2005.

Dyer, Chris. *Plants, Potions & Oils for Horses.* Warwickshire, Great Britain: Compass Equestrian Limited, 1999.

Mcdowell, Robert and Di Rowling.. *Herbal Horsekeeping.* North Pomfret, VT: Trafalgar Square Publishing, 2003.

Morgan, Jenny. *Herbs for Horses.* Addington, Buckingham, Great Britain: The Kenilworth Press Limited, 1993.

Massage Therapy

Meagher, Jack. *Beating Muscle Injuries for Horses.* Hamilton, MA: Hamilton Horse Associates, 1985.

Wyche, Sara. *The Horse's Muscles in Motion.* Wiltshire, Great Britain: The Crowood Press Ltd, 2002.

Stretching

Blignault, Karin. *Stretch Exercises for Your Horse.* North Pomfret, VT: Trafalgar Square Publishing, 2003.

Veterinary Care

Devereux, Sue and Liz Morrison. *The Veterinary Care of the Horse.* London, England, J.A. Allen & Company Limited, 1992.

Pavord, Marcy; Pavord, Tony. *The Complete Equine Veterinary Manual.* Newton Abbot, UK: David & Charles Publishing, 1997.

Glossary

Abduction—a motion that pulls a body part away from the midline of the body or one of its parts.

Acupoint—refers to a specific point that is located on a meridian and can be accessed through acupressure or acupuncture for treatment.

Acupressure—a Traditional Chinese Medicine technique derived from acupuncture; physical pressure is applied to acupuncture points by the hand or elbow; a non-invasive therapy.

Acupuncture—an invasive technique associated with Traditional Chinese Medicine in which fine filiform needles are inserted into specific acupoints on the body for the therapeutic purpose of healing.

Adduction—a motion that pulls a body part toward the midline of the body or one of its parts.

Adhesion—an abnormal joining of adjacent tissues.

Adrenals—something that relates to the adrenal glands, their secretions, or something that is at, near, or on the kidneys.

Alkaloids—organic compounds that are comprised of basic chemical properties found in vascular plants and some fungi; known for their poisonous or medicinal attributes; examples include nicotine, cocaine, and morphine.

Allopathic—refers to the method of treating disease by means of agents that produce effects opposite from those of the disease addressed (opposed to homeopathy).

Alternative Therapy—a form of practice, covering a broad range of healing philosophies and modalities, that is generally viewed as outside of the mainstream of traditional medicine.

Analgesics—remedies or medications that reduce or eliminate pain.

Anti-bacterial—anything that is destructive to the growth of bacteria.

Antibiotic—any of a large group of chemical substances produced by various microorganisms and fungi that have the ability in dilute solutions to repress the growth of or to destroy bacteria and other microorganisms; used chiefly in the treatment of infectious diseases.

Antifungal—agents that eliminate or inhibit the growth of fungi.

Antihistamine—medicines that neutralize or repress the effect of histamine in the body; used in the treatment of allergic disorders and colds.

Anti-inflammatory—medication used to reduce signs of inflammation, tenderness, fever, and pain.

Antioxidants—chemical compounds or substances that repress oxidation and therefore damage cells.

Anti-parasitic—a substance that is used to eliminate or inhibit the growth and reproduction of parasites.

Antiseptic—antimicrobial substance applied to the skin to reduce the possibility of infection by keeping the area free from germs and other microorganisms.

Antispasmodic—a substance that relieves or prevents muscular spasms.

Aromatherapy—a form of alternative medicine that uses essential oils in order to alter a patient's mood or health.

Ascarids—any of various nematode worms of the family Ascaridae, which includes the common intestinal parasite Ascaris lumbricoides.

Astringent—See *styptic*.

Bitters—herbs that are steeped in liquid and are most often alcoholic in nature.

Cast—refers to a situation in which a horse lies down in an area too close to a wall or fence and is unable to right himself without help.

Cecum—a sac-like cavity in which the large intestine begins.

Chakra—one of the seven pools of energy present in the body.

Chakra Therapy—utilizes the healing energy that is found in the seven major energy centers or chakras of the body; the practitioner lays her hands upon each chakra of the horse to transmit healing energy into the area.

Chi—refers to the vital life force (energy) in the body.

Chiropractic Therapy—focuses on diagnosis, treatment, and prevention of mechanical disorders of the musculoskeletal system and their effects on the nervous system and overall health by implementing spinal, joint, and soft-tissue manipulation.

Chromotherapy (color therapy or colorology)—therapy in which the practitioner uses color and light to balance energy in the patient's body in order to alter their physical, emotional, and mental state.

Chronic Obstructive Pulmonary Disease—allergic condition leading to poor pulmonary aeration usually caused by exposure to fungal spores.

Circulatory System—organ system that moves nutrients, gases, and wastes to and from cells, aids in combating diseases and assists in stabilizing body temperature and *pH* to maintain a state of equilibrium.

Color Essences—each associated to a chakra; correlate with energy and healing of mind, body, and spirit; energy and vibrations emitted from each color offer therapeutic value.

Complementary Therapy—a healing treatment of disease or disorders, generally viewed as outside of the mainstream of traditional medicine; used in conjunction with conventional medicine.

Compress—a soft cloth held in place by a bandage that is used to provide pressure or to supply cold, heat, or medication.

Cortisol—a steroid hormone that is produced by the adrenal cortex and used to treat allergies, arthritis, and other systemic conditions.

Coprophagy—refers to eating feces.

Depressives—an agent that tends to lower the function of a specific body part.

Diuretics—substances that tend to increase the discharge of urine.

Element—a single jump that is part of a combination of jumps; also refers to one of the five components that make up The Five Element Theory in Traditional Chinese Medicine.

Entanglement—when muscle tissue twists together or entwines into a mass; a snarl.

Essential Oil—a water-repelling, aromatic oil, or concentrated essence, that is the product of the distillation of a plant.

Expectorant—an agent that promotes the discharge of fluid from the respiratory tract.

Flavonoids—any of a large group of water-soluble plant pigments that are beneficial to health and wellness.

Flexion—refers to the act of bending a limb.

Free-Choice—when a horse is given a constant supply of a product (e.g. hay, water, salt) to ingest at will.

Fructans—sugars found in grass.

Fumonisins—Fumonisin B1 and Fumonisin B2 are toxins that frequently contaminate maize and other crops.

Glycosides—any of a group of organic compounds occurring in plants that yield a sugar and one or more nonsugar substances

Ground Rails—a pole generally constructed of wood that is approximately 10–12 feet (3.1–3.7 m) in length and 6 inches (15.2 cm) in diameter that is placed in front of a jump to aid the horse in locating a proper take-off; can also be used in the construction of jumps, or individually to create exercises for the horse to maneuver through or over.

Herbal Therapy (Herbalism)—is a medicinal practice that is based on the use of plants and plant extracts for the maintenance of health in humans and animals; herbs may be used aromatically, topically, and/or internally depending on the situation and the practitioner.

Herbs—plants that are often aromatic and are used especially in medicine.

Holistic—relating to a theory in which the parts of a whole cannot exist or be understood unless their relation to the whole is considered, most commonly associated within a system of therapy, often thought of as outside the mainstream of scientific medicine; examples include massage and chiropractic treatment.

Homeopathy—a form of alternative medicine which believes that an ill party can be treated using a substance that can produce, in a healthy patient, symptoms similar to those of the illness.

Hyperlipemia—refers to the presence of excessive amounts of fatty substances in the blood.

Immune System—a complex system of interacting cells, cell products, and cell-forming tissues that protects the body from foreign substances, destroys infected cells, and removes cellular debris; the system includes the thymus, spleen, lymph nodes and lymph tissue, stem cells, white blood cells, antibodies, and lymphokines.

Infusion—a liquid extract made by steeping or soaking a blend of substances together; example is tea.

Ingestion—the process of taking a substance (such as food) into the body.

Inhalant—a substance that is inhaled.

Ivermectin—a combination of two drugs that are used in veterinary medicine to eliminate parasitic worms.

Knot—a protuberance on or in a part of a muscle.

Lunge—to work a horse on a long line in a circle while tracking around the person that is holding the line.

Lunging Cavesson—a specially crafted head collar with ring attachments for a lunge line.

Lungworms—any of the parasitic nematode worms, especially of the family *Metastrongylidae*, found in the lungs of horses.

Lymphatic System—the system by which white blood cells are produced in response to inflammation or presence of antigens; in horses, the system includes the lymph glands, vessels, and sinuses through which lymph is carried, and lymphoid tissues.

Macro Minerals—include calcium, magnesium, sodium, potassium, and phosphorus and are needed in the tissues in larger quantities than micro minerals.

Magnetic Therapy (magnetic therapy, magnetotherapy, or magnotherapy)—a practice involving the use of static magnetic (magnetostatic) fields produced by permanent magents that is believed to produce health benefits when applied to certain parts of the body.

Manipulate—to examine or treat by the use of trained hands.

Massage—manipulating, by hand, the soft body tissues (muscles, tendons, ligaments, skin, joints, and other connective tissue) using varied pressure, tension, motion, or vibration.

Meridian—an energy pathway found in the body.

Metabolism—chemical process that takes place within a living organism where substances are broken down to produce energy for vital processes while other substances necessary for life are synthesized.

Micro Minerals—include boron, chromium, copper, germanium, iodine, iron, vanadium, and zinc; also referred to as trace minerals.

Modality—a means of treatment referring to the application of a therapeutic agent.

Mucilage—any of various gummy secretions present in plants.

Narcotics—natural and synthetic agents or drugs that are used in medicine to control pain.

Non-invasive—refers to a medical procedure that does not penetrate the skin or require the removal of bodily tissue.

Organic—a term that refers to products grown with fertilizers or pesticides of animal or vegetable origin and not from manufactured chemicals.

Palpate—to examine by touch for the purpose of diagnosing unwellness.

Pasture Associated Pulmonary Disease—an allergic condition leading to poor pulmonary aeration usually caused by exposure to pollens.

Physiotherapy—refers to physical therapy that aims to maintain and restore maximum movement and functional ability of the body by implementing an appropriate program that includes exercise, stretching, and manipulation.

Pinworms—any of the parasitic small nematode worms of the family *Oxyuridae* which are parasitic on horses; also called threadworms.

Poultice—a soft, moist mass of cloth, herbs, etc., applied as a healing remedy to the body.

Preventative—denotes a drug, therapy, procedure, or practice that is used to prevent disease or injury.

Probiotics—dietary supplements comprised of beneficial bacteria or yeasts.

Pyrantel—an anthelmintic drug administered in the form of its pamoate or tartrate for the purpose of eliminating parasitic worms.

Reflock—to stuff with wool, such as to reflock a saddle.

Reiki—a Japanese healing art in which the practitioners use their hands to move and channel energy to reduce stress, encourage relaxation, and promote healing.

Rejuvenation—the process of restoring something to its former condition or state.

Roundworms—any nematode unsegmented worm possessing an elongated, cylindrical body.

Saponins—any of various plant glucosides that form soapy lathers when combined and agitated with water; used in detergents and foaming agents.

Sedate—to calm, or quiet.

Spasm—an involuntary contraction of a muscle.

Stimulants—an agent that temporarily accelerates physiological or organic activity.

Strongyles—any of the parasitic nematode worms of the family *Strongylidae*, which are often found in the gastrointestinal tract of horses.

Styptic—an agent that serves to contract organic tissue and acts as an astringent to stop bleeding.

Tannins—astringent, bitter plant polyphenols that either bind and precipitate or shrink proteins; used for their anti-inflammatory properties or as a drawing agent.

Tapeworms—any of various ribbonlike, long flatworms of the family Cestoda, which lack an alimentary canal and are parasitic in the intestines of horses.

Titer Test—An antibody titer test is a test that measures the existence and quantity of antibodies in the blood in order to reflect the extent of past exposure to something that is foreign to the body; antibodies are used by the body to attack and remove foreign substances.

Tonify—to give strength to.

Topical—healing remedy applied externally to a particular part of the body.

Trace Mineral—any element that is required in small amounts for physiological functioning; also referred to as *micro minerals*.

Traditional Chinese Medicine (TCM)—encompasses a variety of traditional medical practices originating in China and considered a complementary or alternative medical system in many parts of the world; examples include acupuncture and herbal medicine.

Vital Signs—indicators of essential body functions, including pulse rate, body temperature, and respiration.

Yang—Chinese principle that is attributed to warmth, light, acute, positive and male; exists dually with Yin.

Yin—Chinese principle that is attributed to the presence of cold, dark, chronic, negative, and female; exists dually with Yang.

Index

Photographer Credits

All photography by Glenn Scott Photography with the exception of the following:

Roberto Adrian/www.istockphoto.com, 160

Cynthia Baldauf/www.istockphoto.com, 59

Eric Boegel/www.istockphoto.com, 37; 190

Zuzana Buráňová/www.istockphoto.com, 6 (middle); 60

jeong yoon choi/www.istockphoto.com, 45

David Claassen/www.istockphoto.com, 6 (main image)

Jacques Croizer/www.istockphoto.com, 17

Barry Crossley/www.istockphoto.com, 7 (right); 16; 135

Hendrik De Bruyne/www.istockphoto.com, 62

Jim DeLillo/www.istockphoto.com, 38

Matthew Dixon/www.istockphoto.com, 195

Simeon Flowers/www.istockphoto.com, 179

Karen Pulfer Focht/www.gettyimages.com, 20

Dirk Freder/www.istockphoto.com, 92

Virginia K. Frerk, 109

Giel/www.gettyimages.com, 13

Hedda Gjerpen/www.istockphoto.com, 94

Nick Goldsmith/www.nkgphoto.com, 83; 97

bosco gutierrez/www.istockphoto.com, 42

Nicola Hackl-Haslinger/www.istockphoto.com, 27

Karen Harrison/www.istockphoto.com, 25

Eileen Hart/www.istockphoto.com, 177

Angela Hill/www.istockphoto.com, 41

www.istockphoto.com, 8; 31; 39; 54–55; 63; 98; 182; 186–187; 199–200

Frans Lemmens/www.gettyimages.com, 11

Victor Maffe/www.istockphoto.com, 15 (bottom)

Melissa Anne Galleries/www.istockphoto.com, 131; 167

Dean Millar/www.istockphoto.com, 149

Eastcott Momatiuk/www.gettyimages.com, 35

Mary Morgan/www.istockphoto.com, 15 (top)

Sharon Morris/www.istockphoto.com, 6 (right); 28; 64

Kary Nieuwenhuis/www.istockphoto.com, 43 (right); 53

Thomas Northcut/www.gettyimages.com, 22

Oxford Scientific/Photolibrary/www.gettyimages.com, 5

Jean-Marie Pluchon/ www.istockphoto.com, 85

Angus Plummer/www.istockphoto.com, 6 (left); 180

www.septemberlegs.co.uk/www.istockphoto.com, 40

Robert Simon/www.istockphoto.com, 18

Rob Sylvan/www.istockphoto.com, 7 (left)

Chitra Tatachar/www.istockphoto.com, 7 (middle)

Raymond Truelove/www.istockphoto.com, 132

Drazen Vukelic/www.istockphoto.com, 19

Raphaelle Wavrant/www.fotolia.com, 50

Kent Weakley/www.istockphoto.com, 86

Serdar Yagci/www.istockphoto.com, 129 (right)

Acknowledgments

I would like to offer my most sincere gratitude to those who assisted in their unique ways with the creation and development of this book.

First and foremost, I would like to thank God. I would not have been able to complete this enormous undertaking without his guidance.

Next, my heartfelt appreciation goes to my family and friends. Thank you to everyone who continuously offered support and encouragement along the way.

I would like to thank all of my clients. I am fortunate to work with an outstanding group of souls who want nothing more than to keep their horses happy and well.

Of course, I would like to thank all the horses I have had the privilege to meet, know, and love throughout my lifetime. I have been, and continue to be, amazed at where these magnificent creatures have taken and continue to take me, from riding and competing to travelling and therapy, to business owning and now to writing this book.

I would also like to thank Glenn Scott, the photographer for this project. In addition to being incredibly talented, he was professional, humorous, and a true pleasure to work with—always patient while aiming for just the right shot.

Finally, I would like to say thank you to my pride and joy, Lieutenant. Lieutenant, my horse, is my dream come true. He was his usual handsome, brave self, modeling and performing effortlessly in many of the photographs in this book. Thank you, Lieutenant, for bringing a smile to my face each and every day.

About the Author

Denise Bean-Raymond brings 28 years of experience with horses to her equine therapy practice, Exclusive Equestrian Services. She has worked in a wide range of fields including barn management, instruction, training, and alternative therapy. She is certified in equine sports massage and in equine acupressure therapy from the Animal Acupressure Massage Training Center in Nevada City, California. Ms. Bean-Raymond is a member of the International Association of Animal Massage Therapists and the International Association of Animal Massage and Bodywork.

In addition, Denise Bean-Raymond is a licensed riding instructor who is certified nationally with the American Riding instructor's Association. A lifetime of observing horses working in various disciplines has allowed her to intuitively recognize common movement issues, confirmation flaws, and performance-related problems, and to create suitable treatment plans for them. She also offers equestrian clinics and lectures. Denise lives in Danvers, Massachusetts.